The Primary Teacher's Guide to the New National Curriculum

Edited by

Kate Ashcroft and David Palacio

 Falmer Press

(A member of the Taylor & Francis Group)

London • Washington. D.C.

UK   The Falmer Press, 4 John Street. London WC1N 2ET
USA   The Falmer Press, Taylor & Francis Inc., 1900 Frost Road, Suite 101, Bristol, PA 19007

First published in 1995

A catalogue record for this book is available from the British Library

Library of Congress Cataloging-in-Publication Data are available on request

ISBN 0 7507 0467 5 cased
ISBN 0 7507 0468 3 paper

Typeset in 10/12 pt Bembo
Graphicraft Typesetters Ltd., Hong Kong.

Printed in Great Britain by Burgess Science Press, Basingstoke on paper which has a specified pH value on final paper manufacture of not less than 7.5 and is therefore 'acid free'.

The Primary Teacher's Guide to the
New National Curriculum

Contents

Contents

Section 1

Introduction

1   Introduction to the New National Curriculum

Kate Ashcroft and David Palacio

The new National Curriculum has now emerged and includes many changes to the existing curriculum. It will have far reaching effects on the content and delivery of the primary curriculum. This book is designed to give you a quick and accessible overview of the new curriculum arrangements. Whether you are an experienced teacher in a primary school, a newly qualified teacher or a student in training, you are probably anxious to gain an insight into the new curriculum as quickly and as painlessly as possible. We have tried to create a book that clearly and succinctly identifies the changes and their implications for practice.

The Department for Education (DFE) does not generally produce its National Curriculum material in a form that makes it an easy or enjoyable read, although this version is an improvement on previous ones. You may have put a great deal of effort into understanding and interpreting earlier versions of the National Curriculum and be unenthusiastic about starting this process again. For these and other reasons, we have tried to do much of the initial interpretation for you.

This book is a guide to the essential features of the new National Curriculum, covering all subjects within that curriculum. It also describes the recently introduced curriculum guidelines for religious education and discusses a number of issues that emerge from these guidelines. In order to take you beyond a factual understanding, content and enquiry tasks (a central feature of every chapter) focus upon the development of key understandings and the ways that these may be put into effect in the primary classroom.

At the moment the government intends that schools will be inspected by the Office for Standards in Education (OFSTED) once every four years. Unlike previous inspection regimes, these inspections focus on *judgment* at the expense of *development*. If your school is due to be inspected during or soon after the publication of the new National Curriculum you will wish to be sure you can answer questions about your understanding of the new Orders and your school's response to them. We hope that this book will provide an accessible starting point for this understanding and action.

It is intended that you could use the book either as a means of gaining an immediate understanding of the new curriculum as a whole, or as a reference book should you wish to focus on a particular aspect. In the second case you might refer to the synopsis, that you will find at the end of each chapter, and perhaps read the full chapter when you have more time. We have tried to give the book a practical focus and create 'bite size' chapters that could easily be tackled in an evening. Although the style is practical, we still wanted to retain a clear educational philosophy. The focus of that philosophy is what is called the Reflective Practitioner Model of teaching and learning, and has an emphasis on the exploration of particular values and the principled resolution of dilemmas within any specified curriculum. This model underpins the enquiry tasks at the end of key sections. We hope you will find that the tasks help your reflection and aid the integration of the new curriculum with your own theory of teaching in practice.

Enquiry Task

One of the tasks of the beginning teacher is to get to grips with language that has become associated with the National Curriculum and the organizations that have, or have had, a significant part to play in its development. Some of these organizations are listed below.

What are their full names and what part did they play in the development of the National Curriculum?

- TGAT;
- NCC;
- SEAC;
- HMI;
- SCAA;
- OFSTED?

Do you know how each is organized and run?

Do you know how TGAT, NCC and SEAC related to each other and to SCAA?

Do you know how HMI relates to OFSTED?

If you do not know the answers to these questions, why not find out? It will aid significantly your understanding of the National Curriculum and this chapter.

A Brief History of the National Curriculum in Britain

The modern education system in the UK could be said to date from the 1944 Education Act that established universal secondary education to the age of 15 for all children. It also established the principle of entitlement to an education suited to each child's needs. This education would be varied according to each child's ability, as measured at eleven years of age by pencil and paper tests. The intention was to establish a national system of education, but there was no attempt to prescribe a National Curriculum. Indeed, the only subject to be made compulsory in state schools was religious education.

The concept of the National Curriculum was implemented in the Education Reform Act of 1988. However, it has had a longer history than that. There had been calls for improvements in education since Harold Wilson's 'white heat of technology' had failed to materialize, partly because of a skills shortage in the workforce. The blame for Britain's apparent underperformance – especially in science, technology and mathematics – was attributed to 'trendy' teaching methods that emphasized 'a process approach' at the expense of content. This process began in the Black Papers published by Cox and others (Cox and Dyson, 1971) and became part of the political landscape following James Callaghan's speech at Ruskin College in Oxford in 1976 that opened the 'Great Debate' about education.

The debate about what should be taught and how education should be 'delivered' (a term that was spawned out of the 1988 Education Act) became associated with Conservative politics and therefore it was not surprising that it was the radical Conservative Government in the 1980s that decided to introduce a nationally determined content to the curriculum.

From the conception of the National Curriculum, the various factions in the Conservative Party had different ideas concerning its purpose. Perhaps the most distinguished of the many Secretaries of State for Education during the long Conservative administrations of the 1980s and 1990s was Sir Keith Joseph. He was particularly anxious about the poor educational experiences of the bottom 40 per cent of pupils and the low expectations that teachers had of them, and was eager to find a mechanism to ensure that such pupils had an entitlement to a proper standard of education and a minimum curriculum. Kenneth Baker, who emerged as Secretary of State after the brief and easily forgotten Mark Carlisle, took up this theme of entitlement, but expressed it in terms of a universal (more or less) entitlement to a 'broad and balanced curriculum'.

Others within the Conservative Party had different ideas. Some (including the then Prime Minister and one time Secretary of State for Education and Science, Margaret Thatcher) saw a prescribed curriculum as a means of ensuring that teachers, and especially primary teachers, focused on the basic subjects. Yet others saw the National Curriculum as a means of ensuring that teachers returned to traditional teaching methods. Some saw the introduction of a centrally devised curriculum, together with an attendant common assessment system, as a way of raising standards in schools.

Despite Kenneth Baker's assurance that only the content of the curriculum was being decided, and that teachers would remain free to use a variety of teaching methods, it soon became clear that the two main factions had won separate and contradictory victories. Kenneth Barker had won the argument over a broad curriculum, that led eventually to a nine-subject National Curriculum in primary schools, whilst the back-to-basics faction won all other victories. Thus, the recommendations of the Task Group on Assessment and Testing (TGAT) were initially accepted and then increasingly abandoned as its recommendations came to be seen as unworkable. From that time onwards, a gradual movement of government policy was discernible away from teacher moderation and practical, task-based individual and group assessment and towards pencil and paper tests. These tests came to be used in part to police the curriculum coverage and teaching methods. Because they tested 'old fashioned' knowledge at the expense of 'new fangled' skills, they encouraged more passive forms of learning and transmissional teaching methods. The eventual publication of test results was in part designed to ensure that schools focused on those elements of the full curriculum that were the subject of the tests (mainly the core subjects: English, mathematics and science).

The National Curriculum was drafted by a number of working groups, each responsible for just one subject of the curriculum. In addition to the National Curriculum, schools would have to offer a programme of religious education that accorded with locally determined guidelines. This arrangement had two major effects. The first was to ensure that there was too much content in the curriculum to teach in the time that was available. Any group of enthusiastic subject experts will find much content that they deem 'essential'. This is, of course, predictable, since many subject experts are unlikely to be objective about the place and relative importance of their subject in the overall curriculum. Most will have been deeply influenced by a particular set of concepts, ideas and views about the world and will want others to be influenced similarly.

The second effect of a curriculum designed by a number of independent subject groups, as far as primary schools were concerned, was a move away from cross-curricular towards a more subject-specific teaching approach. This again was entirely predictable (and, one could argue, was part of the government's overall strategy for educational change). Many people in the Conservative Government saw cross-curricular approaches as left-wing and trendy, a point of view borne out by the fact that the Secretary for State for Education failed to set up a working party to look at the National Curriculum as a whole – the sort of thinking that might have made the task of delivering the curriculum manageable.

Enquiry Task

Examine two sets of curriculum documents or guidelines from a particular primary school; one that pre-dates and one that post-dates the introduction of the National Curriculum.

How do they differ?

Categorize the changes you notice in terms of:

- the specificity of objectives;
- the approach to differentiation of the curriculum;
- the specificity of content and how the subject is to be taught;
- the specificity of assessment.

What has been gained and what has been lost by the changes you have noticed?

A number of problems inherent in this subject-based approach emerged with the curriculum proposals. A large number of important, but non subject specific, issues were absent from the proposed curriculum. This led to the notion of the cross-curriculum theme, the cross-curriculum dimension and the cross-curriculum skill. Few teachers ever got to grips with these. As a group, the themes comprised an unconnected set of elements including economic and industrial understanding, health education, education for citizenship, environmental education, careers education and guidance, and health education. Each of these was supported by a short curriculum document. Only the first received substantial government emphasis.

The cross-curriculum dimensions received even less government emphasis and attention. These included equal opportunities, personal and social education, and education for life in a multicultural society. Cross-curriculum skills were identified, including communication, numeracy, study skills, problem solving, personal and social skills, and information technology. Most dimensions or skills were dealt with in a few sentences in the curriculum Orders or in the non-statutory guidance that accompanied the Orders (National Curriculum Council, 1989 and 1990). In consequence, they became peripheral in planning and implementing the new curriculum.

The way the National Curriculum was introduced had the effect of marginalizing the arts and, to some extent, the humanities. This was a victory for the back-to-basics group. It was achieved by the simple expedient of timetabling the implementation of the curriculum so that core subjects (mathematics, science and English) were introduced first, technology next, the humanities (history and geography) next and the arts (music and art) and physical education last. By the time the arts and physical education were considered, staff and course development energies had been expended on other areas of the curriculum. In addition, the evidence of an overcrowded curriculum was growing, as were the protests about assessment loads carried by teachers and pupils. As the humanities and arts subjects emerged, each was subject to 'slimming' and a simplification of the assessment requirements (in the case of the arts, almost to nothing). To make matters worse, two arts subjects, drama and dance, lost their place as separate subjects within the curriculum, and the 'design' element in the National Curriculum subject 'design technology' was dropped, signalling a change away from a creative subject to a more technical one.

During the tenure of Kenneth Clark as Secretary of State for Education, the subject working groups who were writing and rewriting the curriculum were increasingly packed with political appointees, many with little or no experience of state schooling (especially state primary schooling). Some people argued that the idea was to ensure that the curriculum conformed to traditional Conservative values. In the event, the subject working parties mostly worked well and produced an interesting if overcrowded curriculum. Many of their recommendations were overturned on the opinion of the political masters who felt that they did not emphasize traditional 'British' subject matter sufficiently. This led, for example, to substantial changes to the English and history curriculum, including the establishment of a 'canon' of literature to be studied and an emphasis on British history at the expense of world and European history.

The perceived over-politicization of education and the stresses caused to teachers and children by an overcrowded, over-assessed curriculum led to some fairly concerted opposition to the National Curriculum. To make matters worse, much of the content emerging in the statutory Orders did not fit well with the values of many teachers. In addition, many teachers, especially those in primary schools, lacked particular skills, expertise and the personal knowledge needed to teach and assess the new curriculum.

By about the early 1990s, some of the problems became too great to be ignored. Several subject groups (for example, mathematics) were asked to 'tinker' with aspects of their subject. Some subjects, such as science, were subject to a more drastic review. These changes were being absorbed by schools at the same time as other subjects were being introduced for the first time. Teachers started to suffer stress resulting from the increase in workload, the continuous change and the sheer weight of curriculum content and assessment.

These stresses came to a head during the tenure of the next Secretary of State for Education, John Patten. In 1992, Dr Patten published a White Paper 'Choice and Diversity', in which he repeatedly stressed his commitment to the National Curriculum and testing. He insisted there were no long-term problems and that he would continue with the existing system of testing. Unfortunately, this system had largely fallen into disrepute on the grounds of unmanageability and a lack of validity and reliability associated with the assessment programme. When test results were published in league tables, teachers took industrial action because they saw them as crude and inaccurate. In February 1993, despite the fact that the majority of teachers were boycotting the tests, Dr Pattern was still insisting that the National Curriculum was not too prescriptive. However, by Easter 1993, it was clear that the teachers' boycott was too widely supported to be ignored. In April 1993, Dr Pattern invited Sir Ron Dearing to undertake a review of the curriculum and its administrative arrangements. This would be the first time that the National Curriculum had been reviewed in its entirety. A great experiment had been tried on the nation's children and had been found wanting. Perhaps, a holistic view of the curriculum and a more rational approach to the introduction of the National Curriculum – involving pilot work and evaluation *before* whole scale implementation – might have prevented this disaster for a generation of children.

One of the first tasks of the School Curriculum and Assessment Authority (SCAA) was to slim down the curriculum and testing arrangements, simplify the ten-level scale of assessment and improve the administration of the tests. Between April and July 1993, Sir Ron Dearing consulted with around 4,400 schools, other organizations and individuals. He outlined five main ways forward in his interim report (School Curriculum and Assessment Authority, 1994a). These included: slimming down the National Curriculum and cutting the number of statements of attainment; ensuring the core subjects occupied less time and allowing schools to direct the rest of the curriculum; limiting national tests to the core subjects for at least a while, and cutting the teacher and pupil time taken in testing; giving teacher assessments (TAs) and standard assessment tasks (SATs) equal status; and cutting bureaucracy, simplifying documents and delivering materials earlier to schools.

Despite the review, Dr Patten introduced SATs for 11 year olds and retained those for 7 and 14 year olds. Meanwhile, the teachers' boycott continued. Dr Patten then published a glossy folder entitled *National Curriculum Testing: The Facts* (Department for Education, 1994), containing what many teachers saw as a one sided view of the benefits of the existing (i.e., National Curriculum) system of tests. Examples that, for many people, illustrate this bias include: '. . . before National Curriculum tests were introduced, teachers relied on their own individual assessments of children' (Sheet 2); and, 'The benefits of national tests for 7 year olds are well established' (Sheet 3).

In the final report of his review of the National Curriculum, Sir Ron Dearing made the following recommendations (School Curriculum and Assessment Authority, 1994b):

- the equivalent of one day a week should be released for primary schools to use at their discretion;
- reductions in content should be concentrated in non–core subjects;
- reductions in the number of Statements of Attainment;
- the introduction of Level Descriptions to replace Statements of Attainment; and
- all the changes should be made in one go.

Following the acceptance by the Secretary of State for Education of this final report, SCAA set up advisory groups of (mainly) teachers for each subject, the purpose of each group being to identify an essential core of content for that subject, to formulate new level descriptors and to seek solutions to widely reported problems. The responses from subject groups were then published to enable further consultation to take place. The results of this consultation were considered by SCAA during August 1994. The revised National Curriculum, once approved by Parliament, was published in draft in November 1994, and in its final form in January 1995 with a start date of August 1995.

The National Curriculum was an attempt to give all children an entitlement to a broad education, to ensure that standards were established and the progress of individual children charted. In some subjects, such as mathematics and science, the National Curriculum produced a great improvement in typical practice. In other subjects, such as technology and information technology, it ensured at least a minimum exposure for all children, where there was often little or none before.

The National Curriculum, in its original version, foundered under the weight of non-expert political interference and untested assumptions. Finally, in mid-1994 the Prime Minister John Major appointed a new Secretary of State for Education, Gillian Shephard. In 1995, after a period of real and sustained consultation, a new National Curriculum was introduced in which programmes of study and systems for assessment have been looked at as a whole. There is, perhaps for the first time, substantial evidence that teachers who, after all, know about teaching, understand how children learn and who will have to deliver the curriculum and assessment reforms, have been listened to.

Enquiry Task

Examine a 1989 version and the 1995 version of the National Curriculum.

Look in detail at one of the core curriculum subjects – English; mathematics or science (or Welsh if you teach in a Welsh medium school).

How do the two documents differ in terms of:

- the specificity of objectives;
- the approach to differentiation of the curriculum;
- the specificity of content;
- the specificity of assessment?

Select another National Curriculum subject. Examine the 1989 and 1995 versions of that subject.

How do they differ in terms of:

- the way they are presented;
- the level of detail;
- the values and assumptions underpinning the documents?

What has been gained and what has been lost by the changes you have noticed?

The Philosophical and Political Climate for the New National Curriculum

The new National Curriculum has moved from a plethora of detailed Statements of Attainment to simpler and more overarching descriptions of key elements. This represents a reduction of about four-fifths in the number of Statements of Attainment. (Before, you would have had to carry out about 8,000 individual assessments in order to cover your obligation to assess children in an average class of children, applying 966 Statements of Attainment.) You will now be able to make professional judgments about the Level Descriptor that best fits individual pupils in your class. No longer will you have to keep detailed and itemized records on each and every aspect of each and every child's learning. The ten-level scale of attainment has been retained, but it now extends downwards to offer primary school children with special educational needs real targets and real descriptors for their achievement.

The status of the arts does not seem to have improved: they will contain only End of Key Stage Statements. The original cross-curricular themes seem to have died a death, but English has emerged as a cross-curricula dimension.

The new Orders should be helpful to most primary teachers. In particular you may be glad to note that the allocation of similar attainment and subject matter to different Key Stages in different subjects has been eliminated; progression should be easier to follow; and the link between Programmes of Study and Attainment Targets is clearer.

This is not to suggest that the process of devising a new National Curriculum has been free from political interference. For example, John Patten, in a letter to Sir Ron Dearing as late as 15th April 1994, stated his support for an emphasis on team games in the physical education Order for Key Stages 1 to 3. This was perhaps linked to the Secretary of State's belief that a preparatory and public school ethos should be applied to state education. Furthermore, such a view may have been reinforced by some national newspapers relating the failure of the UK national football teams to qualify for the World Cup, and a series of defeats for the English cricket team, with a general decline in 'Britishness' and Britain's standing in the world. In the same letter, Dr Patten insisted upon changes to the proposals for English and history to make them conform more closely with Conservative values. It is unlikely that such interference will have led to improvements.

Many people believe that, and if past experience is anything to go by, government politicians may live to regret interfering too much in a successful and productive process of consultation. It is interesting to note that Dr Patten lost his cabinet post shortly after such interference. Unfortunately, politicians of all political parties have to be concerned about gains in the short term and those achievable during a particular government's time in office, whereas education is about long- as well as short-term opportunities: hence one major difference between politicians and educationalists. This difference in time scale has been at the base of most of the problems with the National Curriculum, but there are signs that Mrs Shephard is not keen to repeat the mistakes of the past.

The Structure of the New Curriculum

The main structural changes in the new National Curriculum involve a reduction in the level of prescription and a simplification in the means of assessment. Unnecessary text has been removed from the Orders and the language has been altered to clarify exactly what should be taught. *What* is to be covered in the compulsory curriculum is prescribed, but you and your school are freer to decide *when* (apart from the Key Stage) and *how* it should be taught. This freedom is, of course, limited by the curriculum. For instance, it would not be possible to cover the science curriculum through teacher demonstrations only, the English curriculum through reading and writing activity, or the mathematics curriculum purely through work from a textbook.

Statements of Attainment have been replaced by Level Descriptions. These are simpler and fewer in number, and will enable you to choose the description that 'best fits' a child's performance. The descriptions show a clearer progression within each subject and a greater comparability across each subject than some of the original Statements of Attainment. There is also a close relationship between level descriptions in subjects that use them and End of Key Stage descriptions in subjects

---

Enquiry Task

Make a list of those people and groups to whom the teachers in your school are accountable, for example:

- parents;
- the headteacher;
- governors;
- government.

Do you know what legal form the accountability takes to each of these groups?

If not, why not find out?

For accountability to be effective, it must be based on the provision of information.

For each of the interest groups you listed above, identify the kind of information your school provides and the form that such information might take, for example:

Interest group	Information required	Most appropriate form
Parents	Details of their child's progress	Yearly written narrative reports Termly meeting with the classteacher.

Share your lists with an experienced colleague, and add to them.

Discuss the ways that reporting and accountability have changed in the last ten years.

What has been gained and what has been lost in these changes?

---

that do not. As the change of name suggests, Level Descriptions and End of Key Stage Descriptions use the same style of language: care has been taken to ensure compatibility of demand between them.

The content of the new National Curriculum is less than that in the original version. At Key Stage 1, the demands of the English curriculum have received particular attention from SCAA. At Key Stage 2 there has been a general slimming down of the curriculum, particularly in history, geography and science. In addition, 'design' is back in favour. It has been reinstated in *design* and technology, resulting in substantial restructuring. The inclusion of design in the title is reflected by a design emphasis in the content, and in information technology becoming a separate subject. The establishment of information technology as a separate subject increases the number of National Curriculum subjects in the primary school to ten. On the other hand, there is less emphasis on prescription, particularly regarding cross-curricular themes. Overall, the new curriculum should provide your school with more opportunity to decide how it will ensure breadth and balance within its particular context.

The new curriculum Orders should also make planning easier. The relationships between what has to be taught (Programmes of Study) and what has to be assessed (Level Descriptors and End of Key Stage Statements) should enable you to identify key objectives for learning. It will be part of your role to ensure that your children are given appropriate opportunities to show what they *know, understand* and *can do*, so that, at the end of each Key Stage (at the age of seven for Key Stage 1 and the age of eleven for Key Stage 2), you can make judgments in terms of the level descriptors.

An important change in the 1995 curriculum is the introduction of access statements for children with special educational needs. This should allow you greater flexibility and enable children with learning difficulties to be catered for better within the statutory framework of the National Curriculum.

The National Curriculum as it is now constructed should release the equivalent of a day a week of curriculum time for you and your school to use at your own discretion. More details of the changes to the National Curriculum, together with a discussion of their major implications are contained in the following chapters.

Enquiry Task

Identify one key objective for the Level Description for a group of very able or less able children that you are teaching for each core subject of the curriculum.

Create a schedule of behaviours that would indicate whether or not a child had achieved each of the objectives:

Subject	*Objective*	*Indicators that objective has been attained*
English		
Mathematics		
Science		
Welsh (if appropriate)		

Use the schedule to monitor the children's learning.

What are the strengths and weaknesses of such an approach?

Discuss this and other approaches to recording children's progress with your colleagues.

The Reflective Practitioner Model as a Tool for Integrating Curriculum Change

In writing this book we assume that you wish to go beyond a factual interpretation of the new National Curriculum and to look at its implications in terms of the values that underpin it, and the relationship of these values to your own practice and that of other teachers in the school in which you work. We believe that the Reflective Practitioner Model as derived by Dewey (1926) and developed by Zeichner and others (for example, Zeichner, 1982; Pollard and Tann, 1988; Ashcroft and Griffiths, 1989), provides an appropriate vehicle for the process of self-critical problem solving and the assessment of evidence that underpins reflection.

In this model, reflection is much more than 'thinking about': rather, it refers to an active process of critical enquiry that becomes possible as the individual develops particular qualities and skills. Among the qualities prerequisite to reflective practice are *openmindedness, responsibility* and *commitment*.

Openmindedness implies that you are willing to actively seek out and consider alternative viewpoints, not to take them on board automatically nor to reject them blindly, but rather to consider how they might apply in your circumstances and how they might affect your practice. (The reflective practitioner knows that feelings are part of reality and that it is irrational to undertake rational planning that does not take them into account.) Perhaps the original National Curriculum might have achieved its intentions had politicians developed the quality of openmindedness.

Responsibility, the second quality prerequisite for reflective practice, implies that you are willing to investigate the long-term, as well as the short-term consequences of your actions. As a responsible teacher, you will understand that you are part of a system, that your relationships with other teachers may be as important to the education the children receive as your relationships with those children. You will be interested in looking at the causes of problems and understanding the issues within current educational change. For example, in dealing with a difficult child, you will be unlikely to say, 'This child is uneducable because of the damage done to them in the past', but rather, 'I have not yet found a way to meet the needs of this child, I will have to investigate the problem further.'

As a responsible teacher you will wish to move beyond intuition to questions of worthwhileness, in order to explore the underlying effects of your actions and values. Thus responsibility implies you consider the hidden curriculum alongside the implementation of the new National Curriculum in your school. It also implies that you consider radical approaches to the organization of the curriculum, rather than less effortful minor tinkering with the existing pattern of your work. Whatever approach you take, responsibility implies you evaluate its effects on all concerned in the long as well as the short term.

Commitment, the final quality prerequisite for reflective action, implies that responsibility and openmindedness are part of your whole life. You will not display particular qualities only in certain contexts, or for personal advantage. It implies that you work hard, but also that you take an essentially moral stance: that you are willing to articulate your personal theory of practice and then to explore your practice and the values that you are transmitting to children and colleagues.

Commitment makes great demands on teachers exhausted by continuous revolution. It means that you must respond to the new National Curriculum with as much energy and enthusiasm as if it was not the most recent of many changes. It also implies that you will seek to make it work for you, for the children and for their parents. This will be in the context of clearly articulated principles that you and your colleagues have examined in the light of this change and have agreed underlie good professional practice. Commitment means that there can be no 'going through the motions'.

The development of these qualities is a lifelong process. Reflective practice is an ideal to work towards rather than to achieve. It requires the persistent development and application of particular skills, such as research skills, interpersonal skills and communication skills. As an openminded teacher, you will not automatically accept the prevailing educational orthodoxy of your school or the national system, but rather you will examine it in the light of your experience and compare it with that of colleagues and other parties to the educational process such as parents, children and governors.

As a responsible teacher, you will also need to develop research skills such as observation, data collection, analysis, and so on. Without such skills it is difficult to see how you will find out about the actual effects that your actions in implementing the new National Curriculum have on those engaged in the process of schooling, and the extent to which these actions are congruent with your own theories of teaching and the aims and purposes of your school. Systematic collection of evidence that is then shared and discussed with others seems to us the only way of ensuring that your intuition is not deceiving you.

In order to build up, and continuously examine a conception of teaching in which attention is paid to its moral, political and social context, you will need skills in critical enquiry (see Zeichner, 1982; Van Manon, 1977; and Ashcroft and Griffiths, 1989).

Implementation of the new National Curriculum will therefore involve you in the negotiation of values and practice. Change that is embedded in its social context, that takes account of the feelings and perspectives of parents, colleagues, teachers in general and the wider educational community, is likely to be more lasting and effective. The process of discovering, sharing and considering these viewpoints will be time consuming and skillful. You will need the opportunity and ability to work effectively as a member of various teams, with all the personal skills and qualities that this implies. None of this will constitute reflective action unless you engage in systematic evaluation.

The process of reflective practice is therefore an active one. In the context of the implementation of the new National Curriculum, it requires you to articulate theory and principles, find out how your ideas stand up to the scrutiny of others and data collected through practice, and to change both your values and practice if either emerge as inappropriate or educationally indefensible.

The Content of the Book

Each chapter in the book explores the values that underpin the way the 'subject' under discussion has been described. Such an analysis can only be the start of a reflective process. Questions and issues that need more consideration than can be managed within the space available are introduced through enquiry-based tasks and

---

Enquiry Task

List the methods you use, or might use, to collect evidence about the long- and short-term effects of your actions on children.

Identify the strengths and weaknesses of each method, for example:

Evaluation method	*Strengths*	*Weaknesses*
e.g., Fly on the wall observation	Good for collecting evidence about actual behaviour	Cannot get at feelings
Unstructured observation		
Analysis of discussion		
Interview		
Diagnostic marking		

Use three of these methods to evaluate the effects of an aspect of your teaching behaviour over a period of time (e.g., the amount and quality of attention you give to different groups, say, to boys and girls).

What did you learn about yourself from this exercise?

How might you investigate the effects of your actions on other teachers?

---

an annotated list of further reading. The enquiry tasks are designed to challenge you further and provide material for reflection.

Each chapter also includes a summary of the main changes between the old and new versions of each subject of the National Curriculum. Issues relating the content to equal opportunities, religious education and drama are also discussed. Also provided are practical examples of how the content may be tackled at the various Key Stages and levels in the primary school.

We do not pretend that the implementation of the new curriculum will be trouble free. We explore some of the threats and opportunities presented by these changes, together with some practical options for teaching and learning, including ways of incorporating the cross-curriculum issues. Also discussed in the various chapters are the main implications for assessment practice. We take Sir Ron Dearing at his word, and include other areas and aspects of the curriculum that might occupy the day-a-week equivalent that will be supposedly free of National Curriculum work.

References

Ashcroft, K. and Griffiths, M. (1989) 'Reflective teachers and reflective tutors: school experience in an initial teacher education course', *Journal of Education for Teaching*, 15, 1, pp. 35–52.

CALLAGHAN, J. (1976) 'Towards a National Debate; Ruskin College, Oxford: 18 October', *Education*, 22, pp. 332–3.

COX, B.C. and DYSON, A.E. (eds) (1971) *The Black Papers on Education*, London: Davis Pointer.

DEPARTMENT FOR EDUCATION (1994) *The National Curriculum: The Facts*, London: Department for Education.

DEWEY, J. (1926) *Democracy and Education*, New York: The Free Press.

NATIONAL CURRICULUM COUNCIL (1989) *Circular Number 6*, October, York: National Curriculum Council.

NATIONAL CURRICULUM COUNCIL (1990) *Curriculum Guidance Number 3: The Whole Curriculum*, York: National Curriculum Council.

PATTERN, J. (1992) *Choice and Diversity: A New Framework for Schools*, London: HMSO.

POLLARD, A. and TANN, S. (1988) *A Handbook for Reflective Teaching in the Primary School*, London: Cassells.

SCHOOL CURRICULUM and ASSESSMENT AUTHORITY (1994a) *Key Stages 1 and 2 Compendium: Draft Proposals*, London: School Curriculum and Assessment Authority.

SCHOOL CURRICULUM and ASSESSMENT AUTHORITY (1994b) *Dearing: The Final Report*, London: School Curriculum and Assessment Authority.

VAN MANON, M. (1977) 'Linking ways of knowing with being practical', *Curriculum Inquiry*, 6, pp. 205–18.

ZEICHNER, K. (1982) 'Reflective teaching and field-based experience in teacher education', *Interchange*, 12, 4, pp. 1–22.

2 The School Context for Curriculum Change

Carolyn Boyd and Peta Lloyd

What Were the Major Issues with the Original National Curriculum?

When a curriculum is prescribed centrally there are the questions of, 'Whose curriculum?', 'How much does it meet the needs of all children in our schools?', 'How much does it reflect the pluralist society in which we live?' We need to remember that the National Curriculum is only one way of organizing a school curriculum. A school's curriculum could be organized in terms of skills; general areas of experience, such as language; topics or themes which span subjects; separate subject areas. For example, HMI (1985) defined nine areas of learning and experience (aesthetic and creative, human and social, linguistic and literary, mathematical, moral, physical, scientific, spiritual, technological). In New South Wales, Australia, the curriculum in the 1980s was organized under the broad headings of expressing, communicating and investigating.

Enquiry Task

The curriculum is never static. Think back to:

- how you worked and what you taught when you first started teaching;
- how and what you were taught when you were a pupil in a primary school.

Compare these experiences with teaching today. Why do you think these changes took place? You may wish to consider some of the following:

- Legislation has greatly influenced what we statutorily have to teach.
- Society is always changing due to factors such as the economy, politics, immigration, etc.
- Views regarding development change over time, for example we hold views of childhood today that are different from those of the Victorians.
- Changes in technology have required changes in education to meet the new needs of society.
- Research is constantly developing our understandings of how children learn.

The early stages of implementing the National Curriculum were problematic. There was confusion over the use of Programmes of Study and Attainment Targets. In the documents sent to schools, the Statements of Attainment were placed in front of the Programmes of Study and made it difficult not to let assessment dominate thinking and planning or outcomes determine the curriculum. That is, planning *from* outcomes rather than planning *for* outcomes.

For the majority of teachers, the most stressful problem was one of overload. Teachers working at Key Stage 1 may have worried about lack of time for the adequate development of reading and computational mathematical skills. Those with a Key Stage 2 class may have found it difficult to cope with the large amount of subject content and knowledge they were meant to cover. They may have even been concerned about their own understanding of the very wide range of content they were now expected to teach. Previously, much planning had not been in terms of the subject areas now specified in the National Curriculum.

Links between subjects were not made explicit across the curriculum through the National Curriculum documentation, although there were random overlaps of content and process. This was largely due to subject groups working independently of each other with different starting points and time scales. The cross-curricular themes and dimensions, which were written later and appeared to be very much an afterthought, were difficult to thread into a curriculum rooted in subject knowledge and often became artificial or marginalized.

How Were these Issues Addressed?

Many of these issues were overcome by teachers through teamwork. Through this approach, teachers became familiar with what was required. Each teacher developed detailed knowledge of how to comply with the statutory requirements.

Alexander (1992, p. 35) found that 'schools used a wide range of strategies for curriculum development'. He found the most frequently used strategies were:

- 'Defining school and teacher needs:
    staff meetings;
    GRIDS[1];
    appraisal interviews.
- Delegating responsibility:
    establishing coordinating teams or working parties;
    drafting of guidelines or policy statement by staff member.
- Extending expertise:
    attending courses;
    requesting support from the advisory service;
    visiting other schools;
    inviting outside experts to talk to/work with staff.

[1] a method of helping staff to prioritize school development – see McMahon *et al.*, 1984.

- Staff discussion:
  staff meetings;
  workshops;
  training days;
  informal discussion;
  structured small group discussion;
  collective formulation of guidelines or policy statements.
- Classroom activity:
  collaborative teaching;
  year-group planning.'

Enquiry Task

- List strategies that are frequently used in your school to support curriculum development.
- Which strategies are still in the development stage?
- List new ones which you believe may be useful to try.

The New Curriculum

It was reported in Chapter 1 that while teachers have grappled with these issues, they have also been recognized by both the National Curriculum Council (1989) and Office for Standards in Education (OFSTED) (1993). In separate reports these organizations agreed that Key Stage 1 and 2 were unmanageable, too complex and over prescribed. The School Examination and Assessment Council (SEAC) Review (1993) and subsequent Dearing Report (Dearing, 1993) endorsed these beliefs. The Dearing Report suggested that the primary curriculum be slimmed down to free 20 per cent of school time, the equivalent of one day per week. It was not a simple percentage cut within each subject: curriculum Orders have been divided into statutory and optional material, with only statutory material retained in the Orders; essential content, skills and processes have been defined for each Key Stage in the Programmes of Study.

You will have also noted from Chapter 1 that although the basic content of the Programmes of Study has not changed, the number of Attainment Targets has been reduced. The Statements of Attainment are now replaced by Level Descriptions, which are broad statements about expected outcomes across a level. They contain a range of information on which to base your judgment. For example, the Level Description for the Geography Attainment Target at Level 3 states:

> Pupils describe aspects of physical and human processes in different localities and show an awareness that places can have both similar and different characteristics. They offer reasons for some of their observations and personal preferences. They use a range of appropriate skills and information to pursue set tasks. (NC geography, 1994, p. 12)

Music, art and physical education have End of Key Stage Statements which describe the types and range of performance that children should demonstrate by the end of a Key Stage, rather than at particular levels.

Both Level Descriptions and End of Key Stage Statements are meant to be used holistically to guide your overall judgments. They are intended as a basis for summary assessments for reporting purposes; they are not intended to guide children's work. This means that you need to plan from the Programmes of Study and keep ongoing records throughout the year that can be passed on to the child's next teacher. These records are most helpful when based on observation and sampling rather than simple tick lists – involving children in collecting samples of their work and reflecting on their own progress helps support their learning and provides them and their teacher with useful information on their development. All of this will enable the teacher at the end of each Key Stage to make considered professional judgments about each child's progress. The School Curriculum and Assessment Authority (SCAA) has provided exemplars of level descriptions to help standardize assessment in the new National Curriculum.

Thinking about Learning: Coping with Change

Some people would argue that the National Curriculum is concerned with the acquisition of knowledge and understanding, that there is no dictation over the pedagogy (how to teach it). Perhaps this view is grounded in simplistic ideas of teaching and learning. It implicitly carries the view that teaching is about delivery of knowledge and relaying content (an unarticulated view of learning in itself).

Many teachers are pleased to have the chance to reflect on their own beliefs about learning and plan for ways to meet the statutory requirements, while being true to their beliefs about teaching and learning. Yet content cannot be dictated without the possibility of it affecting teaching styles. For example, because the first Attainment Targets in mathematics (using and applying) and science (experimenting and investigating), are concerned with the processes by which data is collected, interpreted and conclusions are reached, it is impossible to meet the statutory requirements without adjusting your teaching to incorporate this view of the nature of the subject in question.

Teachers have, on the whole, worked conscientiously to make each curriculum change work. Perhaps the teachers who managed to hold on to what they considered best in their practice are the teachers who had already reflected on and articulated most explicitly their views of teaching and learning.

We live in times where the political climate has tended to suppress discussion on theory and the nature of learning. Such things are taken as self-evident, 'common-sense' and therefore not relevant for discussion. The danger is that common-sense is nothing more than a theory, or a view of the world that has not been made explicit or tested against systematically collected evidence. Yet it is important to realize that all practice is informed by theories — ideas, values and assumptions — of some kind, and the notion of theory-free classroom practice is essentially a contradiction, since practice, of course, is no more and no less than ideas in action. (Alexander, 1992, p. 172)

Alexander goes on to state that the best theory is carefully thought out in relation to knowledge about children's development, views of learning, curriculum and how to teach effectively.

Teachers must be able to justify their views and articulate how it relates to the classroom. For example, Holdaway (1979) initiated the use of enlarged texts to support children who are learning to read. In a recent interview (1992), he once again stressed the dissatisfaction with practice current at that time, the thinking that brought about the change, the discussions of effective learning and what it meant for practice:

Our first responsibility as professionals was to determine with great detail and precision those strategies of teaching which led to success in becoming literate and to try to explain why this was so in each case. (1992, p. 3)

He stressed the need to rearticulate the aims and underlying learning potential of the activity. As professional practice gains wider currency in the educational world and commercial ventures, such as publishing, become involved, it is necessary to reflect on the thinking behind the activity and not just the activity itself.

Being able to talk about practice is important. It is easy to use terminology, but what is needed is to explain what each person means when they use it. In education there are lots of terms and jargon that imply views of learning. When teachers use jargon such as 'the child is not ready for the next stage', 'group work', 'differentiation', 'child centred', they are all alluding to views of learning that have been incorporated in their thinking. But not everyone means the same things by these terms. We are arguing for the role of dialogue as an important factor in the effective management of change. We are using the term to imply time for reflection and time for discussion. Reflection allows teachers to take the position of researchers of their own teaching. This can be an empowering process that may point the way to teachers gaining control of their own practice and the profession, to an extent compatible with the political context. Such a position will allow us to move beyond defending our teaching in a polarized way, and towards detailed, focused discussions that will make a difference to practice. This may make it easier to take on board curriculum changes as they arise, whether these are imposed or self-initiated.

School Development Plan

A school's development plan is a key to implementing change. It is focused on the aims of the school and brings together aspects of a school's planning by listing, prioritizing, pacing, and organizing development. As schools are accountable to their governors, governors need to be involved in planning. A development plan turns

Enquiry Task

If you look more closely at the term 'group work', what does this term mean?

- Write down your definition of group work.
- Do you use group work?
- Why or why not?
- If you do, list the circumstances when you use it.
- Do the children work *in* groups or *as* a group?
- How big is a group? Why this size?
- How do you plan to develop collaboration?
- Are the children supported in developing the ability to work together?

Make a list of the terms relating to group work that you and your colleagues use most frequently.

- What do you mean by them?
- How have you developed these notions?

long-term vision into a series of short-term goals. It is useful to have detailed priorities for one year and outlines of the subsequent four years.

Schools will need to prioritize in their development plan a timetable for a review of the curriculum and prepare to implement any changes arising from the new (i.e., post Dearing Report) curriculum.

Enquiry Task

- Has your school's development plan provided for time to review the curriculum?
- List the steps that you think are needed for such a review.
- Provide your ideal timetable for implementing the outcomes of this review.

Whole School Versus Individual Planning

The National Curriculum means that teachers can no longer plan in isolation. In order to ensure that all children have the possibility of progressing through the Key Stages, teachers needed to plan as a whole school and across a Key Stage. This was a particular concern at Key Stage 2 which covers four years of schooling.

The issue of planning for an entire Key Stage has generally been addressed in recent years so that schools can plan to meet the requirements of the National Curriculum. Teachers have had to take the discrete subjects of the National Curriculum and form a coherent curriculum. Mapping the curriculum at both a whole school and Key Stage level has helped ensure continuity and progression. Team planning at a year-group level has helped share expertise and work load.

Developing a 'Broad and Balanced' Curriculum

A 'broad and balanced curriculum' has become a common phrase as if 'broad' and 'balanced' are synonymous terms. Yet they mean subtly different things. They have often been looked at in terms of time allocation. This in itself is not an indicator of the quality of the teaching or likely learning. It may be more helpful to think of the diversity and challenge for which you need to plan.

The National Curriculum highlighted areas of the curriculum which were not being addressed or were covered inadequately; for example, science was not generally taught in as much detail as the National Curriculum required. This led to science becoming a focus for schools' inservice training. In the new National Curriculum there is not as much required content as in the original. This will help reduce work overload, but you will still need to plan for breadth across the curriculum.

The original National Curriculum with its emphasis on a broad range of subject knowledge led to a lack of focus on literacy and numeracy. It was hard to cover all the content in all subjects at Key Stages 1 and 2 without skimming the surface. The new National Curriculum is characterized by an emphasis on the core curriculum. Now the danger is that the curriculum might become too narrow and heavily weighted towards the core curriculum. Schools will need to plan to effectively teach the core curriculum while keeping a balance across the range of subjects.

Enquiry Task

- What do you mean by *broad* and by *balanced* when used in the context of a school's curriculum?
- What steps does your school take to ensure that the curriculum for all pupils is both broad and balanced?
- Does your school offer a broad and balanced curriculum?

Equal Opportunities

The National Curriculum is an entitlement curriculum. All children are entitled to a broad and balanced curriculum. Pupils have the right to participate in a common range of experiences. Children with special needs are entitled to follow the same curricular path as all other children. National Curriculum documentation does not make equal opportunities an explicit issue in every subject. The National Curriculum Council (1990) referred to equal opportunities as a 'dimension' of the curriculum, but did not provide any guidance. The Runnymede Trust (1993) filled this gap, with regard to issues of race, with a useful publication *Equality Assurance in Schools*. In some instances, such as children for whom English is not their first language, no recognition is given in the curriculum of the important place their first language plays in their identity and development. It is often how we teach and not what we teach that influences children's access to the curriculum. For example, the way we approach mathematics will influence girls' and boys' views of their ability to be mathematicians (Walkerdine, 1989)

Enquiry Task

- How do you ensure high-quality education for *all* pupils?
- How do you support the development of cultural and personal identities?
- How do you prepare pupils for full participation in society?
- List the actions you take on each of the issues above.
- Discuss your list with a colleague.
- Identify one area where you might do more and list actions you might take.

Planning for Differentiation

Attainment varies widely amongst children. Most children's attainment varies from subject to subject and within each subject. Differentiation is not a new idea although the term has only recently become widely used. Teachers have been used to the idea of matching tasks to children's needs. Teachers influenced by the Plowden Report (1967) matched the curriculum to the child. Now we are being asked to match the child to the curriculum. It may be unhelpful to talk about a differentiated curriculum as it is not the curriculum that needs to be differentiated but children's learning. Differentiation means:

> planning, resourcing, and implementing a curriculum which is sufficiently relevant and coherent to interest challenge and advance the intellectual growth of a class of individual children. Savva (1991, p. 2)

Enquiry Task

- How do you plan for differentiation?
- Find out how two colleagues plan for differentiation.
- How do your views compare with those of your colleagues?
- Compare your practice with those implied in your school's policy documents.

Subject versus Topic Organization

There has been a debate for many years about subject as opposed to topic organization. Since the Plowden Report (1967) there has been a move from subject to topic teaching. Teachers were concerned to make links between subjects in order to teach in a holistic way and help children (especially young children) make connections, rather than see learning as fragmented pieces of knowledge. This led to topic webs and flow diagrams as a form of planning. When topic planning was done well, useful links were made across areas of knowledge and understanding. These links need to be made explicit so that children understand the connections in the teacher's planning. By asking children what understandings they are making, teachers can gain insight into whether children are making the same connections to the ones intended by the teacher.

Alexander, Rose and Woodhead (1992) suggested that teachers should review their thinking about topics and subjects. While they support the view that a topic approach in skilled hands can produce work of high quality, they also believe it is important to consider subject teaching where appropriate. For example, stories should be read even if they are not relevant to the topic because they are of value in their own right. OFSTED (1993) outlined factors associated with successful topic work. These included an agreed system of cooperative planning which took careful account of National Curriculum requirements and were tightly focused.

Enquiry Task

- List the types of learning that you feel are effectively taught in topics?
- How tightly focused are these topics?
- Define the kinds of meaningful connections that can be made in a topic.
- What types of learning do you feel can be taught effectively in subjects?
- In what ways has your, or your school's, approach to topic work changed over the past five years?

Many schools have found it useful to plan in terms of:

- broad themes, e.g., ourselves;
- topics led by one or two curriculum subjects, e.g., the history of the local area;
- subject teaching in tightly focused units e.g., electricity;
- regular daily or weekly work, e.g., paired reading.

Resources

Schools are now responsible for maintaining their own budgets. Planning for resources needs to be part of a whole-school approach. It involves a long-term view, aimed at achieving high educational outcomes, which reflect equal opportunities and current views on learning. Schools need to assess whether spending priorities match educational priorities. Resources come in many forms. We tend to think first of classroom materials. Central resource areas and classroom-based materials need to be reviewed regularly in order to ensure they meet the needs of the children.

Making the best use of the expertise of teaching and non-teaching staff (for example, through team planning, team teaching, INSET and curriculum coordination) encourages the best use of human resources and also develops expertise across the staff. Parents and people in the community are valuable human resources that need to be incorporated in the school development plan so that the school is firmly rooted in the community in which it is located.

Time is a precious resource which needs to be managed effectively. The length of time spent on an activity is not necessarily an indication of its quality. The complexity of the organization of the children and curriculum activities influences the amount of time you have to engage with children's learning. For example, a teacher who encourages children to become independent learners, through the labelling and displaying of resources, will need to spend less time allocating materials.

Enquiry Task

- Do you know the school's policy for overviewing, updating and deploying resources? If not, find out what it is.
- How do you set out your classroom for learning?
- How are areas in the school used to support learning?
- List the ways that you ensure that equal opportunities are reflected in your resources.
- List the ways you manage human resources.
- Discuss your list with a colleague.
- Are there other ways you could optimize your use of resources?
- Design a method to find out how much of your time is spent managing organization and behaviour rather than focusing directly on learning.

The Learning Cycle

Many people view learning as a complex, recursive process. Such a view is at odds with a linear system of learning, such as a National Curriculum based on levels of attainment. Teachers have to find ways of helping children revisit areas of learning with increasing depth. For example, rereading a picture book such as *Not Now, Bernard* (McKee, 1987) may encourage further readings beyond the literal.

Teaching and learning are not synonymous terms. Children do not always learn what teachers think they have taught. All learners bring their own experience to a given situation and construct meanings which incorporate these prior experiences. For teachers, this involves finding out about children's present understandings and knowledge. For example, when starting a unit of work, you could ask the children what they already know (see Chapter 5 for more details of how you can do this). As work progresses, it is important that you regularly assess what has been learned in order to gauge the children's new level of understanding. If you refer to your initial brainstorms, you and the children can reflect on what has been learned. This will supplement your understanding of the children's development that you are also gaining through your observations and sampling of children's work.

Children need time to engage with practical activities and, more importantly, time to develop concepts. Although concept development is a long-term process, concepts, as well as knowledge and skills, need to be stated in lesson planning. Concepts are important since they help children to make connections in their learning. Children need to be helped to construct links between previous and new learning. For example, a child may have noticed the sequence of colours which appear when sunlight shines through a fish tank. She will almost certainly have noticed the rainbow that can be seen sometimes when sunlight shines through rain. However, unless encouraged to by the teacher, she is unlikely to have made any connections between these two, apparently, quite separate events.

Involving Children in Planning

The National Curriculum is to a large extent prescribed and so there are difficulties in involving children with planning. Indeed, planning should not be left until you are actually sitting in front of the children. This presents us with the dilemma of helping children feel ownership of the work without us abdicating our responsibility as teachers for planning. For example, one of us was asked to team-teach a unit of work on Britain since the 1930s and took the opportunity to investigate the extent to which the children could be involved in the planning. After asking children what they knew, she then asked the children what they would like to know about the topic. When she compared the children's contributions with her planning and with the National Curriculum, she were pleasantly surprised by the extensive overlap. She realized that she had to add work on World War II of which the children were unaware. In addition to indicating their knowledge of the subject, by being asked to contribute to the planning, the children had a clear understanding and commitment to the unit of work.

Planning also needs to be flexible enough to be able to accommodate spontaneous occurrences: children's interests need to be recognized and valued. The time taken in responding to this may vary. You may wish to respond immediately with the whole class, for example, to a sudden hail storm. You may allow a child or group of children time to find information about an object that has been brought into the classroom. You may wish to gather resources with the children to do a mini-focus the following week. When teachers felt the curriculum was overloaded, they found it difficult to allow time for this. With the new curriculum it should be possible to incorporate such flexible teaching into the 20 per cent discretionary time.

Assessment

Assessment must be an integral part of the teaching and learning cycle. When assessing, you need to refer to the lesson aims in your planning. It is important to remember that the purpose of assessment is to help you gain insight into children's understanding that will influence your future provision. You need to continually monitor and assess the activities as they take place in the classroom. Teacher assessment should include observation and sampling in order to construct a detailed picture of each child's development over a period of time.

Children need to be involved in evaluating their own learning. Parents and others concerned with the child's education have a role, too, in building up a whole view of the child's learning. If children's first language is not English, their understandings in all their languages should be recorded.

Ongoing teacher assessment will inform statutory assessment at the end of each Key Stage. Thus a whole-school overview of the learning cycle and record keeping are crucial.

Enquiry Task

- In your school, how is assessment part of a whole school view of planning?
- Make a list of information that should be passed on to the next teacher.
- How do you assess the effectiveness of your own planning as well as children's learning?
- List ways your evaluation and records might be improved.

Using the Discretionary Time

The changes outlined in the 1993 review of the curriculum (Dearing, 1993) are aimed at reducing prescription and allowing you to have greater day-to-day control of your work. However, Dearing (1993) has stipulated that:

> The first priority for discretionary time must be to support work in the basics of literacy, oracy and numeracy . . . Schools should be accountable to their governing bodies for using the time released effectively. The school's decisions should be recorded and available for inspection. (p. 7)

Enquiry Task

In order to decide what to include in the 20 per cent discretionary time you may wish to consider the following issues:

- What strategies do you consider important for developing literacy, oracy and numeracy in your classroom? Which of these strategies are in place at the moment?
- What areas of learning not currently present in your school's curriculum do you feel are important to include now?
- How much of what has been removed from the statutory orders do you wish to reinstate?

Over the past five years, schools have become much more experienced at implementing change, reflecting on practice and delivering a broader curriculum. The critical question is one relating to how schools, and in particular your school, will review their curriculum. Will your school stay within the narrow confines of what it now feels to be familiar, if not comfortable with, or will it use the latest legislation to reconsider its philosophy and views of learning and in doing so rethink its approach to the planning of the whole curriculum?

Enquiry Task

At each level of planning (whole school, Key Stage, year group, class) review:

- What do you want to keep of your present plans?
- What needs to be changed?

Summary

This chapter has focused on issues related to defining a curriculum.

- No curriculum is value free. Decisions on what a curriculum is, how it is determined and organized have to be ongoing discussions.
- Whole school planning is an important element in supporting change.
- While curriculum changes are imposed, it is important for you to root these changes firmly in your views of the teaching and learning cycle.
- Being able to provide a rationale for why you teach in a particular way is part of being an effective professional. Any rationale needs to be based in understandings about learning, rather than a mere reciting of current jargon.
- Being able to outline explicitly such views is ultimately empowering for teachers as individuals and collectively as a profession.

References

ALEXANDER, R. (1992) *Policy and Practice in Primary Education*, London: Routledge.
ALEXANDER, R., ROSE, J. and WOODHEAD, C. (1992) *Curriculum Organisation and Classroom Practice in Primary Schools: A Discussion Paper*, London: DES.
DEARING, R. (1993) *The National Curriculum and its Assessment: Final Report*, London: SCAA.
HMI (1985) *The Curriculum from 5 to 16, Curriculum Matters*, London: DES.
HOLDAWAY, D. (1979) *The Foundations of Literacy*, London: Scholastic.
NATIONAL CURRICULUM COUNCIL (1989) *A Framework for the Primary Curriculum*, London: NCC.
NATIONAL CURRICULUM COUNCIL (1990) *The Whole Curriculum: Curriculum Guidance 3*, London: NCC.

OFFICE FOR STANDARDS IN EDUCATION (1993) *Curriculum Organisation and Classroom Practice in Primary Schools: A Follow-up Report*, London: DFE.

PLOWDEN REPORT (1967) *Children and their Primary Schools: Vol. 1*, London: HMSO.

RUNNYMEDE TRUST (1993) *Equality Assurance in Schools: Quality, Identity, Society: A Handbook for Action Planning and School Effectiveness*, Trentham Books.

SAVVA, H. (1991) 'Differentiation,' unpublished paper, London Borough of Kensington and Chelsea.

SCHOOL EXAMINATION and ASSESSMENT COUNCIL (1993) *The National Curriculum and its Assessment: An Interim Report*, London: SEAC.

WALKERDINE, V. (1989) *Counting Girls Out*, London: Virago.

Further Reading

BOURNE, J. (1994) *Thinking Through Primary Practice*, Milton Keynes: Open University/Routledge.

POLLARD, A. and BOURNE, J. (1994) *Teaching and Learning in the Primary School*, Milton Keynes: Open University/Routledge.

The Subjects in the New National Curriculum

3   English

Helena Mitchell and Jenny Monk

Introduction

The new National Curriculum for English has only three Attainment Targets: Speaking and Listening, Reading, and Writing, in place of the original five. This has been achieved through combining the original Attainment Targets: Writing, Spelling and Handwriting, so that spelling and handwriting are incorporated into Writing.

There is an increased emphasis on the Programmes of Study for both planning and assessment; each Programme of Study is clearly and consistently structured so that the document is more readily accessible to its readers. For the purposes of this chapter we have chosen to use this structure as our basic framework. Each section therefore develops certain themes; these are: Range, Key Skills, Standard English and Language Study.

As for some of the other National Curriculum subjects, there are eight Level Descriptors for each Attainment Target; for English, each descriptor is termed synoptic, in that it is a composite description made up of three or more distinct skills or aspects.

Professional judgment is emphasized; the synoptic descriptors are intended to provide a useful basis from which you can work. It is clear that your school will need to have a clear and consistent policy for language development supported by ongoing staff INSET and professional development if this approach is to be successful. The Programmes of Study for English need careful unpacking if they are to form a valid and cohesive curriculum. You need to bear in mind that this is a curriculum intended for seven years' work. With this in mind, this chapter can only be an introduction to the complex and multifaceted field of language and literacy. We have attempted to provide some practical tasks which can be used either individually or as part of a whole staff development programme.

Speaking and Listening

The general requirements for Speaking and Listening foreground the importance of children learning to use standard English. As teachers, you will recognize that this is a developmental process that can be achieved only, as the document states, by introducing it with 'appropriate sensitivity'. The Programmes of Study suggest many activities to promote the development of talk: used in conjunction with materials produced by the National Oracy Project, for example, *Teaching, Talking, and Learning at Key Stages 1 and 2*, (NOP/NCC, 1990), a worthwhile curriculum can be planned. A chapter of this length cannot do justice to the importance of the language variety present in schools, and in the wider, multicultural society. Proficiency in other languages should be seen as an advantage; most of the world's population is at least bilingual. If you are working with bilingual children you will be able to build upon the facility with which these children can use and discuss language.

Speaking and Listening at Key Stage 1

Range

It is clear from the wealth of ideas provided in this section, that purposeful talk is best developed through an integrated programme of activities. The importance of providing real and meaningful talk opportunities cannot be overemphasized. It is only through these that the subtle differences of register required in different situations will become apparent. Opportunities are needed for imaginative play and drama. Regular thematic play situations will need to be built into your planning so that children can rehearse a range of roles from real–life situations, e.g., café, doctor's surgery, museum.

Key Skills

Skills of turn-taking, confidence and precision can only be achieved through children being given the opportunity to work in small groups on focused tasks with clear outcomes. Involving adults – e.g., parents, learning support assistants, and visitors – will provide children with a range of different views, role models, and the opportunity to rehearse and clarify their ideas with adult support. Wells (1986) has demonstrated the crucial role of the adult in furthering language development. There is also a clear link in this section of the National Curriculum Order between children's talk and the range of writing required by the Programmes of Study. Until children have been given the opportunity to rehearse ideas orally, they will find it very difficult to write -coherently. Differences between spoken and written English can be identified and discussed in a meaningful context.

Standard English and Language Study

All people have the facility to use an appropriate repertoire of language forms if given the opportunity to do so. Defining what standard English is presents difficulties; Stubbs, (1983), calls it 'fluid, shifting and ill defined'. You need to know what is appropriate, and this can only be learned through a wide range of experiences that provide the opportunity to practise, to reflect and to become familiar with the repertoire of language in use.

Enquiry Task

Take any nursery rhyme, e.g., Jack and Jill. Discuss with your children the different roles they might play:

- mother talks to Jack about the incident;
- television reporter talks to camera recounting the event;
- Jill returns with her version of the events;
- mother talks to the doctor.

Taking on a range of roles in this way develops children's awareness of the choices they can make in their use of language.

Speaking and Listening at Key Stage 2

It is important to recognize both the interrelated nature of the Programmes of Study and the specific demands of the section on speaking and listening. In addition to the work of the National Oracy Project, publications from the Leverhulme Project (Carre, 1990) provide many helpful suggestions for developing the skills of questioning and explanation through a variety of teaching situations.

Range

The range of speaking and listening activities outlined in the National Curriculum Order is clear and concise. Your planning needs to take account of the following questions:

- How can I ensure that I am building upon the work begun in Key Stage 1?
- Am I developing this range in all areas of the curriculum, and, if so, how is it planned for and recorded?
- How do I ensure that all children have the opportunity to participate?

A variety of role-play situations could be explored as a follow-up activity to reading a text. For example, using *The Highwayman* (Noyes, 1913), children can discuss in groups the roles of the different characters and then devise questions to elicit their motives and the reasons for their actions. These characters could then be interviewed (or hot-seated) in role.

Key skills

Key skills in speaking and listening are complex and interrelated, and will need to be developed across the curriculum and over time. To benefit fully from activities you will need to allocate sufficient time for children's talk to move from exploratory and tentative comments to reasoned and reflective conclusions or actions. For example, using an issue current in the media, children could first explore the main arguments as they are presented in a variety of sources, and then assume roles in order for these arguments to be challenged in interviews conducted by their peers. In this way, children will be listening, questioning, justifying and clarifying their points of view. This will also form part of an integrated programme of speaking, listening, reading and writing.

Standard English and language study

Activities such as those outlined above will provide many opportunities for discussion and use of both standard English and other dialects, and for explicit discussion of the features of both written and spoken forms. Drama and media education have a very significant role to play in enriching and extending language repertoire. They provide a wealth of opportunity for experiencing the richness of our language in its many and varied forms.

Reading

Reading at Key Stage 1

Reading at Key Stage 1 is primarily concerned with the early stages of reading, but emphasizes the need to ensure that you take full account of individual children's development. The Programmes of Study should be used flexibly, both for children who start school and are already reading fluently, as well as for those whose experience of literacy is limited. Clearly, you cannot start at the same point with every child.

The purpose of this section is to look at the sort of activities that you could use to promote the development of reading in the early stages. It needs to be emphasized, however, that some children may already be working at levels beyond this. Although children at Key Stage 1 will need to focus upon developing a knowledge and understanding of print, the alphabet, and the beginnings of sound symbol correspondence, they should be doing so with meaningful texts that conform to the criteria in paragraph 1c of the order. If such texts are not being used, children will be unable to use grammatical knowledge and contextual understanding to check for meaning. Furthermore, as the Programme of Study demands that children are given 'extensive experience' of children's literature in the range of their reading, you will be able to meet this criterion to a greater or lesser extent, through the texts you make available to the children.

Range

The most crucial concern, and the thread which runs strongly through Key Stage 1 Reading, is the importance of teachers using good-quality literature extensively in order to promote and to teach reading. Non-fiction texts, presented traditionally and also on screen, need to be included within this definition of literature. All texts can be used through reading and discussion to stimulate imagination and enthusiasm.

You will need to ensure that you present children with as wide a range of literature as possible, both drawing upon children's own experience and also presenting them with vicarious experience. The importance of rhyme and rhythm is emphasized, as is the use of visually stimulating illustrations. The categories of literature are clearly set out in the new Order, and should include the familiar and the fantastic, folk and fairy tales, and stories and poems from a range of cultures.

Enquiry Task

Developing knowledge of organizational and presentational technique (paragraph 2c)

- Select five or six narrative texts (possibly all picture books, or some picture books, and some longer texts).
- Read the first one or two sentences of each.
- Write each one down on a large flip chart.
- Consider similarities and differences between each.
- Ask children to predict what they think will happen in each story.
- Choose one to read entirely (through consensus).
- Discuss whether outcomes matched predictions and consider the text's ending.

Activities such as these might also focus upon the development of characterization and plot in the text.

Key skills

The Programmes of Study place an increased emphasis upon word recognition and the development of phonic and graphic knowledge. However, these need to be placed within a balanced and coherent programme so that children are not expected to learn these relationships in isolation, nor with meaningless texts. The importance of rhyme and rhythm is recognized, as shown by Bryant and Bradley (1985) and Goswami (1993). Such an approach allows us to utilize collections of poetry and rhyme to promote the development of phonic and graphic knowledge through amusing, interactive texts. The use of big books, such as the *Storytime Giants*, (Oliver and Boyd, 1989) will enable you to promote the recognition of alliteration and rhyme.

Enquiry Task

Developing phonological awareness

- Select two or three rhyming or poetry books, (Dr Seuss books are excellent, as is poetry by the Ahlbergs and Michael Rosen).
- With a group of five or six children, read selected entries.
- Ask the children if they can hear any words which sound the same.
- Make a list of the words they identify.
- Ask the children to suggest any others that they know which sound similar and could be added to the list.
- Share the words with the rest of the class at a class discussion time.

This activity is best done with big books of rhymes if available; if not, you could make your own class versions.

Tasks, such as the one above, also allow you to develop understanding and response by discussing with the children your enjoyment and response to the texts. You might use such activities to promote a range of reading knowledge, rather than simply focusing upon single aspects of the key skills. This notion of balanced and flexible approaches to the teaching of reading was highlighted by HMI (DES, 1990). You will need to draw upon various methods and not overemphasize one approach. Parental involvement in reading has been shown to be of great benefit when well organized, but needs to be undertaken with commitment, concern and interest on the part of both parents and teachers. You will need to be prepared to listen to parental concerns as well as to inform and guide them.

Reading at Key Stage 2

Reading at Key Stage 2 focuses upon enthusiasm, independence and response. These were key features of the Cox Report, (DES, 1985) and are fundamental to the development of reading from the initial stages through to GCSE and beyond. The purpose of this section is to develop your confidence in planning for reading at this stage and to suggest ways in which children can become critical readers.

Enquiry Task

Carry out an audit to ascertain whether your collection of reading material contains:

- books for inexperienced readers who still need support;
- books for newly independent and independent readers who are developing confidence and reading stamina;
- books for the experienced and fluent readers;
- a wide selection of poetry.

Range

In order for the full range of texts to be available to, and read by pupils, the collection in every classroom at Key Stage 2 should reflect diversity, sophistication and complexity and, in addition, cater for the differentiated needs of all children. In providing this range of reading material, you will be able to develop the important ideas of understanding and response.

Understanding involves much more than old style comprehension. It embodies notions of:

- confidence in choosing, discussing, and summarizing texts;
- appreciation of both the major points in a text, and its subtleties and ambiguities;
- familiarity with reference material and retrieval strategies.

Response is complex and difficult to describe. It involves the reader in:

- expressing opinions with references to the text;
- being aware of themes and images and considering the structure of texts and the use of language.

Enquiry Task

Developing a range of reading

Consider the following as they relate to your classroom:

- How do pupils learn to choose a text to read?
- How are the books organized, e.g., by author, genre, in sets?
- Is there a poetry collection?
- How is progression monitored?
- What reading records are kept and how do these reflect both the programmes of study and personal response?

In developing group discussions of texts you may wish to consider some or all of the following issues:

- Your role in modelling and demonstrating the process of critical reflection.
- In what ways group discussion can develop children's critical response to their private and personal reading of fiction, non-fiction and media texts.
- How can learning-support staff and parents be included in reading related activities?

Detailed accounts of the implementation of booktalk activities can be found in three articles in *Language and Learning* (Davies, Karavis and Monk, 1993)

Key skills

In developing the key skills, and in particular those outlined in paragraph 2b of the orders, it is important to bear in mind that the reading of any new text will be influenced by previous experience. Therefore, a whole school policy on the teaching of reading must be central to this development. The HMI Report on the *Teaching and Learning of Reading* (DES, 1990), highlighted the importance of the leadership of the head, the quality of teaching, and the organization and management of work on reading as being 'strongly associated with pupils' achievements in reading', (paragraphs 2 and 54). Thus, ideally, each of the suggestions outlined below should be discussed with your colleagues, in the context of your school's reading policy.

You may wish to consider the following description of response in the light of your own reading and in relation to planning for the key skills for reading at Key Stage 2. It is adapted from *Teaching of Reading 2*, one of a series of papers on the teaching of reading produced by Oxfordshire County Council (OCC, 1993).

Initial response	An immediate reaction to what has been read or heard; the reader may consider alone or with others and this may lead to an informal recommendation.
	(This can be achieved in the classroom through: oral book reviews, story swaps, top ten lists, etc.)
Considered response	A reflection on an initial response; the reader questions alone, or in discussion with others, what is suggested or hinted at in the text and/or illustration.
	(You will need to promote the discussion of: story openings, scene setting, mood and character introduction; character actions and motives; story structure and plot development.)
Reconsidered response	A more conscious exploration of possible meanings; the reader thinks beyond the literal meaning to what is implied; the reader may make associations with past experiences or previous reading.
	(You will need to draw attention to inferential meanings within a text, e.g., through consideration of a character's actions. Comparisons can be made between different tellings of folk and classic tales in traditional and modern settings, e.g., *Arthurian Legends, The Odyssey*.)
Critical response	In challenging and questioning the values embedded in the text, the reader questions the author's intentions and is required to make a viewpoint explicit to others.
	(Your pupils will need time to discuss and compare texts; to make links across a range of texts; to reflect on initial impressions of their reading to justify their opinions with reference to details in the text and/or illustrations, and to

consider thematic links, e.g., bravery, jealousy, a view of the future. An excellent framework for booktalk can be found in *Tell Me* (Chambers, 1993)

Reading across the curriculum

When faced with a text dealing with a subject about which we know little, we become novice readers once more. Every kind of reading requires different reading strategies. The Programmes of Study identify this and outline a comprehensive list of strategies required to read and learn from non-fiction texts (paragraph 2c). The difficulty in school with regard to this issue is that, as a rule, children learn to read through fiction and they experience difficulty in adjusting their reading behaviour to non-fiction texts. The work of Littlefair (1991), Mallett (1992) and Neate (1992) has begun to outline some of the challenges and solutions. Pupils need a clear purpose and a structured opportunity to extract and absorb information and to *use it purposefully for a known outcome* (OCC, 1993).

A successful way of helping children to achieve this is through the representation of information as a documentary sound-bite, a newspaper report or an interview. To support this you will therefore need to: read aloud to pupils from non-fiction texts; discuss text organization and page layout; discuss vocabulary and word usage, particularly with regard to subject specific vocabulary; demonstrate and provide activities that help pupils to read and extract information, e.g., underlining, high-lighting, and; demonstrate how to represent information in chart, diagrammatic or tabular form, or in any of the ways outlined above.

There are many other suggestions in the work of Neate (1992) and Mallett (1992), and new developments can be found in the work of Lewis and Wray with the EXEL Project (1994).

Standard English and language study

By linking an understanding of text structure with knowledge about language, it is possible to develop schemes of work that include work on the following important areas of language study:

* explicit discussion of the features of certain texts;
* comparisons of texts to show how authors exploit creatively the features of a genre;
* awareness of how language changes over time;
* discussion of word derivation, root words and loan words to aid under-standing;
* discussion of the differences between fact and opinion.

An ideal way of developing this knowledge is to focus on different tellings or versions of one fairy tale. For example, in a recent study, children have compared an Anthony Browne version of *Hansel and Gretel* with that by Tony Ross and then compared these with the range they found at home, at school and in the library. The work is recorded in 'Becoming a Reader 2', (Davies *et al*, 1993).

Writing

This section will focus upon the importance of an understanding of form, audience and purpose in the writing process. For a clear perspective on this, it is important that the whole issue of the writing curriculum is studied in the context of recent research. The research referred to has its roots firmly embedded in classroom practice.

The Cox Report differentiated clearly between the compositional and secretarial aspects of writing. The former encapsulates knowledge of form and purpose, an awareness of reader or audience, and increasing control over organization and language features. The latter is concerned with spelling, punctuation, handwriting and presentation. In combining these two distinct elements, the new Order is in danger of returning us to the state of affairs that was typified in the Assessment of Performance Unit's (APU) research, where children could discuss improving their writing only in terms of their spelling and handwriting, i.e., its surface features.

Chapter 17 of the Cox Report, 'English 5–16', (DES, 1985), is essential reading for all teachers. This chapter outlines clearly the function of written language and the relationship between spoken and written language. The teacher has an important role to play in planning a writing curriculum, where a range of writing is produced, where there is growing attention to the differences between speech and writing, and where the teacher intervenes in the child's learning most often by carefully structuring the context for learning.

To this end, the work of the National Writing Project (1987), the APU (1986), the Language in the National Curriculum (LINC) Project (1992), and writers such as Czerniewska (1992) and Perera (1984), have all contributed to the growing confidence with which teachers are planning, evaluating and assessing the writing in their classes.

Writing at Key Stage 1

Writing at Key Stage 1 emphasizes that writing is for communication; children need to be writing for real purposes and audiences that they can identify for themselves. The integration of punctuation, spelling, and handwriting is outlined clearly, but needs to be developed alongside composition skills, and not separately.

Range

Children need to be given opportunities to write for a range of audiences; to identify who these audiences are; to be aware of the purpose for their writing and where the particular type of writing may be found in the world outside school.

In order to provide a range of purposes, you will need to plan for a range of different activities which stimulate writing. In providing such a range, you will need to give your children the opportunity to use a variety of different forms for their writing. These forms should include narrative, notes, records, and messages. A classroom writing area will help to provide opportunities for writing. Such an area could include postcards, writing paper, and scrap paper for lists, etc., as well as individual books in various shapes and sizes, all of which children can use for different writing tasks. Chronological writing, such as stories, can be developed more easily if children are given the opportunity, and support, to write an entire book (perhaps a 'zig zag') of their own. Writing such as lists, signs, and recipes, needs a different format. All writing needs to be prefaced, and accompanied, by the chance for children to discuss content and format, and to consider how they can extend their writing.

Enquiry Task

Developing a range of writing

- Choose a picture book with a strong, clear storyline, e.g., *Suddenly* (McNaughton, 1994).
- Read the book and discuss the story with the children, focusing especially on the different characters, e.g., Mum, the wolf, the pig.
- What happens to each of them in the story? How does each of them feel at the end?
- Suggest that each child writes a letter to a friend with their version of the story. Provide the children with a list of what would need to be in each letter.
- Let children work collaboratively in composing one of these.
- Other types of writing could also be discussed and developed, e.g., a poster for the wolf's capture, a menu in the wolf's café, the little pig's shopping list.

Key skills

Independent writing should be part of the classroom, and children need to be given opportunities to write independently in a range of situations. You can provide these through creating role-play situations in the classroom, e.g., travel agent, café, and also by encouraging writing in a writing corner, such as that described above. Other parts of the classroom, such as the construction area, can also provide opportunities for developmental writing.

Children using independent writing are approximating to the standard form, and therefore need to be given support in the classroom with word lists, notices and signs, and the chance to use the knowledge gained from their reading in their writing. Word processing programs, such as Flexiwrite, can help children to develop appropriate formats for their writing, and can enable children to concentrate on the construction of their writing, rather than on the secretarial skills. In order to create the best outcome for their purpose children must be able to write directly onto the screen, and to experiment with moving text around to create the best outcome for their purpose. Using word processing solely for the purpose of presenting writing that has been written by hand already does not enable children to make full use of the technology that is available to them. Working collaboratively can be especially beneficial at this age; children can support each other and develop their ideas more appropriately through discussion. Many children will also need you to scribe for them, providing a writing model, and enabling them to focus on the composition of their writing.

The difference between spoken and written English will need to be emphasized, so that children begin to take on written forms of language, to acquire literary language, and to discriminate between the two. Punctuation can only be taught effectively through a focus upon children's own writing; discussing where there are pauses, and which punctuation fits where. Reading text aloud enables children to hear where the text needs punctuation in order to facilitate meaning.

Spelling needs to build upon the knowledge of the writing system that children bring with them to school; the promotion of independent writing will allow this and also give an indication of how children know. In addition, children need to know about common letter strings and patterns, and to look for words within words. With very young children, their own names can provide a starting point for such work; identifying the letters which compose it, looking for similarities between names, looking for words which occur within names. The development of spelling may be linked effectively with handwriting (see Cripps and Ede, 1991). If children are taught to write cursively from the beginning, practice in handwriting can reinforce common spelling patterns and help to establish them.

Handwriting needs to be practised regularly and systematically, but briefly. Again, resources are important with a range of suitable writing materials including thick and thin pencils, well sharpened and of sufficient length.

Standard English and language study

The links between spoken and written English are especially pertinent when considering standard English. Reading aloud from a wide range of texts, and discussing its format and features, will help to draw children's attention to the different ways that language can be constructed. With children's own writing, they can be encouraged to edit their work, and to consider changing its construction in order to make it more effective. Working with a writing partner can also be very productive here, enabling children to discuss the features of their writing that need change and development.

Writing at Key Stage 2

Writing at Key Stage 2 is characterized by pupils' progress in the writing of a range of forms for a variety of purposes. It is essential to consider this element because from that experience will come the knowledge about language and language use. The Cox Report (DES, 1985) in its insistence upon both chronological and non-chronological forms of writing, undoubtedly helped to broaden the writing curriculum. Heated debate centred around this issue but, as a result, teachers did begin to differentiate more knowledgably in their planning, and were also able to articulate explicitly what they had known implicitly. In this context, and with a clear understanding of the differences between compositional and secretarial skills, you can consider the key skills in the new Order.

Key skills

The grammar of a text is dependent upon its form and purpose. Awareness of this on your part, leads to a recognition of the need for pupils to know about language so that they can use it appropriately. The new Order for English over-simplifies this and suggests that differences are to do with degrees of formality. This does not do justice to the complex process involved in the transition that writers make from spoken to written language. In acquiring new forms, as the Cox Report, (DES, 1985) states so clearly, '. . . the language competence acquired is additive: it does not replace earlier competencies. . . . written language is not just spoken language written down' (paragraph 17.6).

In your planning do you consider the following points?

Immersion	Until children have heard a range of texts read aloud, read them for themselves *and* discussed them, they will be unable to write text similar in style for themselves.
Demonstration	Children need to see how a text is constructed. You can do this through shared writing, with you as their scribe, if necessary, and go through the process of planning, drafting and revising with the children.
Focusing	In making some of the features of text differences explicit on print to the children, you can focus on aspects of *text organization, word order, vocabulary, style, punctuation and spelling*. It is a waste of valuable time to look, separately, at these through exercises devoid of context. The most effective way of developing competence in written language, as outlined in the section on key skills, is in the context of the children's own writing.

In working with students, we have found the following table helpful in identifying the types of text and the forms writing might take. For example, letters can persuade, describe or narrate. In planning the writing, you may wish to refer to the very useful framework produced by the National Writing Project (SCDC, 1987) in *Reasons for Writing* (pp. 14–15). It asks the following questions.

- What do we use writing for?
- Who do we write for? Who reads it?

- What happens to the writing when it is finished?
- What makes for effective writing?
- What are the different formats for writing?
- How do we develop writing capabilities?

Assessment

The new Programmes of Study offer little guidance on assessment and recording, but with teacher assessment being of greater importance, it is even more important for everyone in your school to introduce agreed methods that truly reflect the developing abilities of each pupil. Reading interviews held once or twice a term, for example, can focus on range, preference and response, and provide you with information to inform your planning for individuals, groups, or the whole class. The

Table 3.1: *Identifying types of text and the forms writing might take*

Form	Type	Purpose	Examples
Poetry	Narrative	to entertain, to challenge	*Hiawatha* Longfellow
	Description	to create an impression or image	*The Highwayman* Noyes
	Recount	to retell, to entertain, to frighten	*Eddie and the Gerbils* Rosen
	Argument	to present opinion, to challenge	*Veteran's Dream* Heaney
Letters	Instructions	to get something done	route map/directions
	Description	to create an effect, to inform	a journey, an occasion
	Argument/Discussion	to get something changed, to persuade	letter from bank manager letter to newspaper/MP
	Narrative/Recount	to inform, to entertain, to retell	holiday escapade/incident
	Report/Explanation	to inform, to summarize	state of affairs/findings
Poster or Notice	Information	to give details or facts	floor guide in department store
	Instructions	to get something done	cash machine
	Argument	to persuade	anti-smoking poster/ cigarette advertisement

Enquiry Task

- Using the grid, identify the types of writing that the work your children are doing at the moment lends itself to.
- Consider the range of texts produced by the class in any one week, half term or term. Does it reflect breadth and balance?
- Look across the curriculum to identify the types of writing that dominate the children's work. Is this a true reflection of the range required by the new Order? If not what are the implications for planning?

extended use of the running record for the assessment of reading in the early stages has heightened teachers' awareness of the need for a diagnostic approach.

It is good to see progress in writing characterized by a growing awareness of form, purpose and audience. Within that context, and with the support of the assessment frameworks for writing provided by the School Curriculum and Assessment Authority in the Key Stage 2 SAT materials, a wealth of information exists now on which to draw.

In addition to the framework for narrative writing, there is also, from 1995, a framework for the assessment of information/report writing. The Primary Language Record (Barrs, 1988) offers excellent frameworks for the assessment of all three language modes. Teacher assessment is central to the new Order and with increased confidence and professional development, assessment can be central to the planning of an integrated language curriculum that is both challenging and rigorous.

Conclusion

There is now the opportunity for a period of reflection and stability. For this new Order to be successful, however, it must become dynamic. Teachers need to gain ownership of it through a process of developing manageable schemes of work. Good teaching is central to the successful implementation of an English curriculum. English has discrete elements and cannot therefore be delivered solely through a topic. There is much work to be done on the teaching of reading at Key Stage 2, for example, and in developing a range of writing that will ensure equality of opportunity.

In this brief review of the new Order for English, we have attempted to put some flesh onto a very lean skeleton. Teachers and students need support and guidance; only then can their judgments become informed and truly reflective. The reflective practitioner seeks to adapt her practice in the light of experience and evaluation; a statutory document has no life without enthusiastic teachers.

References

APU WHITE, J. (1986) *The Assessment of Writing*, Windsor: NFER-Nelson.

BARRS, M. (*et al.*) (1988) *The Primary Language Record*, London: CLPE.

BROWNE, A. (illus.) (1986) *The Brothers Grimm: Hansel and Gretel*, London: Methuen.

BRYANT, P. and BRADLEY, L. (1985) *Children's Reading Problems*, Oxford: Blackwell.

CARRE, C. (ed) (1990) *Leverhulme Primary Project: Classroom Skills Series*, London: Routledge.

CHAMBERS, A. (1985) *Booktalk*, London, The Bodley Head.

CHAMBERS, A. (1993) *Tell Me*, Stroud: Thimble Press.

CRIPPS, C. and EDE, J. (1991) *A Hand for Spelling*, LDA.

CZERNIEWSKA, P. (1992) *How Children Learn to Write*, Oxford: Blackwell.

DAVIES, P., KARAVIS, S. and MONK, J. (1993) 'Becoming a reader', (3 articles) in *Language and Learning*, Birmingham: Questions.

DES (1975) *A Language for Life*, (Bullock Report), London: HMSO.

DES (1985) *English from 5 to 16*, (Cox Report) London: HMSO.

DES, HMI (1990) *The Teaching and Learning of Reading in Primary Schools*, HMSO.

GOSWAMI, U. and BRYANT, P. *Phonological Skills and Learning to Read*, Hove: Lawrence Erlbaum Associates Ltd.

LEWIS, M. and WRAY, D. (1994) EXEL publications from Exeter University School of Education.

LINC (1990) *Language in the National Curriculum Materials for Professional Development*, Nottingham University.

LITTLEFAIR, A. (1991) *Reading All Types of Writing*, Milton Keynes: Open University Press.

MALLETT, M. (1992) *Making Facts Matter: Reading Non-Fiction*, London: Paul Chapman.

MCNAUGHTON, C. (1994) *Suddenly*, London: Andersen Press.

NATIONAL ORACY PROJECT/NATIONAL CURRICULUM COUNCIL (1990) *Teaching, Talking and Learning in Key Stages One and Two*, York: NCC.

NATIONAL WRITING PROJECT (1987) *Reasons for Writing*, London: SCDC.

NEATE, B. (1992) *Finding Out About Finding Out*, Sevenoaks: Hodder and Stoughton.

NOYES, A. (1913) *The Highwayman* (in several anthologies).

OLIVER, and BOYD, (1989) Storytime Gaints, Edinburgh: Longman.

OXFORDSHIRE COUNTY COUNCIL (1993) *OCM 8 Papers on the Teaching of Reading*, Oxford: OCC.

PERERA, K. (1984) *Children's Writing and Reading: Analysing Classroom Language*, Oxford: Blackwell.

ROSS, T. (1992) *Hansel and Gretel*, London: Red Fox.

SCAA (1994) *Key Stage 2 National Pilot: English Teachers' Guide*, London: SCAA.

SEUSS, DR. *The Cat in the Hat Series*, London: HarperCollins.

STUBBS, M. (1983) *Language, Schools and Classrooms*, London: Methuen.

WELLS, G. (1986) *The Meaning Makers*, Sevenoaks: Hodder and Stoughton.

4   Mathematics

Pat Booth and Margaret Jones

Introduction

The changes to the mathematics Order are those of an alteration in structure and format, rather than content. No new non-statutory guidance has been commissioned. The new mathematics Order will fit just as well alongside the existing non-statutory guidance as did the 1991 Order. The emphasis on Key Stages in particular is a new aspect for mathematics.

In this chapter we have been at pains to indicate not only the changes to content and structure, but also, where possible, to use evidence and tasks to give life to the new Order consistent with messages from Her Majesty's Inspectorate and the Office for Standards in Education. There are many ways of using this chapter but we have designed it with the intention that, if you follow it all the way through, you will become familiar with the new Order. The enquiry tasks are central to this process.

Summary of Main Changes

There are six significant changes to the 1991 Order for Mathematics.

1   The number of Attainment Targets has been reduced from five to three at Key Stage 1. These are: Using and Applying Mathematics; Number; Shape, Space and Measures. At Key Stage 2 there are four Attainment Targets. These are the same as those for Key Stage 1 with the addition of Data Handling.

2   The levels that were a feature of the previous Programme of Study no longer exist and have been replaced by a Key Stage Programme of Study. For each Attainment Target the Programme of Study is set out in sections which describe the opportunities to be given to pupils and specify what should be taught. Each section is further subdivided in order to cluster together related aspects of mathematics.

3   Some of the content has been omitted and some deferred to the next Key Stage. Despite the disappearance of Algebra and Data Handling as separate

Attainment Targets at Key Stage 1, the content which could formerly be found in Levels, 1–3 is now incorporated into the Attainment Target for Number. This does not include the section on probability which was formerly included in Data Handling. The start of work on probability has been deferred to Key Stage 2 and there is a consequent slippage of content into Key Stage 3.

4   In line with overall policy, individual Statements of Attainment have been replaced with Level Descriptions. This allows the teacher to decide which Level best describes that at which the pupil is working.

5   In the main, Key Stage 1 now covers work from the former Levels 1–3 instead of 1–4 as in the 1991 Order. Similarly, Key Stage 2 now covers, in the main, work from the former Levels 2–5 rather than, as previously, Levels 2–6. This brings mathematics in line with the other subjects of the National Curriculum.

6   For all Key Stages there is a requirement to provide an appropriate curriculum for the individual child, which might mean using material from another Key Stage.

There have been very few changes to the content of the mathematics Order. However, since the document is very different in style and no longer looks familiar, it might be thought that the changes are more drastic than in fact they are. The Programme of Study is introduced through a section called *Common Requirements*. This outlines the *Access* for pupils to the Programme of Study, the *Use of Language* and the place of *Information Technology* (Department for Education, 1995). Each attainment target is introduced by a section entitled, *1. Pupils should be given opportunities to*. These sections give guidance on the experiences that pupils should have and bring some of the philosophy of the former non-statutory guidance into the statutory Order. For example, Key Stage 1, Number, the first statement in this section is:

a   develop flexible methods of working with number, orally and mentally;

This links closely with the advice given on *Pupils Doing Calculations* outlined in pages E1–E6 of the non-statutory guidance (National Curriculum Council, 1989) which was provided for the original Order for mathematics.

Enquiry Task

Read through sections B, D, E and F of the non-statutory guidance (NCC, 1989) for the previous Order and section 1 for each of the attainment targets in the new Order.

Identify overlaps which change status from advice (formerly non-statutory guidance) into statutory Order (now).

The introductory sections which are common to all Attainment Targets are followed by further sections which group the content under broad headings. These headings are similar in style to those used on the Strands Poster that was distributed to schools in 1991. However, the poster linked groups of Statements of Attainment and showed progression through these. The sections in the new document facilitate planning because they are part of the Programme of Study and group concepts together in a way which allows progression to be identified, within these related aspects of mathematics.

However, progression is not as clear as it was in the former document. This is both because the ten levels are no longer indicated within the Programme of Study and because the Statements of Attainment have been replaced by Level Descriptions. The Level Descriptions are separated from the Programme of Study and the intention is that they will be used only at the end of a Key Stage to make summative judgments of each child's achievements. This loss of detail is deliberate, since the intention is to focus your attention onto the requirements of the Programme of Study and to allow you to make judgments about the appropriate material for individual children rather than trying to teach to a level.

Under broad headings are lettered sections *a, b, c*, etc. These sections group together related areas of concepts but they do not indicate a progression through the sections; that is, it is not intended that you should teach section *a* before section *b*. This becomes clear if you look at Number, Key Stage 1, where under the broad heading, *2. Developing an understanding of place value*, there are two statements which clearly need to be linked whilst teaching:

a   count orally up to 10 and beyond, knowing the number names;

and:

b   read, write and order numbers, initially to 10 (Department for Education, 1995a, p. 3),

Section *a* goes on to talk about counting in steps of different sizes and recognizing sequences, amongst other skills, and it is clear that you wouldn't be introducing those further skills, before the children could 'read, write and order numbers, initially to 10'. These two statements would be being developed concurrently, despite being found in different sections.

Enquiry Task

In a group, focus on the Attainment Target for Number for your Key Stage. Try to find similar links across broad headings and sections which group statements together in terms of their teaching. You can then go on to try other Attainment Targets.

Key Stage 1

As stated already, at Key Stage 1 the number of Attainment Targets has been reduced to three. Across the whole document phrases relating to IT capability have been removed. IT capability should still be taught within the context of mathematics, since it is a cross-curricular theme, but you will now be planning for and assessing it through the IT documentation.

There have been no changes to the Attainment Target for Using and Applying, except for the change of layout and the rephrasing of some of the statements. The Programme of Study covers the content formerly identified in Levels 1–3. Under the Opportunities section, the emphasis is on the development of pupils' abilities to:

 a   use and apply mathematics in practical tasks, in real-life problems and within mathematics itself;
 b   explain their thinking to support the development of their reasoning (Department for Education, 1995a, p. 2).

You will find Number covers the content formerly found in Levels 1–3 of the 1991 Order; however, there has been substantial rephrasing. Algebra has been integrated into Number. Handling Data has also been partially integrated: those aspects concerned with Data Handling can now be found as section 5 of Number, although, as formerly mentioned, those aspects relating to IT capability have been deleted. The start of Probability, which was the third strand of Data Handling, has been deferred to Key Stage 2. Shape, Space and Measure now contain all the work on measures, including linear measures, which was to be found formerly in Number.

Key Stage 2

At Key Stage 2, again you will find all reference to IT capability has been deleted and the number of Attainment Targets has been reduced to four. The major change being the loss of the Attainment Target for Algebra as a separate entity; the content still exists and can be found in the Attainment Target for Number. In Handling Data, those statements which related to continuous data have been moved to Key Stage 3. Other items of content which have been deferred to Key Stage 3 are:

- all material currently specified at Level 6;
- the treatment of continuous data;
- trial and improvement methods;
- using index notation;
- using coordinates in all four quadrants;
- finding areas and volumes using formulae;
- angle properties associated with intersecting and parallel lines;
- constructing pie charts.

Using networks to solve problems has been deleted totally from the document at all Key Stages. If you look at the Level Descriptions it is clear that much of the previous Level 4 content now forms part of the Level 5 descriptions and similarly some of the former Level 5 content can be found within the Level 6 descriptions and thus has been moved out of the Programme of Study for Key Stage 2. This has allowed for a more balanced approach to the content and defers some of the more difficult mathematical ideas to a later stage.

Enquiry Task

Read through levels 4 and 5 of the old documents, both the Statements of Attainment and the Programme of Study for Number, and compare with the new level descriptions for levels 4, 5 and 6 for Number which can be found in the new document on pages 25 and 26. (Note: for the purposes of the level descriptions this is called Number and Algebra not just Number.)

Write down any changes of level that you can identify: e.g., from the Programme of Study of the 1991 Order at level 4: solving addition, subtraction, multiplication and division problems using numbers with no more than two decimal places.

In the new document, this is contained in the level 5 description: they use all four operations with decimals to two places.

When you have found all the changes for Number repeat this for the other attainment targets.

Challenges and Opportunities

Can we construct a different mathematical experience for our pupils from the new mathematics Order? The mathematics Order has, in substance, changed very little. In fact the core curriculum has remained the most stable; it is the foundation subjects which have been changed and reduced the most. This means that mathematics now represents a greater proportion of the total statutory curriculum than before. At Key Stage 2, in particular, we know from Office for Standards in Education publications (e.g., OFSTED, 1993) that in general pupils were not felt to be succeeding especially in Years 3 and 5, and that, '... typically, the pupils in Year 3 ... worked on their own from printed material almost all the year ... (OFSTED, 1993, p. 5).

You now have a slimmed down statutory mathematics curriculum, together with less overall pressure on time. However, more time available for mathematics will not, of itself, affect pupils working on their own from printed material; less pressure might, however, enable you to think more deeply about the learning processes in place in your classroom.

Enquiry Task

Photocopy Attainment Target 1 Number in the old Order and the Number Attainment Target in the new Order. Compare the two by taking each bullet point one at a time. Tick off common concepts/skills.

Write in on the new Order any exemplar material that helps your understanding. Repeat with the remaining Attainment Targets

for example:

b extend their understanding of the number system to negative numbers in context, and decimals up to 2 places in the context of measurement and money from the new order (DFE, 1995a, p. 7)

matches with:

Read a thermometer, a stopwatch, ruler, the dial on kitchen scales.

copied from the old Order.

The Leeds Primary Needs Study (Alexander, 1992), which was carried out just before the introduction of the National Curriculum, found that mathematics was more commonly taught as a separate subject than other subjects, involving little collaborative activity between pupils and little discussion with the teacher. Research originally commissioned by the National Curriculum Council also indicates a heavy reliance on commercial schemes, with mathematics being regarded by some teachers as more difficult to approach through a cross-curricular topic than other subjects (Schools Curriculum and Assessment Authority, 1994, p. 4). Robin Alexander in his later article (1994, pp. 24–35) also argues that the time devoted to mathematics is less efficiently used than in other curriculum areas.

Enquiry Task

Are the findings of the Leeds Primary Needs Study, that mathematics is more commonly taught as a separate subject, appropriate to mathematics as described in the new Order?

Consider this finding firstly by yourself, and then with one or two colleagues.

How will you address the OFSTED findings, that pupils typically worked on their own from printed material almost all the year (HMSO, 1993, p. 5)?

Key Stage 2 contains less material than previously. Also some of the more difficult mathematics in Handling Data has moved upwards into Key Stage 3. For example:

Ma 5   • designing and using a questionnaire to survey opinion (taking
Level 6   account of bias);

is now in Key Stage 3. You could be enabling more pupils to succeed now at Key Stage 2; what you are expecting of them could now be said to be more realistic. No material has moved the other way!

Another aspect of the changes is that material already stated elsewhere has been omitted. There are two ways in which this has happened: external repetitions and internal ones. Examples of external repetitions giving rise to deletions are as follows:

Ma 4   • using and understanding compass bearings   geography
Level 3   and the terms 'clockwise' and 'anti   Order
            clockwise'.

Ma 5   • inserting and interrogating data in a computer   information
Level 4   database.   technology
            Order

Similar examples exist relating to movements from the mathematics Order to the physical education Order.

This gives you both the opportunity to make cross-curricular links, and simultaneously, in a sense, allows you to forget those links. They were after all made explicit previously. This is true in a similar way for the 'internal' repetitions. An example of this kind of deletion would be:

Ma 3   • dealing with inputs and outputs from simple function machines.
Level 3

This is presumed as being implied here:

f   understand and use the relationships between the four operations, includ-
        ing inverse;

Again, this both allows you to make connections but relies on you to make explicit what is now only implicit.

The arrangement and resulting clear structure of the mathematics within Key Stages, together with the provision and hence flexibility for those small number of pupils who might need the provision (DFE, 1995a, p. 1), allows you to select material from an earlier or later Key Stage, and gives the opportunity for each Key Stage to develop a particular culture. This 'culture' could then relate to the developmental needs of the pupils. For example, '3. *Understanding and using properties of position and movement*' at Key Stage 2 has a particular 'flavour' to it; this 'flavour' is one which seems to suggest pupils engage in practical work, in visualizing, using and talking about their movement skills to perform 'real' tasks. The 'flavour' of the same section in Key Stage 3 seems more graphical and diagrammatic. However, in developing such a 'flavour', the needs of those pupils working outside of the Key Stage should not be overlooked; so a pupil should not be stopped from developing a more graphical approach when she or he is ready. The opportunity to create a different 'flavour' for each of the two Key Stages could also threaten the integration of the mathematics.

Algebra is now part of Number. This might at first glance seem appropriate for at least Key Stage 1. However, despite the fact that introduction to Key Stage 2 contains these words, 'Algebraic ideas of pattern and relationships should be developed in all areas of mathematics' (DFE, 1995a, p. 6), the benefits from the reminder that algebraic structure underpins all number work is lost, as is the opportunity to acknowledge the 'roots' of algebra during Key Stages 1 and 2, for example, at Key Stage 1:

3a using repeated patterns to develop ideas of regularity and sequencing;

and at Key Stage 2:

3a . . . using simple relationships; progress to interpreting, generalising and using simple mappings, . . .

We are also, in a sense, in danger of returning to a previous time when algebra was only recognized as such in secondary schools.

Last but not least, there is no mention of standard algorithms for number work at either Key Stage 1 or 2, for example, teaching subtraction through decomposition. Instead, such phrases as (pupils should be given opportunities to):

a develop flexible and effective methods of computation and use them with understanding (DFE, 1995a, p. 7);

give plenty of scope for children's own methods. Similar principals underpin the introduction to Key Stage 2: there is continuing emphasis on wide ranges of methods and flexibility in their use.

Assessment

The aim of the review has been to make the assessment process easier. It is no longer possible to produce easily tick lists for items of content. Attention is now focused on the Programme of Study for the Key Stage, rather than a series of statements which may have been seen as hurdles. This puts the emphasis on the teaching of the mathematics and the successful formal and informal methods of assessment used by teachers. There may also be less temptation to teach towards particular outcomes, such as those described in Level Descriptions. In fact, there is a danger in so doing since the SAT tests will be drawn from material contained in the Programme of Study. The Level Descriptions are just place holders for this content and do not contain all the content of the Programme of Study. However, the work on Data Handling at Key Stage 1, which you will find within the Number Attainment Target, will not be assessed at Key Stage 1, and this is the only exception within the Programme of Study. There is still a statutory obligation to teach this content for Data Handling even though it will not be assessed within the requirements of the National Curriculum.

The document has Level Descriptions which are separated from the Programme of Study, thus intentionally distancing the formal assessment procedures from the taught programme. In fact the School Curriculum and Assessment Authority (SCAA) will be releasing guidance on the process of setting teaching and learning objectives based on the Programme of Study. It is intended that teachers' own objectives will be used to assess the progress of children for formative and diagnostic purposes.

The Level Descriptions are only required to be used at the end of a Key Stage and provide a much less precise method of measuring achievement than the former Statements of Attainment. The Level Description which describes most closely a child's performance is the level which that child achieves. It is not expected that any given child will understand all the concepts described at any one level, but rather most of them, and that the description chosen fits most closely what you know about the child's learning. It is expected that you will find first the Level Description that fits your pupil best; then look both up and down to the Level Descriptions on either side. This is to check that content below is all known and some of that above has also been understood. This process will verify the accuracy of your choice of Level Description.

It may be that schools will want to use the Level Descriptions at the end of each year for the purposes of communicating to the next teacher each child's progress; however, Level Descriptions would seem to be too blunt a descriptor for this purpose. The receiving teacher will want to know details of successes and problems. Level Descriptions are not a tool for formative or diagnostic assessment. Your informal methods will be more useful for this purpose. SCAA is encouraging you to decide on your own objectives for each lesson, the content of which will be drawn from the Programme of Study, and to decide on your own record keeping system in the light of this. Once again the emphasis is on evidence rather than record keeping and SCAA, along with OFSTED, are to release guidance on this during 1995.

Since the assessment process is quite different and requires a global judgment, it will be crucial that evidence is kept in order to make judgments. If you already keep pupils profiles, you will know that it is not necessary to keep every single piece of work to evidence a pupil's achievement. You need only keep a sufficient cross-section of work to support your judgments. You might simply keep pupils' workbooks which have been annotated rather than just ticked.

Practical Tasks

The process of learning mathematics varies very little across the Key Stages. There is a need to develop the language and notation within a concrete context and to continue to practise the skills gained in both abstract and real contexts.

Enquiry Task

Ask colleagues to share supporting work and to talk about a child's achievements. Together, look at and listen to the evidence available for a child and match what you see and hear with the Level Descriptions, on an individual basis.

- Are there differences?
- Observe yourselves in action: how is a consensus arrived at?
- As you go through the process can you identify any learning points for you and your school?

Finding the activities which allow this to happen can be time consuming. There are now many publications produced both commercially and by local education authorities that can provide you with activities of this type. Those activities that allow for differentiation across a wide range of ages and abilities are especially useful. A practical activity which seems to fit with all Key Stages and which incorporates many features of the Programmes of Study, including Attainment Target 1, can be found described in the journal for *Educational Studies in Mathematics* (Streefland, 1984, pp. 327–45). You might like to try this activity with your children.

I begin by telling a sad story:

Last night I went out for the evening and when I arrived home I discovered that my house had been burgled. My video, my television and my box of jewellery had all been stolen. The police came and were very nice. They had a good look around and discovered a very large handprint on the window. They wondered if we could tell them something about the person who had left this print.

I have a large picture of a handprint – this is usually my hand enlarged by placing it on the photocopier. What happens next will depend on the children.

At Key Stage 1 and Key Stage 2 the children might explore some of these possibilities:

- How large is the hand? Can something be found to measure its area?
- Who has larger/smaller hands?
- What is its length? What can we use to measure it? Will 'my hand' fit onto it, once, twice, three times?
- If this is the hand, how big is the foot? Can I draw it? Could I find the size of the foot for any size of hand?
- Can I tell anything about the size of other parts of the body? The length of the legs, arms, body . . . ?
- What might be the size of the head? Could I make a hat?
- Can you reproduce a 2-D model of the burglar?

Before you read on you might like to try the following enquiry task.

Enquiry Task

Make a list of those elements of the Programme of Study, in the new Order, that you think might be covered whilst working on this task.

What might your objectives be for this work?

At Key Stage 1 what are the elements of the Programme of Study that might be addressed by such an activity? Certainly, Using and Applying, in that it relates how children apply existing knowledge in daily activities to real and imagined situations. The children will be explaining, talking, asking questions and will be encouraged to find different ways of solving problems. They will be using simple fractions, 'my hand is less than half the size of this', and collecting and recording data linked to the activity. They will also be comparing objects, using appropriate language, and standard or non-standard measures.

What is being addressed for Key Stage 2? In Using and Applying, the children will be developing mathematical language, selecting and using mathematics and materials, and developing mathematical reasoning. In Number, they will be understanding and using fractions in context – to estimate, describe and compare proportions of a whole. In Shape and Space, they might be choosing appropriate standard units and making sensible estimates with them. In Handling Data, the children could be finding averages – some groups have been known to work out their average hand size and height and use this to compare the hand and the unknown height.

Whenever this activity has been used with groups of both children and adults, they have tended to use non-standard measures and estimations rather than accurate measurement. They will be working with quite complex notions of ratio but in a comfortable and stimulating way.

One infants' teacher decided to use the activity with a group of reception/year 1 children. She chose a time when both the classroom assistant and some parent helpers were available. Having told the story, she split the children into small groups and asked them to try to find out how tall the burglar was. In each group they discussed ideas. One group wished to go outside, so that they could stop passers by and test the hand against the photocopy, thus finding someone who might match the burglar for height. All groups eventually came up with a notion of comparison and ratio, and produced a burglar from paper to make an interesting classroom display.

The idea is rich in that it is practical, interesting and stimulating. It will provide for differentiation by outcome, provided the children have been given some freedom to choose their own strategies. It encapsulates the essence of working on Using and Applying mathematics.

Enquiry Task

To catch a burglar genuinely requires a collection of cross-curricular skills. With a colleague (or several), explore the possibilities that the 'burglar task' offers for cross-curricular development. Start with broad connections on a large sheet of paper, gradually increasing in detail until you get to the stage of referencing the appropriate National Curriculum programmes of study. Highlight any other mathematics that arises.

Cross-Curricular Dimensions and Themes

There seem to be three themes which permeate the mathematics Order. There is a strong sense of the place of language in mathematics and the social context of the classroom; there is emphasis on explaining 'their (*pupils'*) thinking' (DFE, 1995a, p. 2); pupils are asked to 'understand the language of number' (*op. cit.*) and 'ask questions' (*op. cit.*). This shows, too, in the explicit encouragement of pupils to find their own ways of recording their work (*op. cit.*, p. 6).

A second theme is 'connected mathematics'. In direct contrast to the well-known Cockcroft comment (*Mathematics Counts*, HMSO, 1982) to the effect that that mathematics lessons were not about anything, there is a strong sense coming through this Order: good mathematics is meaningful mathematics.

Meaning is added and emphasized in at least two ways: answers to problems should make sense in relation to those problems and pupils should learn to check for accuracy and appropriateness; there is an emphasis throughout on contexts for the mathematics, often with 'real' stated explicitly. At Key Stage 2, the introduction to Attainment Target 1 includes the phrase 'use and apply maths . . . in real-life problems' (DFE, 1995a, p. 6). Number work is linked to phrases of the kind 'in context' and 'realistic data'.

Enquiry Task

With colleagues discuss the following two questions:

- What real-life situations do you/could you use with your pupils?
- How do these situations 'connect' with the new Order?

References to the use of IT are ubiquitous. This includes specific mention of calculator use, as in:

> *g* . . . using a calculator as appropriate;

and;

h understand and use the features of a basic calculator, (DFE, 1995a, p. 8);

and more general references to IT and computers. This 'generality' also serves to prolong the life of the Order so that it does not become out of date too quickly. The emphasis throughout (on calculators, IT, or computers) is on their use as tools to enhance pupils' mathematics.

There is also an apparent intention to giving the Order a cross-curricular dimension. Handling Data includes the words 'formulate questions about an issue of their choice' (DFE, 1995a, p. 10), thereby giving scope for cross-curricular work. Space, Shape and Measures could be used to make purposeful links between mathematics with art, technology, science and physical education; map references (DFE, 1995a, p. 9) are used as an example.

Enquiry Task

In a group, share out the Attainment Targets for your particular Key Stage. Write down phrases from your Attainment Target that denote a cross-curricular dimension or theme. Next to each, give an example of one way you could be obtaining, in your classroom, evidence for the theme/dimension, for example:

Phrase   **Practical example**

Key Stage 1

3a copy, continue and make   4f organise sound in simple
    patterns (DFE, 1995a)   structures (DFE, 1995b, p. 3)
                                      4a pattern . . . in made forms
                                          (DFE, 1995a, p. 2)

Key Stage 2

2c recognise the reflective   2b emphasise change of shape
    symmetries of . . . 3-D shapes   (DFE, 1995c, p. 4)
    (DFE, 1995a, p. 5).

Share your list with your group members. Consider how you will introduce examples such as these to your pupils.

The Practical Options for Teaching and Learning Methods and Resources

As indicated previously, there is no substantial change in mathematical content. The 1989 non-statutory guidance has not been superseded and remains – not least – an important source of guidance for teaching and planning.

Other evidence from HMI (HMSO, 1989) and research (SCAA, 1994) – commissioned originally by the National Curriculum Council – raises concerns over the effectiveness of learning where there is over-reliance on text books and published schemes. The evidence suggests that where:

> Children embarked on problem solving or investigative work using their existing skills and knowledge, the need to adapt and add to these quickly became apparent. It was here that more formal direct methods of teaching often proved very effective. (p. 24)

This means that your pupils' problem-solving and investigative work provides a rich source of guidance as to how and what to teach more formally, and so might often precede more formal teaching.

Enquiry Task

Consider how you might proceed to more formal teaching specifically based on observations of your pupils during problem-solving and investigative tasks.

What implications might there be for resources?

Conclusion

We have been fortunate in that the changes to the mathematics Order have been minimal, and ones principally related to format and structure. There is no apparent message to change teaching style, to redefine what constitutes mathematics, or to change the definition of 'good practice'. Cockcroft (HMSO, 1982) gave us this definition in the famous paragraph 243:

> Mathematics teaching at all levels should include opportunities for:
>
> - exposition by the teacher;
> - discussion between teacher and pupils, and between pupils themselves;
> - appropriate practical work;
> - consolidation and practice of fundamental skills and routines;
> - problem solving, including the application of mathematics to everyday situations;
> - investigational work.

Subsequent messages have been more or less consistent. The information derived from inspections and reports not only identifies good practice in schools, but also provides both detailed supporting evidence and a consistent message. The passage below encapsulates this message and outlines the features of good practice:

... there was considerable discussion of the work; the children showed a lively attitude towards mathematics; they were accustomed to predicting outcomes and giving consideration to the efficiency of the methods they were using and the degree of accuracy appropriate to a particular case. The content of the lesson was carefully planned to extend pupils' knowledge, develop their skills and stimulate them to think logically. The skillfulness of the teaching showed the way tasks were matched to the different abilities of the pupils to provide a progressive challenge to their mathematical thinking. (HMSO, 1987, p. 20)

This describes not only the implications for planning, but also the types of pupil outcome to be looked for. It has been our intention in this chapter to give exemplars and activities consistent with these intended outcomes and to examine the changes within this perspective.

Enquiry Task

Share with colleagues, activities that you think encapsulate the above description of good practice.

How do these activities relate to the Programme of Study in the new Order?

References

ALEXANDER, R. (1992) *Policy and Practice in Primary Education*, London: Routledge.

ALEXANDER, R. (1994) 'What primary curriculum? Dearing and beyond', *Education*, 3, 13 March pp. 24–35.

DEPARTMENT OF EDUCATION and SCIENCE (1991) *Mathematics in the National Curriculum*, London: HMSO.

DEPARTMENT FOR EDUCATION (1995) *Key Stages 1 and 2 of the National Curriculum*, London: HMSO.

DEPARTMENT FOR EDUCATION (1995a) *Mathematics in the National Curriculum*, London: HMSO.

DEPARTMENT FOR EDUCATION (1995b) *Music in the National Curriculum*, London: HMSO.

DEPARTMENT FOR EDUCATION (1995c) *Physical Education in the National Curriculum*, London: HMSO.

DEPARTMENT FOR EDUCATION (1995d) *Art in the National Curriculum*, London: HMSO, p. 2.

HER MAJESTY'S STATIONERY OFFICE (1982) *Mathematics Counts*, London: HMSO.

HER MAJESTY'S STATIONERY OFFICE (1987) *Primary Schools: Some Aspects of Good Practice*, London: HMSO.

HER MAJESTY'S STATIONERY OFFICE (1989) *Aspects of Primary Education: The Teaching and Learning of Mathematics*, London: HMSO.

National Curriculum Council (1989) *Mathematics: Non-Statutory Guidance*, London: HMSO.

Office for Standards in Education (1993) *Mathematics Key Stages 1, 2, 3 and 4, Fourth Year, 1992–93*, London: HMSO.

Schools Curriculum and Assessment Authority (1994) *Evaluation of the Implementation of the National Curriculum Mathematics at Key Stages 1, 2 and 3: Summary Report*, London: HMSO.

Streefland, L. (1984) 'Search for the roots of ratio: some thoughts on the long-term process', *Educational Studies in Mathematics*, Vol. 15, pp. 327–48.

5 Science

Cliff Marshall and David Palacio

Introduction

The focus for this chapter is twofold. In the first instance we shall try to examine the changes that have occurred in the National Curriculum for Science as the 1991 Order has been replaced by the 1995 Order. These changes will be analysed in order to identify those which are true omissions or additions, and those which are simply re-presentations of existing content. The implications of the new Level Descriptions and the reduced direct inclusion of cross-curricular subject matter will also be discussed. The second major focus will be on the issues that arise in implementing the science curriculum in your school and your classroom. Ways of finding out about children's existing ideas, and then building this knowledge into teaching and learning processes, will be examined along with an analysis of how the new National Curriculum can be used to help you make decisions in your planning for progression and continuity. Throughout, we shall be emphasizing the need to sustain the growth of experimental and investigative skills alongside the development of science knowledge and understanding.

Changes to the Science National Curriculum

The so-called 'Dearing Review of the National Curriculum' (SCAA, 1994a) heralded the second revision of the Science Order since its introduction at the start of the 1989 school year. Fortunately, and as one might hope, the changes arising from the Dearing Review have been small in scope, being associated mainly with a reduction in content of the Programmes of Study (PoS), together with the replacement of Statements of Attainment by Level Descriptions (as explained in Chapter 2). However, the Dearing Review did, in addition, provide an opportunity for some 'tidying up' of the prescribed curriculum; for example, magnetism, previously associated with electricity (Attainment Target (Sc) 4, PoS i) has been moved within the same Attainment Target but is now associated with force. More importantly, 'tidying up' has been used to address the issue of progression within the documentation, both within a Key Stage and between one Key Stage and the next. For example, progression within the concepts associated with *force and motion* has been clarified by rewriting the Key Stage 2 Programme of Study as a sequence of eight separate ideas centred around the two themes of *types of force* and *balanced and unbalanced forces*. The title for Attainment Target 2, *Life and Living Processes*, was considered to be inconsistent with sections in the new Programme of Study. As a consequence this Attainment Target has been renamed, *Life Processes and Living Things*.

Three important general points emerge out of the Dearing Review. Firstly, the review is unlikely, of itself, to require your school to rewrite, or even modify, its policy document for science; overall aims and methods of teaching need not change. Secondly, although teacher assessment is still a statutory requirement in science, as it is for English and mathematics, you will no longer be expected to keep *detailed* records of each child's progress; the keeping of extensive tick lists encompassing each Statement of Attainment is a thing of the past. Finally, non-statutory guidelines have been provided in the Interim Report (Dearing, 1993) concerning how much time, on average, needs to be devoted each week to science; for Key Stage 1 the recommendation is one and a half hours per week, and for Key Stage 2 the recommendation is two hours per week.

The reduction in curriculum content has been achieved through:

(i)   specifying more clearly the *limits* of the content that has to be taught;
(ii) removing the *overlap between Key Stages* by assigning areas of study to one or other Key Stage. For example, 'temperature' and the 'Earth and beyond', which now are in Key Stage 2 rather than in Key Stages 1 and 2 as before (although the 'effects of heating common materials' remains in both Key Stages), and *explicit* reference to energy, which is not covered now until Key Stage 3;
(iii) removing the *overlap with other subjects*, e.g., weather (to geography) and electronics (to technology).

Reduction in the Order has been achieved not only by addressing 'content' but also by paying particular attention to 'presentation'. For example, PoS are presented now as a series of brief lettered bullet points. Although these reductions will be welcomed by many teachers, they may well present you with difficulties when you try to translate the PoS into individual lesson plans. Furthermore, reduction in content brought about by removal of the overlap between one subject and another, that is assigning overlap in content to just one subject, makes it all the more difficult to see potential cross-subject links. When the 1991 Order (DES/WO, 1991), which in itself is a reduction in content of the 1989 Order (DES/WO, 1989), was first introduced, teachers at the time had difficulties deciding what depth of understanding pupils might be expected to reach; a similar situation is likely to arise with the 1995 reduction (DFE/WOED, 1995). The 1995 revision is likely to prove even more problematic to implement than the one in 1991, since teachers coming to grips with the earlier revision did at least have quite detailed Statements of Attainment to act as a guide. Level Descriptions are much broader in nature, and far fewer in number, than the Statements of Attainment they replace. Moreover, they are expressed in terms of pupil achievements rather than, as for Statements of Attainment, a detailed description of an individual piece of work.

The Main Changes: A Summary

In this section the main differences between the 1991 and 1995 versions of the National Curriculum for Science will be outlined.

Key Stages 1 and 2 – Science 1: Experimental and Investigative Science, Previously called Scientific Investigation

Although subject to a major revision in terms of focus, the PoS for Attainment Target 1 – Science 1 (Sc 1) – remain basically unchanged. Pupils are still expected to undertake whole investigations. However, the notion of 'flexibility' has been built into the new PoS so that practical work not carried out in the context of a whole investigation may now be incorporated into the overall procedure for assessing children's progress.

The previous three stage, sequential model of scientific enquiry (hypothesizing, observing, and interpreting/drawing conclusions) has now become less important in determining the overall approach to science and, in particular, the type of work that you can undertake as part of your scheme of work for science. In planning lessons it is no longer necessary for you to attempt to apply in a mechanistic way this three stage model to all the science work that your children do. The new model for science investigation (planning experimental work, obtaining evidence, and considering evidence) lays emphasis on the *ways in which scientific evidence is obtained and evaluated.*

Due to the change to an information/data gathering and processing model of scientific enquiry, the hitherto emphasis on the identification and control of variables has been reduced. In the new Order the word *variable* has been replaced by the word *factor*. Factor has a broader, less precise, meaning than variable, and has been introduced into the PoS so as to enable something to be included in an investigation, which must be recognized and allowed for, but which cannot necessarily be controlled. Therefore, credit can now be given to a more diverse range of investigative features than has hitherto been the case. In certain areas of science, for example, biology, earth science, and some aspects of chemistry, this change should allow you to plan for a wider range of work than was possible previously. The procedures associated with 'fair-testing', although still important, need only be carried through *in their entirety* as, and when, it is appropriate to do so.

Finally, when considering the likely effect that the Dearing Review will have on your school's science curriculum you should also bear in mind that lessons may be planned around material selected from either earlier or later Key Stages where this is necessary to enable individual pupils to progress and demonstrate achievement.

Although changes to the content of the PoS for Sc 1 have been minimal, changes of a more significant nature begin to emerge from a study of the PoS for the 'concept' elements of the new National Curriculum for Science, Sc 2, Sc 3 and Sc 4. Tables 5.1 and 5.2, which follow, describe the main omissions and additions for each of these elements, one at a time, first for Key Stage 1 and then for Key Stage 2.

Table 5.1: Summary of the omissions and additions to the 1995 Science Order: Key Stage 1

Omissions	Additions
Science 2: Life Processes and Living Things	
• care for living things • decay and care for the local environment • human influences on the environment • plants as the ultimate source of all food • survival of species (extinction)	• differences between living and non-living things
Science 3: Materials and their Properties	
• awareness of materials which are manufactured • direct reference to dissolving and pouring • dissolving as an example of a physical change • weathering	
Science 4: Physical Processes	
• dangers of electricity • work with magnets • conductors and insulators • natural forces – gravity (weight) • floating and sinking • energy – 'hot and cold', temperature, fuels • light – shadows, reflection and colour • echoes • road and water safety • the whole of PoS (v) – Earth in Space	• effects of an incomplete electrical circuit • forces can change the direction of objects • darkness is the absence of light

At first sight the list of omissions in Tables 5.1 and 5.2 looks quite long and detailed; this was to be expected given that one major aim of the Dearing Review was to slim down the prescribed curriculum. (Given the slimming down focus to the review, the scale of the additions in the Order was, perhaps, unexpected.) Based on the number of omissions and additions you might be tempted to draw the conclusion that you, and your school, will be involved in major, and therefore, time-consuming, revisions. This is not the case. Many of the items included in the lists above are there because *explicit* reference to them either has now been included, or has now been omitted, from the relevant Programme of Study. For example, the measurement of similarities between plants and animals (omission) could be included in Sc 2 Life Processes where children are to be taught *the life process common to animals and*, separately, *plants*; acidity and alkalinity (omission) could be included in Sc 3 Grouping and Classifying Materials where children are to be taught to *compare everyday materials on the basis of their properties*.

In a similar fashion, some of the ideas which you have now to include may be included already in your scheme of work. For example, you may teach already that food chains start with a green plant (addition to Sc 2) under *green plants use energy from the Sun to produce food and that food chains are a way of representing feeding relationships*, or that some materials are better electrical conductors than others (addition to Sc 3) under *investigating the effects of using different components . . . in a (electrical) circuit.*

Table 5.2: *Summary of the omissions and additions to the 1995 Science Order: Key Stage 2*

Omissions	Additions
Science 2: Life Processes and Living Things	
• similarities and differences between plants and animals	• human skeleton and muscles
• competition between living things	• pulse rate affected by exercise
• defence systems of the body	• model of heart and how it functions
• heredity	• life cycle of plants
• care of living things	• food chains start with a green plant
• decay (although breakdown of waste is retained)	
• safe handling of food	
• personal hygiene	
• waste disposal	
• human influences on the Earth	
• fossils	
• measurement of environmental changes using a variety of instruments	
Science 3: Materials and their Properties	
• acidity, alkalinity and chemical indicators	• understanding of the concept 'solubility' and how this may be measured
• mass, volume and solubility as criteria for classifying materials	• naturally occurring and manufactured materials
• dangers associated with the use of everyday materials	• some materials are better thermal insulators than others
• combustion, energy release and waste gases	• some materials are better electrical conductors than others
• chromatography	
• weather, seasons and associated fieldwork	
• geological events	
• rocks and soils in the local environment	
• soil formation	
Science 4: Physical Processes	
• heating and magnetic effects of an electric current	• light – sources and how we see
• parallel circuits	• lunar month
• all work involving micro-electronics	• shape of Earth, Sun and Moon
• dangers of mains electricity and appropriate safety measures	
• measurement of force (newtons) but see *measurements* – Sc 1	
• belts, levers and gears	
• strength of structures	
• all work where 'energy' is mentioned specifically, e.g., fuels, 'hot and cold', energy transfer	
• reflection of sound, echoes and the obtrusive nature of sound in the environment	
• comparison of speed of light and sound	
• brightness, colour and shade of light	
• seasons and phases of the Moon	
• eclipse	
• planets	

However, some additions may require you to modify your programme of work in order to fulfil the new requirements. For example, in Sc 3 you probably cover already the idea of 'solubility', applying the criterion soluble/insoluble as a means of grouping and separating materials. What you may need to do now is to extend these activities so as to encompass the idea that *there is a limit to how much of a solid can dissolve in a given amount of water.*

Some omissions, such as human influences on the Earth, chemical indicators, chromatography, and comparison of speed of light and sound, are real omissions from the prescribed curriculum for science. You may well decide to omit these from your scheme of work. However, now is an opportune moment to give some detailed consideration to what you might like to include in the 20 per cent non-prescribed time.

Perhaps the biggest, and in some ways most unexpected, change concerns Sc 4 and the omission of any *explicit* reference to energy and energy transfer. Don't be fooled, this omission is not real. Think about energy transfers that take place when:

- a battery operated electric circuit is switched on – see the new Sc 4, Electricity;
- either food is eaten or you run upstairs – see the new Sc 2, Humans as organisms;
- water melts or a candle burns – see the new Sc 3, Changing materials;
- plants use sunlight to produce sugar (food) – see the new Sc 2, Green plants as organisms.

Enquiry Task

Take the list of 'omissions' for the Key Stage appropriate to your class. Match each item in turn to your current programme of work and then answer the following questions.

- Is it a real omission?
- If it is, are you still required to cover it as part of another Programme of Study?
- If the omission is real, and, therefore, can be left out, do you want to do so, or is the idea/topic so important that you feel you want to leave it in as part of your 20 per cent discretionary time?

Now consider each of the 'additions'. Match them to your programme of work, and answer these questions.

- Is it a real addition?
- Have you been dealing with it already in some other aspect of your teaching?
- If the idea is a real addition, how will you accommodate it into your existing programme of work? (Since some of your 'additions' may be linked, for example those in Sc 2, you might find it better to determine the total changes necessary before you try to incorporate them into your programme of work.)
- What additional resources will you need, and how will you obtain them?

Science in the Primary Classroom

Have you used the 'helicopter' activity with your class? Just in case you haven't, this activity requires children to make helicopters, usually out of A4 size pieces of paper, and then to investigate ways in which they can affect how the helicopter falls to the ground. For example, the children could investigate what effect changing either the wing size (width as well as length), or the weight attached to the body of the helicopter, has on how well the helicopter flies. If you have used this activity already the chances are that you will have done so as part of a science lesson. If this is the case then pause awhile and consider the enquiry task below. If you haven't tried the activity, then, before reading on, have a go at it yourself; to start off you will need some paper, a pair of scissors and a few paper clips.[1]

Enquiry Task

Why is the work on helicopters generally considered to be 'good' science?

Make a list of your reasons.

Did you answer the question by suggesting that the activity requires children to:

- select (possibly) and then use measuring instruments so as to gather some data?
- interpret the data they have collected so as to produce answers to the question originally posed?
- suggest a question that is open to scientific investigation?
- set up an investigation?
- identify, and then control, variables?
- carry out an investigation?

Or, did you answer the question by stating that the activity requires children to:

- apply their existing knowledge and understanding about gravity, and the way things fall to the ground, in order to address the original question?

Within the framework of the National Curriculum for Science, either answer to the enquiry task above, *by itself*, is not sufficient for any activity to be considered science. You need to be able to justify the activity in terms of it providing the children with experience of both the process/procedure (Sc 1) and knowledge (Sc 2–4) domains of science. Science is both a way of working, which enables people to collect information about the world, *and* a body of knowledge, understanding and ideas that has been obtained through the previously mentioned procedure of systematic enquiry. Dropping helicopters and then simply timing how long they take to reach the ground, interesting as this activity is, is not science.

In order to make the helicopter activity 'good' science you might encourage your children to think about how they would explain, why a heavier helicopter takes less time than a lighter one to reach the ground even though both have the same sized wings, why the helicopter with wide wings take longer to reach the ground than one with narrower wings, and why some helicopters spin in different ways to others. It is by trying to explain situations like these that your children will be helped to develop further their scientific understanding of the world.

However, the explanations that your children give to situations such as the ones described above could well lead you to some disturbing conclusions about the ways in which children's scientific understanding develops. You may well come to the conclusion that what the children have learnt does not match up very well with what you have taught them, that it was not what you intended they should learn, and that the ideas about force that you hoped the children would use in their explanations were not the ones that they did use; some of their ideas might be correct scientifically, others might not.

When planning work you may find it useful to start from the children's existing understanding. You might like to spend a little time reminding yourself of the methods that you use to find out what your children actually understand already. You may decide that it's no good looking in your record book, or even asking the children's previous teacher since doing this will simply tell you what the children have experienced. Unless you, or the previous teacher, undertook a formal assessment at the end of the work, and recorded it, you will have little idea about your children's understanding. And, even if you did assess the children their understanding may well have changed in the intervening time. Therefore, your picture of the children's understanding at the end of the work, yet alone now, is likely to be incomplete. You may need to find out the children's understanding *now*, that is as you begin to introduce the new work. There are various ways to do this, for instance:

1   You could ask questions, either orally or in writing:
    * Who can explain . . . ?
    * What do you think will happen when . . . ?, and then,
    * Why do you think this will happen?
    * What do you think happens to the electricity in the batteries when you switch on your Walkman?
    * What do you think happens to your breakfast after you have eaten it?

2   You might ask the children to sort (group/classify) 'objects', such as (pictures of) animals. This activity is very appropriate to use with quite young children, and with older children who have difficulty with their writing. Once the children have sorted the animals you will need to ask them why they have grouped the animals in the way that they have. Asking the children in this way helps prevent the danger of drawing wrong inferences about their reasons simply from the observed composition of each grouping. What's more, you may find that you need to ask them to sort the animals in more than one way before you get a complete picture of their understanding.

3 The children might draw what they think is happening during an event. Once again this is a very good activity for children who have difficulty with their writing; but with young children, especially, you may experience some difficulty initially interpreting some of their drawings! Older children can annotate their drawings so as to explain more fully *what* they think is happening and *why* they think it is happening. You could ask the children to:

• Draw what they think happens to the sugar after a cube of it has been dropped into a cup of water.

(You may need to explain that you're interested in what happens after the cube has settled at the bottom of the cup and that it may be more appropriate to produce a sequence of drawings rather than to attempt to put everything on the one drawing.)

You can also use drawings to probe children's understanding of, for example, night and day, the solar system, and simple electrical circuits. Here, you might ask your children to make drawings to show:

• Why it is light during the day time and dark at night.
• How to connect up the wires between the bulb and battery so as to make the bulb light up.

Finding out children's ideas *about* science, a slight digression at this point, is well worth the effort since it enables you to gain some awareness and appreciation of what the children think science is. You might ask the children to:

• Draw a scientist so that you can see that they are a scientist; or
• Draw a scientist at work.

What you are likely to get is a stereotypical image of a scientist – male, dressed in a white coat, old, balding, and with horn rimmed glasses. That is the sort of image that can be seen portrayed on television, in either children's cartoons or advertisements, even those advertisements directed at an adult audience. The children's first attempts may be misleading. To get at their real understanding you may need to ask a further question.

• Do you think scientists are really like the person in your drawing?

4 You could ask the children to write down their answer. This is an alternative approach to simply asking them to tell you their answer and, as such, you can use it to best effect with older children, working either singly or in groups of two or three.

• What happens to your food after you have eaten it?
• What happens to the petrol in a car after the engine has been switched on?
• Explain why a ball comes back to the ground after you have thrown it up into the air.

5 You could organize your class into discussion groups. This is a similar technique to the one mentioned first of all, except that here the interaction is not between teacher and pupil(s) but between pupil and pupil(s).
   - Why do you think the ball of plasticine sunk when it was placed in the tank of water yet floated when the plasticine was made into a boat shape?

   (Clearly, beforehand you will need to have provided the children with a tank of water, some Plasticine and the task of trying to make the plasticine float.) Once the children have discovered that the plasticine ball sinks you could ask the children to discuss ways in which they might get the plasticine to float.

6 You could ask the children to draw *concept maps*. The 'concepts' to be explored can be expressed as either pictures or words. Therefore, children of all ages, working individually or in small groups, can undertake this type of activity very successfully. First of all, you, your children, or best of all, you and your children, supply the words/pictures to be used. Then the children connect up the words/pictures with arrows and, in addition, provide one or two word 'explanations' over their arrows. The children will need to be shown how to complete their map, so provide them with some practice beforehand but remember to use a completely unrelated set of words or drawings.

Here are some concept words which you could use to find out your children's understanding of solid, liquid and gas, what scientists call the three states of matter:

Gas, Liquid, Particle, Solid, Energy, Boil,
Condense, Evaporate, Melt, Solidify

For example,

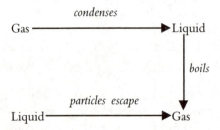

(You might like to try out this activity yourself but we suggest that you do so before you give it to your children to do.)

These 'finding out' activities are particularly appropriate at the beginning of a programme of work. Their purpose is to enable you to find out your children's understanding *before* you introduce them to some new work. Equally, these same techniques can be used at the *end* of a scheme of work, that is when you want to find out the gains that the children have made. In other words, these techniques can be used for both planning and assessment purposes.

As the activities we have just considered will show you, regardless of their age, across all Key Stages children have their own ideas and understandings about the world. As teachers of science you will be involved in trying to help your children develop their ideas toward the more generally accepted scientific viewpoint. Since science concepts are abstract you need to place the work you plan to do in science with your children in a tangible context. Children in Key Stage 1 sorting a collection of objects with a magnet to see which are attracted to it are unlikely to be able to explain in scientific terms what gives rise to the magnetic force. It is sufficient for them to explore the phenomenon and to begin to realize the pattern that emerges: most objects that are attracted to magnets are made of metal. By the end of Key Stage 2 those same children may be able not only to predict which objects are more likely to be attracted to a magnet but also to be able to talk about magnets exerting forces of attraction and repulsion. In addition, they may recognize the usefulness of this in relation to finding directions using a compass. They are moving towards a fuller conceptual understanding yet still need to use their immediate experience of the behaviour of magnets to be able to explain what happens.

It is this progressive changing and developing of understandings that good planning of teaching in science should aspire to. However, as the structure of the National Curriculum for Science makes clear, it is not just the development of understanding and knowledge about science concepts that constitutes science education. Children also have ideas about what scientific enquiry is and, as their response to the draw a scientist task may show you, some children may have better formed ideas than others about the processes of science. In planning for science in your classroom, the understanding of the concept of what it is to be scientific as well as science knowledge and understanding, will need to be planned for. Being an active scientist requires the progressive development of key skills and attitudes. The new Order retains the emphasis, in Key Stages 1 and 2, on the attention you need to give to promoting these process skills. Assessment at the end of Key Stage 1 and Key Stage 2 continues to place 50 per cent of the weighting on Sc 1.

It is important not just to ensure that the lessons you teach are aimed at developing science understanding and skills but, also, to appreciate that the demands made by the activities you provide need to be appropriate to the children's learning needs. The biggest challenge facing you as a science teacher is to try to match the lessons you teach to the science and other learning needs of the children. In order to achieve this matching there are a number of factors you will need to try to take into account. These factors are considered, as two sets of questions to be answered, in the enquiry task below. One set of questions relates to your knowledge of your class, the other set relates to your knowledge of the science curriculum. You may be able to answer some of the questions in the enquiry task by making use of the wider resources available to you. Research into children's learning in science in recent years has led to a number of useful sources of knowledge about the way

Enquiry Task

Consider the science aspects of your next half-term's work. Write down answers to the following questions.

Questions about your children
- What do I know about the children's present ideas?
- What skills do they have already?
- How proficient are they at key skills such as measuring?
- What do I know about individual children's ideas and needs?

Questions about your science curriculum
- What science ideas do I want to teach?
- What skills and attitudes do I want to help the children to develop?
- What activities will give experiences that will link into children's current experience and introduce the science ideas effectively?
- What activities will provide good opportunities to use and develop particular skills?
- Which activity will I use to give the children the opportunity to use and develop their skill in carrying out a whole investigation?
- What resources are most likely to be helpful for these activities?
- What will I as the teacher need to do to enhance the children's learning?

children think about key ideas.[2] Published resources for science are beginning to draw on these findings and provide one way to identify activities that are well focused on their content and demand (Nuffield, 1993). Other questions will need you to refer to the policies and guidelines for science in your school. There is no order laid down in the National Curriculum to determine when different aspects and ideas in science should be taught. The overall approach to curriculum planning in your school may specify that science is approached through the use of cross-curricular themes or topics. The themes chosen will ensure that there is a progressive coverage of the curriculum in general. On the other hand, science may be identified as a subject on your timetable with a science specific programme of topics designed to achieve the coverage of all of the Programmes of Study. Finally, some questions lead to the need to identify the science demands of particular activities in order to decide if they are right for *your* children in *your* classroom at the time proposed.

These questions can be seen as arising from a 'model' (see figure 5.1) of the science teaching and learning process which emphasizes the roles of the teacher and the pupil in the classroom setting. Science learning occurs successfully if the learning activity leads to new ideas and skills that are more scientifically 'acceptable'. If your awareness of the children's ideas and skills is not well developed the chances are that your teaching activity, your lessons and how you teach them will not lead to productive learning activity. In other words, however exciting and interesting your lesson was, the child's ideas may not have changed or, perhaps, they may have changed to take a new form which is no more scientifically acceptable than before.

Figure 5.1:   A 'model' of science teaching and learning

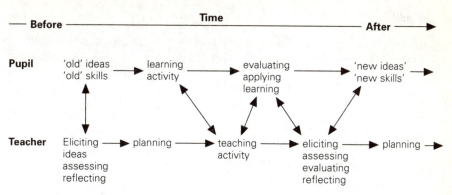

The upper 'line of action' shows the pupil's activities while the lower line tries to summarize your activities as the teacher.

Unproductive learning activity is an example of a mismatch occurring between learning needs and learning activity. Clearly what is needed ideally is a close inter-action between the teacher's and the child's line of action. The two need to progress together so that the child's understanding and skill progressively develop as you and your colleagues provide a programme of work that meets both the needs of the children and those of the science curriculum. If the lines drift apart it may be possible for your lessons to have little real effect on the child's science learning at all – he or she retains the old ideas and level of skill.

We have already explored some of the ways you might try to elicit your children's ideas and we need now to turn to that vitally important next step; the planning and achievement of good lessons in science. As we have seen, good lessons will be those which enable children, through effective teaching, to engage in productive learning activity. We have identified some of the important questions that you need to try to answer as you plan. Amongst these are specific questions about *what* the science ideas and skills to be covered are, *when* such ideas and skills should be introduced and *how* these ideas and skills may be taught. It is to these three questions that we now need to turn for examination in relation to the new National Curriculum for Science.

What are the Key Ideas and Skills?

The new Order for Science has a structure to the Programmes of Study (PoS) that is intended to make much clearer the important ideas and skills that you need to teach. The accent, too, is on teaching rather than learning, the PoS attempt to clearly identify teaching objectives, e.g.,

Pupils should be taught . . . that both pushes and pulls are examples of forces. (KS 1, Physical Processes, 2. Forces and Motion)

Enquiry Task

Look at *all* of the Programmes of Study for Key Stages 1 and 2 including the overall statements. List the section headings:

Life Processes and Living Things
Life processes
Humans as Organisms
Green Plants as Organisms
Variation and Classification
Living Things in their Environment
etc.

Remember to look at the 'Common Requirements', the overall section at the start of each Key Stage and Sc 1, Experimental and Investigative Science. The lists you have compiled give you the key science skill and conceptual areas that are now identified as appropriate for study at Key Stages 1 and 2. Another useful way to get a general overview is to look at the statement made in the 'box' at the head of each PoS.

Scrutiny of the lists of what should be taught, what might be called teaching objectives, within each of the numbered sections of the Programmes of Study will show you the range of study within each skill or conceptual area. You may find that some of these statements challenge your own understanding. The planning of successful lessons will depend on your confidence and knowledge in the area of science you are teaching. As you gradually work through the science curriculum, you may need to refresh your own understanding so that you can appreciate the learning that your children are trying to achieve.

Many people feel unsure about some of the ideas of physical science. If you take a look at the Key Stage 2 PoS for Physical Processes, you may find it useful to consider, in the light of what you thought about the helicopter activity, how you feel concerning the statements made about forces. Different people will have uncertainties about different science concepts; we are as individual in our ideas as the children we teach. Research into primary teachers' ideas in science has indicated that they can develop their understanding by identifying and reflecting on their own and children's ideas,[3] and there are a variety of resources available to help you develop your own understanding about science concepts and skills, (NCC, 1992, 1993a, 1993b, 1993c; SCAA, 1994b, 1994c).

In planning a particular lesson for children you will need to consider many issues, but one of the most important will be the focus the lesson brings to bear on the ideas and skills of science. The more general the lesson's focus the less likely you are to challenge and develop ideas. The degree of emphasis you place on ideas and skills in any particular lesson will affect the possibilities for learning. If you wish your children to think about, say, the fact that some substances dissolve in water and some do not, the activity you provide will need to focus on this with a structured experiment to test the idea. This would be an *illustrative activity*. The demands on the children's investigative skills would be low, enabling evaluation to centre on the dissolving issue. This activity might be followed by another where the notion of soluble substances is already known, but now the activity focuses on skills more centrally. New substances might be presented and the children asked to predict if they will dissolve, given the chance to decide some of the important factors, and which of these to keep the same, which one to change, and which to 'measure'. This activity can be seen as more *investigative*, enabling the children to consider variables, and identify the independent (changing) and dependent (measured) variables. As a teacher of science, clearly, you need to plan consciously for both kinds of activity. This will involve you in analysing and developing activities to achieve the purpose of enabling learning about ideas and skills. We shall return to this issue later when we consider *how* to approach teaching science in greater depth.

When Should Ideas and Skills be Taught?

There are two main issues to be addressed in seeking to answer this query, and they are interconnected. Your school's policy for science will determine the particular approach to overall science curriculum coverage to be used. Many schools adopt a 'spiralling curriculum' for science topics or for wider themes within which science is covered. Typically each of the three content PoS will be touched on twice in each Key Stage. Published teaching materials and schemes, and guidelines produced by Local Education Authority Science Advisory Teams, will normally seek to achieve a balanced coverage.

Enquiry Task

Select a set of published materials or LEA guidelines. Look carefully at the materials for one Key Stage. Match the themes or topics identified in the published materials or guidelines to the National Curriculum PoS headings and the list you drew up for the key ideas.

• Is there a good match?
• Would the published materials be a sound basis for planning a scheme of work that covered the whole science curriculum?
• What would be the strengths and weaknesses of the materials in assisting such planning?

The way in which different authors present their suggested structuring of the science curriculum can vary considerably and yet still be useful.

As we noted earlier the National Curriculum does not specify the order in which you teach the different concepts. However, if your children's learning in science is to build progressively there is a need to discern the development of ideas and skills over time. This whole area is fascinating and the focus for much research. Just the deceptively simple teaching objective

> *Pupils should be taught. . . . that the Sun, Earth and Moon are approximately spherical* (KS 2, Physical Processes, 4a)

will require children to achieve major conceptual understanding[4] that cannot be directly based on their first-hand experience. Careful thought needs to be given to how this understanding can be achieved, how children can explore the distant phenomena through the use of models. It will be important to know what your children's ideas are before you start your teaching. We gave ideas about how you might gather this information earlier. It will be interesting to contrast your children's views with those found in the research study.

In a broad sense the National Curriculum Order provides support in looking for this progression in ideas and skills through both the PoS and the Level Descriptions. The Level Descriptions are useful in this context as they give an indication of how a child's understanding can be envisaged as developing over time.

Enquiry Task

Choose one area of science skills, for example, obtaining evidence.

Note the progression suggested by the teaching objectives from Key Stage 1 to Key Stage 2.

Compare with the relevant sentences within the Level Descriptions from Level 1 to Level 5.

Note that the quality of the skill goes from simple to more complex, from direct observation to the careful, and repeated use, of measuring equipment.

Compare this progression with the Mathematics Order and you will get a fuller picture of how a skill like measuring can be developed progressively through practical science activity. Clearly you will need to bear in mind both the scientific and the mathematical progression when planning. Similar issues arise in the area of data handling and communication.

Now select some science concept areas and track them in the same way. Try choosing one from each of the three 'content' Programmes of Study.

Comparing statements in the same Programme of Study across the two Key Stages enables you to get a sense of how continuity between them can be envisaged. The development of a progressive set of activities over a period of time is what you will need to try to achieve to help the growth of your pupils' understanding of science ideas and skills. Furthermore, real science understanding requires the linking of learning in science with the wider experience of the everyday world. Science is part of life, it is not something that only happens in school or in the laboratory of the stereotypical balding, bespectacled, white-coated male scientist. So your planning for science will need to lead children *on* in their understanding and skill but also *outwards* in their ability to make connections between the central ideas and their wider applications.

One way to do this is to look for and take opportunities offered in other curriculum areas. In Chapter 11 examples are given of several activities that develop design and technology understanding. In some cases the activities draw on quite specific scientific ideas. For example, the work on yoghurt is linked to the idea that micro-organisms cause changes in milk. Children involved in this work will be learning about the 'good' uses of micro-organisms and the way milk can undergo a change that cannot be reversed. The work on the construction of effective tea-cup cosies gives the opportunity to explore the control of the flow of heat by the material of a tea-cup cosy. Children here will be considering heat as a form of energy and the thermal insulation properties of the materials used. Explicit recognition of the science being used in the technological activity will help your pupils both understand the science better *and* help them to be more effective technologists. Such activities may also enable you to assess the children's understanding as you note the way they are able to apply their learning in science to a new situation.

Enquiry Task

Suppose you have been given a class of Year 3 children and have chosen to do some work on forces with them. You look at Key Stage 1 and Key Stage 2 Programmes of Study and decide to build on the idea *that both pushes and pulls are examples of forces* by introducing the fact that *forces act in particular directions*.

- Identify a range of activities that you could use to allow the children to explore these two notions. What everyday situations might you be able to draw on to illustrate these aspects of force in action?

In thinking about forces you might consider, for example, a building site, or a vehicle. Another fruitful area for children to explore is their own world in which their toys, games and leisure pastimes play a large part. A selection of simple mechanical toys provides a good resource for this work. Whatever you decide, children need many experiences through which to explore science ideas before they can move on to a higher conceptual level of understanding.

The same is true of the acquisition of scientific skills. One opportunity to study a flower through a hand lens will not mean the child can use a hand lens correctly let alone effectively. You will need to provide many opportunities in differing settings for the child to acquire a good understanding of the appropriate, and effective, use of that particular aid to observation. Furthermore, in planning to try to develop a particular skill you should also keep in mind the need to identify other opportunities in other areas of scientific learning for reinforcing the skill through practice. Learning of science skills and ideas progresses on a broad front. The new emphasis on Level Descriptions as summary statements of a child's achievement underlines this notion. One swallow does not make a summer nor does one attempt at a fair test indicate real competence as a scientist. You would need more instances of the same kind of achievement, but set in different contexts, to be convinced!

How Should Ideas and Skills be Taught?

The new National Curriculum for Science offers no more guidance on how to teach science than the previous two. The non-statutory guidance which accompanied the original Order offered ideas on ways to approach both planning and teaching. HMI Annual Reports and the Annual Report of the Chief Inspector for Schools, all provide food for thought, backed by varying kinds of evidence, on the ways you might tackle your science teaching. What is clear in science is that your approach needs to:

- enable the development of science knowledge;
- enable the development of science skills;
- promote science as a systematic means of enquiry;
- enable children to relate their understanding to their own lives and the wider environment in which they live;
- promote the development of key communication, research and IT skills;
- develop the children's ability to consider their own health and safety, and that of others.

Your school is required to establish schemes of work in science and these will need to identify the teaching approaches to be used. Any approach worthy of being called scientific will, almost certainly, have a significant practical element to it. Your role is to plan programmes of work for your children that put the scheme of work into practice.

These programmes of work need to identify:

- the Programme of Study elements to be taught;
- the range of activities the children will carry out in your lessons;
- the teaching resources that will be required;
- the way these activities will link to the Programme of Study, to other areas of the curriculum, and to cross-curricular issues such as Health Education or Economic and Industrial Understanding;
- the way these activities will acknowledge the special needs of the children;
- the way these activities may be of use in contributing to the assessment of the children's progress.

At the heart of a good programme of work, though, lies the basic approach you adopt in your individual science lessons. As we have noted earlier, the selection of the actual activities you are going to teach will be governed by their relevance to, and clarity of focus on, the ideas and skills to be taught. They will also be subject to the availability of suitable resources. However, good lessons, once chosen, still need your skill and knowledge of science *and* your skill and knowledge of working with your children for them to be successful. The order you choose to teach the lessons may make the difference between helping the children to progress in their understanding and skill and simply experiencing a range of interesting but apparently disjointed activities. The balance you strike between the illustrative and the investigative focus will similarly help or, perhaps, hinder the children's growing understanding of science as both a body of knowledge and a set of processes and procedures.

Investigations explore ideas and phenomena as well as requiring application of particular skills. A programme of work needs to develop both knowledge and skills to the point where meaningful investigation can occur. This in turn will help to extend both skills and understanding. Some programmes of work will lend themselves less to full scientific investigation than others. Compare, for example, the opportunities in work on the Earth and Beyond with those in work about Changing Materials.

The way you teach your lessons will determine the effectiveness of the link between the teaching activity and the child's learning activity that we identified earlier. Introductions to lessons that enable the children to feel included, where their views are valued by the questioning you have employed, and teaching that makes clear the way the subject matter is relevant to the real world, will be vital in helping the children to see the science as theirs rather than yours. Activities that enable the children to work at their level (because you have thought in advance about their needs), recognizing where written instructions may pose a barrier or the likely positive interaction of particular groupings of children, will be essential to promoting productive work. Providing prompts to assist the children's investigative approaches, either through written planning guides, or by your involvement in the process alongside the children, using questions to stimulate and guide thinking about ideas and use of skills will be important not only to enhance the likelihood of learning but also to enable you to observe and assess the children's achievements. Finally, and importantly, allowing your children the opportunity to try to draw conclusions and communicate what they have found out, to evaluate and relate their findings to what they already know, and their methods to other possible approaches will be essential if their 'old' ideas are to be challenged and replaced where appropriate by 'new' ones.

Summary

In this chapter we have tried to outline the major changes to the National Curriculum for Science in the 1995 Order when compared with the 1991 Order. The purposes of the new National Curriculum for Science are described as giving directions on what you teach in science and how to judge your children's progress. As we have indicated, it provides a framework for study of experimental and investigative exploration of the three key content areas of science knowledge and understanding, Sc 2, 3, and 4. What we have tried to explore here is the way in which you might make effective use of that curriculum in planning for and teaching science in your classroom and school. We have also attempted to make clear the challenges you need to meet in order to make the enjoyable and constructive learning of science by the children in your class a reality.

Notes

1   For more details of how to undertake this activity have a look at the Autogyros workcard from the series entitled, On the Move, part of *Learning Through Science*, Macdonald Educational, 1983.
2   The work of Driver *et al.* (1985) and the Science Processes and Concept Exploration (SPACE) project (1990–92) repay close attention in this respect.
3   A number of publications from the Primary School Teachers and Science project (PSTS) give further insights in this area (Summers *et al.* 1989, 1990, 1992) as well as providing resources to help teachers develop their own understanding (PSTS 1991a, 1991b, 1992, 1993a, 1993b).
4   For further reading on children's acquisition of ideas about the Earth in Space see J. Nussbaum, *Earth as a Cosmic Body* in Driver *et al.* (1985).

References

DEARING, R. (1993) *The National Curriculum and its Assessment: An Interim Report*, School Examinations and Assessment Council: London.

DEPARTMENT OF EDUCATION and SCIENCE/WELSH OFFICE, (DES/WO) (1989) *Science in the National Curriculum*, HMSO: London.

DEPARTMENT OF EDUCATION and SCIENCE/WELSH OFFICE, (DES/WO) (1991) *Science in the National Curriculum (1991)*, HMSO: London.

DEPARTMENT FOR EDUCATION/WELSH OFFICE EDUCATION DEPARTMENT, (DFE/WOED) (1995) *Science in the National Curriculum*, HMSO: London.

DRIVER, R., GUESNE, E. and TIBERGHIEN, A. (ed) (1985) *Children's Ideas in Science*, Open University Press: Milton Keynes.

KRUGER, C. and SUMMERS, M. (1989) 'An investigation of some primary school teachers understanding of changes in materials', *School Science Review*, 71, 255, pp. 17–27.

KRUGER, C., PALACIO, D. and SUMMERS, M. (1990) 'A survey of primary school teachers conceptions of force and motion', *Educational Research*, 32, 2, pp. 83–95.

NATIONAL CURRICULUM COUNCIL (NCC) (1992) *Knowledge and Understanding of Science: Forces*, NCC: York.

NATIONAL CURRICULUM COUNCIL (1993a) *Knowledge and Understanding of Science: Energy*, NCC: York.

NATIONAL CURRICULUM COUNCIL (1993b) *Knowledge and Understanding of Science: Electricity and Magnetism*, NCC: York.

NATIONAL CURRICULUM COUNCIL (1993c) *Teaching Science at Key Stages 1 and 2*, NCC: York.

Nuffield Primary Science (SPACE) (1993) 11 Teacher's Guides and 22 Pupils' Books for Key Stage 2, Teacher's Guide and 11 Pupils' Books for Key Stage 1, Teacher's Handbook and INSET Pack, Collins Educational: London.

Primary School Teachers and Science Project (PSTS) INSET Materials: 1. *Understanding Forces* (1991a); 2. *Understanding Energy* (1991b); 3. *Understanding Plants and the Gases They Need* (1992); 4. *Understanding Materials and Why They Change* (1993a); 5. *Understanding the Earth's Place in the Universe* (1993b); Oxford University Department of Educational Studies/Westminster College: Oxford. (PSTS INSET Materials are available from Association for Science Education (ASE), College Lane, Hatfield, Herts AL10 9AA.)

School Curriculum and Assessment Authority (SCAA) (1994a) *The National Curriculum and its Assessment: Final Report*, SCAA: London.

Schools Curriculum and Assessment Authority (1994b) *Knowledge and Understanding of Science: Chemical Changes*, SCAA: London.

Schools Curriculum and Assessment Authority (1994c) *Knowledge and Understanding of Science: Genetics and Ecology*, SCAA: London.

Science Processes and Concepts Exploration (SPACE) Research Reports, *Evaporation and Condensation* (1990), *Growth* (1990), *Light* (1990), *Sound* (1990), *Electricity* (1991), *Materials* (1991), *Processes of Life* (1992), *Rocks, Soil and Weather* (1992) Liverpool: Liverpool University Press.

Summers, M. (1992) 'Improving primary school teachers understanding of science concepts – theory into practice', *Int. J. Science Education*, 14, 1, pp. 25–40.

6   History

Paul Taylor

Introduction

History has long been a controversial subject in its own right and the debate over its place in the curriculum of schools has been just as argumentative. This chapter does not dwell on the political and philosophical issues raised by the study of history as such, but rather concentrates on areas of practical and immediate concern.

In the first part of this chapter I will look at the changes from the old to the new curriculum, and highlight significant changes and differences, as well as noting those aspects of continuity. In the next section I will pay attention to some of the fundamental aspects of the teaching of history in primary schools in order to ascertain what is important and significant for the pupil when studying the subject. Finally, I will outline a way of implementing change to meet the requirements of the new Order and suggest strategies for action in terms of planning and classroom delivery.

Overall, my aim is to indicate a positive and reflective approach to the subject that can result in a purposeful outcome for pupils and meet the specific requirements of the statutory Order.

National Curriculum in History – Old and New

The key change in the revised National Curriculum for History is a significant reduction in the prescribed content required at Key Stages 1 and 2. The Order at each Key Stage has been restructured to specify the essential knowledge, understanding and skills elements that constitute history. The three Attainment Targets have been reduced to one, called History, with Level Descriptions replacing Statements of Attainment. These Level Descriptions (LDs) are summative statements of characteristic pupil performance in a range of historical tasks undertaken during each of the two Key Stages. There is a strong content emphasis on national British history, though local, ancient, European and wider world history are not ignored. This is in line with the original document and takes practical account of the resources schools have accumulated.

Key Stage 1

In Key Stage 1 the number of time periods to be taught drops from three to two. The section dealing with change in the way of life of British people since the Second World War has been removed. However, the emphasis on British History is maintained through having to look at aspects of the way of life of people in Britain in the past beyond living memory, having to use examples of famous British men and women over time, and events from British History. The study of myths, legends and fictional stories, and use of music and computer-based material is no longer required. The total time it is presumed might be spent on history would be in the region of thirty-six hours a year; seventy-two hours across the Key Stage, which is about an hour per week on average.

Enquiry Task

Consider how far the changes described so far are likely to affect the teaching of history at Key State 1 in your school.

Take the emphasis on famous British people, the lives of ordinary people in this country, and particular events in British history. Now develop a scheme of work which seeks to show how these can be integrated into a meaningful approach for your pupils, e.g., Guy Fawkes, Gunpowder Plot, Lives of people at the start of 17th Century.

Key Stage 2

In Key Stage 2 the number of study units has been reduced from nine to six. Within the six units the prescribed content has been cut and what is left is now made clearer in relation to the focus of the unit itself. The units are Romans, Anglo-Saxons and Vikings in Britain, Life in Tudor times, Victorian Britain (or Britain since 1930), Ancient Greece, local history, and a past non-European society. For instance, in Victorian Britain the focus is on men, women and children at different levels of society, and the importance of changes in industry and transport. The content that follows specifically outlines the industrial and transport effects and looks at work, home, leisure and school. Total time to be spent on history at Key Stage 2 may be in the region of forty-five hours a year; 180 hours across the Key Stage, which is just over an hour per week on average.

Layout of the New Order in History

There is a common format for both Key Stages. An introduction to each Key Stage; the historical content for each Key Stage; the key elements. The introduction

---

Enquiry Task

How does the reduction of the study units affect the organization and timing of history at Key Stage 2 in your school?

Take one of the six units and decide on the concepts you wish to develop from the study and which of the key elements are to be given prominence. Remember to check that your school has at least 'visited' each of the key elements during the Key Stage.

---

provides a focus for the whole Key Stage and summarizes the development required in knowledge, understanding and skills. The historical content identifies the basic requirements to be taught, while the key elements characterize areas of progression over the Key Stage.

The key elements cover five common areas at Key Stages 1 and 2. Chronology is highlighted including sequencing, dates and time words. There has to be a range and depth of historical knowledge and understanding involving overview and in-depth studies of historical issues, the significant features of historical periods and encompassing a range of peoples' experiences. Interpretation of history is called for, looking at motivations over time. Historical enquiry is to be delivered through using a wide range of sources to facilitate active discovery of the past from the evidence available. Organizational and communication skills are to be enhanced through a variety of mediums. None of these are new additions to what was already expected in the existing National Curriculum. At Key Stage 2, emphasis is given to teaching history from a variety of perspectives, political, economic, technological and scientific, social, religious, cultural and aesthetic. This can be described as the PESC formula, for short.

The content studied and key elements covered should allow a Level Description to be ascertained for the single Attainment Target. The Level Descriptions (Levels 1–3 by the end of Key State 1, Levels 2–5 by the end of Key Stage 2) cover the following factors of pupil achievement, namely, the range and depth of factual knowledge attained; the knowledge, understanding and perception of periods, events and issues acquired; the ability to communicate historical knowledge and understanding; the analytical and interpretive skills the pupils have achieved.

These factors are the essence of the paragraph given for each Level Description at Levels 1–5 and in effect subsume in one statement the old three Attainment Targets and their Statements of Attainment. You will judge which Level Description fits a pupil most appropriately for his/her stage of development in general, and ultimately the Level reached at the end of each Key Stage. Level Descriptions seek to be a balanced, if somewhat generalized, description of where a pupil has reached. The idea is that the overall planning for history is driven by the demands of the Programme of Study, and not determined and directed by the Level Descriptions. The latter should reflect what has been achieved through the planned and focused work in history.

Enquiry Task

Take either Levels 1–3 or 2–5 of the Level Descriptions and outline for at least one of these levels, initially, what form and type of pupil work would be appropriate to meet the criteria outlined. Use samples of past pupil work, where available, to see how the criteria used to match it fits the new descriptions.

Using the Non-Statutory Guidance to Support the New Order

There is a good deal of useful information in the non-statutory guidance (*NSG*), which came with the original Order, to support the planning and implementation of the revised Order. Listed below are those that you may find particularly useful in implementing the new Order; page references come from the Non-Statutory Guidance. Experienced teachers will already be familiar with these. On page B1 of the NSG, the purposes of school history shown remain valid propositions, while in C1 an outline curriculum plan for implementing history covers all relevant areas. Pages C9–C11 show, with examples, how to plan links with other areas of the curriculum. The cross-curricular elements are given attention on pages C12–C13. On C14 there is a list of potential teaching methods and on pages C15–C16 the importance of enquiry and communication in history are noted. Broader areas, such as equal opportunities, multicultural education, special educational needs and exceptionally able pupils are covered on pages C18–C20. There is a range of useful sources to consider and how to plan progression through their use on pages C20–C23. Pages C26–C27 deal with the teaching of sensitive issues such as disagreements about political, social and moral questions and how to approach these. Section F, with its breakdown of the old Supplementary Study Units between F1 and F16 is still useful for showing the kind of information you might include when teaching local history (F7–F9) or a past non-European Society (F11–F16). The bibliography in H1 can still be an appropriate guide. Section D, on planning schemes of work, can be adapted for the new Order as will be shown in a later section of this chapter.

The Fundamental Aspects of Teaching History

History is about knowledge, understanding and skills. In any teaching of the subject these elements should be included in lesson planning and the approaches that are adopted, irrespective of the content matter of the topic itself.

You decide which knowledge and level of understanding is appropriate to your pupils and then you select information accordingly. You may be seeking to build up a picture of a period in history and to develop conceptual awareness of the essential elements of that period. In essence an 'image' of the period is being strived for. The PESC formula referred to earlier may be useful in determining your approach to reading. The 'Political' element requires you to be clear on the main events, what happened and when; the 'Economic' element focuses on issues such as how people made their living, the food they grew, the work they did, their means of transport, the machines and inventions they used and the importance or otherwise of money and trade. With the 'Social' element you need to be looking at how people lived, their clothes, houses, furniture, the different social classes and their religious beliefs, festivals and gods. The 'Cultural' element requires exploration of the buildings, paintings, music, theatre, recreation, sport and stories. From the accumulated information you have acquired and the resources available or obtainable you can then confidently think about what you want the pupils to learn.

There are four skills that are very specific to history, namely developing a sense of time, understanding language of the past, empathetic understanding and the importance of how we know.

With a sense of time, history can introduce pupils to the concept of time through words and phrases such as 'long ago', 'age', 'period', 'century', 'decade', etc. and therefore the means of measuring time. Sequencing is important in understanding 'when' an event took place and to locate it correctly in time. You need to create an image of a particular period to help pupils grasp what fits together and is part of a particular time, such as clothes, houses, transport and technology. Once the essentials of time are grasped the relationship to change and continuity, similarity and difference can be tackled, such as what made things change and how it is different from now.

Enquiry Task

For Key Stage 1 or 2 collect and collate a series of sources which help to create an image of a particular period in time. Repeat the exercise for a different time period. Decide how you would use the material to demonstrate to your pupils ideas of continuity and change.

Pupils need to know something of the language of the past so that words which may have no modern meaning, or whose use has changed, such as Danelaw, Caravel, Board School, Blitz, can be used in relation to past events or people. This not only extends pupils' vocabulary, and can be a source of fascination to pupils in itself, but it is essential to an understanding of the context in which people in the past lived. The words, phrases and sayings used by these people can illuminate a period and give it shape and substance.

Empathetic understanding is the ability to put yourself in the place of another and see their point of view. It is a crucial part of understanding situations belonging to the past to see if it is possible to gauge what people thought and felt. This is not the case of indulging your pupils in imaginary exercises along the lines of 'I am a Roman soldier on Hadrian's Wall' or 'I am a slave in Ancient Greece' – both may well lead to excellent examples of written or spoken English but may not lead to any further direct historical understanding or awareness. The use of imagination in exercises which ask pupils to consider a given situation, after discussion and some research, and possibly the use of drama, is a long way from just 'making it up as you go along'. Though there is much argument about empathy as such, for the primary school pupil it remains a valid focus of activity.

Pupils can be introduced to 'How we know' by, for example, exploring what they can see for themselves and what they can find out from books, pictures and objects; then they can begin to differentiate between fact, fiction and what is likely to be true. There is immense scope here for a wide range of resources to be used and a great deal of discussion to take place. 'Talking time' is crucial if children are to develop the understanding required.

History is fundamentally about telling a series of stories and there is so much opportunity to bring the subject alive through the stories you choose to tell. The subject should be instructive but also fun. Though the allocation of hours has been cut back in terms of the formal teaching time available, the basics of the subject remain unaltered. The subject matter is now less prescriptive and the strategies you employ can now be based on covering a smaller amount of material. What follows is an examination of how to achieve the essentials of the subject through specific examples.

Enquiry Task

For either Key Stage investigate the range of storybooks you have available to identify those that may help to develop a particular historical skill, concept or empathy with the history you are intending to teach.

Implementing the New Order

Many schools already have their school plan for history in place, and have developed planning strategies and tasks, as well as considered and devised teaching approaches. In this section, the aim is to show how existing planning, resources and ideas already being used can be fitted successfully into the new requirements. There will also be three practical examples shown of activities which cover the demands of the revised Order.

Planning Strategies: An Overview

In planning history work you may find it is helpful to focus on four main questions.

- What are your aims?
- What learning objectives do you hope the pupils will achieve?
- What resources are available to deliver the objectives?
- How will the pupils' learning be assessed?

By using these fundamental questions as the basis of your planning the content can evolve in a structured format. You may find it more productive to regard learning objectives from a pupil's perspective hence, 'Pupils will. . . .', 'Pupils can. . . .', 'Pupils should. . . .', etc.

Once you know what you are doing, and what the pupils will be required to do to meet that outcome you need to ascertain what resources you have, or will need, to meet them – written, pictorial, audio–visual, oral. You may have to create/discover some resources of your own.

Having done all this you need to decide what outcomes you are hoping for. Whatever they are, for instance, display, workbook, folder, play, they should be assessed in some way, though not necessarily using National Curriculum Level Descriptions on every occasion. How will you do this? At what stages during the work will you look for specific awareness of pupil development in the areas of knowledge and skills? Are you going to compare pupils with each other directly? (norm-referencing). Are you going to define assessment against a designated learning objective? (criterion referencing). Are you going to pinpoint particular areas of a pupil's work? (diagnostic). How much will be on-going assessment? (formative). How much will be based on end of topic assessment? (summative).

Enquiry Task

Select the main facets within a Level Description. Now identify through initial planning the point at which each of these facets will be assessed through pupil end 'products'. How will you be sure that there is sufficient evidence to support the 'awarding' of a given level?

There will not be formal, nationally set, assessment and evaluation exercises in history, either during or at the end of Key Stages 1 and 2. Therefore any assessment you do is part of your professional need to know where the pupil is, and your school's commitment to providing parents, governors and OFSTED advisers with sound judgments concerning pupil development.

Obviously, you will need to build in assessment at the start of your planning and this assessment will need to occur at various stages in the learning process. In history, on-going assessment is probably the best way to judge the effectiveness of the work from a pupil's perspective since this enables both you and them to reflect on what they are doing. There may be, however, a place for seeking to summarize the range of learning undertaken at the close of the work.

Whole School Planning

At both Key Stages it is important to show what will be studied and where. With Key Stage 1 there is a lot of integrated work in which history may figure. For example in Year 1, pupils could look at Clothes and People Who Help Us. In Year 2, they might explore Light, and then the Victorian Farm.

This fits with the new curriculum, in that Year 1 focuses on changes in the children's own lives and those of their families or adults around them. 'Clothes' fits neatly into an examination of changes in style and use over the recent past, while 'People Who Help Us' allows a study of the changing role of the school secretary, the task of the ancillary helper, and the place of the teacher. With Year 2, the pupils move on to a wider focus to look at aspects of the life of people beyond living memory through a study of light in which methods used in the past will be explored, and through the specific example of a Victorian Farm.

At Key Stage 2 an example of how the revised Order could be implemented covers:

- Year 3: Romans, Anglo-Saxons and Vikings in Britain and a Study on Ancient Egypt;
- Year 4: Life in Tudor Times;
- Year 5: Victorian Britain and Local History;
- Year 6: Ancient Greece.

Under the new Order the units can be taught much as before.

Specific Planning Strategies

In this section, ways of designing tasks to fit the learning objectives identified in the new Order will be explored. In providing this guide, the topic 'light' will be used as an example for this kind of planning at Key Stage 1 (see Figure 6.1).

A sense of chronology should be developed. This might be achieved by giving pupils a selection of pictures, photographs, drawings, etc., and asking them to sequence using words such as old, new, before and long ago. Stories connected with the topic such as Florence Nightingale, 'the lady with the lamp', can be developed.

Children need to become aware of why events occurred and what the results were. For instance, why gas replaced candles and oil as a form of street lighting; electricity replacing gas in the home illustrates how people did things and how these changes affected peoples' lives.

The exploration of artifacts is an important part of the history curriculum, for instance candles, oil, gas and paraffin lamps, bulbs, and torches. This exploration allows a discussion of how we take for granted modern ways of doing things. For instance, during the War Years, 1939–45, there were long periods of blackouts which many grandparents may still remember and in the 1970s there were similar periods of blackouts during the Miners' strikes, which many of your children's parents may recall.

Pupils do not learn in isolation and therefore history can form significant links with other curriculum subjects. The aim should be to blend appropriate subject areas, such as science and basic principles of light, or art with visual displays of light medium, along with the teaching of history.

Figure 6.1: Key Stage 1 history element study unit on light

Focus/Key Questions	Concepts	Activities	Resources
What forms of light have been available to people in the past?	Variety of light sources	Through discussion, pupils consider why certain types of light were the only ones available.	Pictures of people in different buildings over time to facilitate the discussion of light
When, where and how would the light sources available (see resources) have been used?	Use of light sources	In small groups pupils place pictures/artifacts into chronological order, writing a sentence for each one about 'when, where, and how'.	Pictures and artifacts of light mediums
Why were some light sources better than others?	Improvement	Discussion based upon which of these is best, and why.	Photographs showing ease/difficulty of providing light, e.g., gas lamp lighters, electricity supply
How, particularly in the recent past, have changes in light sources affected people's lives?	Continuity and change	By using a selection of resources, children can explore the ways in which all forms of light still have their uses.	Possible videos, stories, photographs

---

Enquiry Task

Construct an area of study from the Key Stage 1 Programme of Study and consider the following points:

- How does my area of study fit into the overall Key Stage 1 provision?
- Which of the key elements do I need to focus on particularly?
- What learning outcomes am I expecting?
- What questions are going to enable the pupils to research these outcomes?
- What resources are available which will enable me to provide activities to support the main learning objectives?

The next example, (see Figure 6.2) shows how Study Unit 3a, Victorian Britain, and Study Unit 5, Local History, can interrelate. It therefore acts as a model for what you might look at, just as in your area there might be the canal, the road or the airport as an aspect of local history.

The plan starts with a general overview of Britain at the start of the Victorian period. This leads into a detailed examination of the processes of economic change. At this point – having covered inventions, innovations and steam power – it would be appropriate to examine the first key local issue, namely a field study visit to the railway station to look for evidence of its Victorian origins. From this the pupils could move on to question why the railway came. Having studied various economic reasons for the railway's arrival we then return to our main focused look at the impact of that change on society at large. With a general overall knowledge it would then be sensible to return to a local issue, e.g., the impact of the railway on the community.

It would be important to examine how the lives of people changed once the railway had been built, for example new houses and public buildings. Before summing-up, it would be worthwhile to explore how the wealth generated by the railway influenced the local community, in a direct sense through new buildings, both public and private, and indirectly through the power of 'railway money' on the town's development, e.g., political influence on the town council. Overall the local history element here should be a dynamic and flexible vehicle which can be adapted to your local area.

The final example (see Figure 6.3) is of a unit based on the Development of the Car Industry in Oxford since 1930. It highlights numerous aspects of Study Unit 3b: Britain Since 1930, particularly changes in technology and transport, which is one of the three emphasized areas in this study unit. There is obviously strong use of local resources, and the over-arching theme of Economic and Industrial Understanding as a National Curriculum cross-curricular theme is addressed.

As can be seen from the plan there is an investigation of an important historical issue, namely the growth of a new industry and its effects on society and the environment. Local developments are related to national trends and events, such as the Second World War, over a long period of time. There are a range of pupil tasks here which show the variety of approaches to the subject.

Interpretation of maps of the area, and of the large factory, along with the reading of written accounts from the time of development are called for. There is a good deal of comprehension of information required from structured worksheets which relate to the resources made available to the pupils. By bringing individuals in to describe their previous work at the factory and to discuss present day environmental concerns in a historical setting, children's questioning skills will be enhanced. There is exploration of the local housing to see the impact of new developments regarding site and location.

Pupils have to design a car, sketch and draw it using a computer. They then discuss their car designs having looked at past examples. The lives of significant individuals such as William Morris are given attention to emphasize the personal role in bringing about change. Obviously a visit to the factory encapsulates the links between present reality and the past which has forged it.

This outline plan can be used in a variety of ways and hopefully shows, once again, the possibilities inherent in any area, irrespective of the local industrial opportunities.

Conclusion

The essence of what history is all about and the needs of the revised National Curriculum are not incompatible. History is a foundation subject in every sense. It

Figure 6.2: Key Stage 2 study unit on Victorian Britain with local history

Key Issues	Concepts	Content	Resources and Types of Sources	Activities	Organization
What was Britain like on the eve of the Victorian period?	• Period	• PESC overview of Britain	• Maps showing Britain & British Empire, 1837, • TV broadcasts	• Brainstorm PESC elements in groups. • Read section from 'Oliver Twist'. • Watch relevant TV programme	• Group/class discussion • Individual • Class
What were the processes of economic change?	• Invention and innovation: • Steam power • Factory production	• Steam engines, railway engines • Child labour • Market expansion	• Pictures, posters • Pupil reference books	• Find out about steam power and factory production. • Look at changes.	• Class • Individual
What evidence is there that the local railway station dates to Victorian times?	• Change and continuity	• A study of aspects of the local railway, e.g. architecture, decorative features	• Railway station • Photographs, newspaper cuttings	• Visit the local railway station. Make observational notes/sketches of any features thought to be Victorian. • In classroom look at photographs of station as it was, and newspaper accounts of it opening	• Work in pairs at station. • Groups of six in class. • Whole class summary
Why did the railway come?	• Market, Profit Trade	• Specific reasons for local railway development	• Newspapers, local histories, railway prospectuses	• Looking at a variety of primary sources. Putting forward arguments based on evidence to show why some people wanted the railway and some did not. • Debate/role play for and against the railway.	• Small group activity followed by whole class participation
What was the impact on society of economic change?	• Urbanization • Class	• Living conditions and Public Health • Three sub-divisions on class	• Various video material	• Talk about urbanization. • Look at Public Health, e.g., in Birmingham. • Find out about factory work, mass production • Talk about poverty and wealth in relation to urban society.	• Class • Individual

Key question	Concepts/themes	Content	Resources	Activities	Organisation
What was the impact of the railway on the local community as it developed?	• Cause and consequence • Growth	• How the town changed lives of the people • Specific Victorian industry/commerce affected by the railway	• O.S. maps • Census material • Diaries	• Examination of maps/census showing impact of railway development, e.g., site and location of new buildings, such as houses, warehouses, factories	• Observation/discussion in small groups
How did the lives of the people change during the Victorian period?	• Factory work • Mass education • Poverty • Wealth	• Factory Acts • Workhouses • Schooling	• Relevant TV broadcasts • Posters, e.g., of fines on workers	• Contrast farm and factory work. • Examine changing hours of work through Factory Acts. • Explore changes in education before 1870 and after 1891.	• Class • Group
How important was religion in the times of the Victorians?	• Worship	• Middle class/working class • Religious practices	• Reference/topic books	• Find out about how different classes worshipped and numbers going to church. • Look at different religious groups, e.g., Salvation Army.	• Individual • Class
What was the cultural achievement of the Victorians?	• Mass literacy • National identity	• Popular culture, e.g., football and holidays • Public buildings	• TV broadcasts, photographs, novels, pictures	• Talk about the idea of more people doing the same thing, e.g., reading newspapers, travel, holidays, national events, e.g., Great Exhibition, Jubilees.	• Group • Class • Individual
What was the impact of the railway money on the community?	• Power	• Study of buildings and institutions	• Newspaper accounts of town buildings showing pride in the wealth of the town • Observation of the buildings today	• Pupils use evidence of buildings, e.g., houses, shops, hotels, public buildings to show how railways brought prosperity by examining the structure and uses of what they can observe, e.g., size of building, design, ornate decoration, function. • Class discussion on the buildings to elicit categorization and visible opulence associated with wealth and its display.	• Small groups perhaps working in various parts of the town. Reporting back to whole class for discussion
What was Britain like at the end of the Victorian period and what was its legacy for today?	• Continuity and change	• PESC overview of Britain in 1901 and 1990s	• Map of Britain and its Empire 1901	• Discussion as in first part of planning	• Class

Figure 6.3: Key Stage 2 local history study unit/elements of study unit on Britain since 1930. The development of the car industry in Cowley, Oxford, 1931–1994

Key Issues	Concepts	Content	Resources and Types of Source	Activities and Teaching and Learning Methods	Links with Other Subjects
Cowley before the coming of the car. What transport existed?	• Continuity and change	• The existing forms of transport; their type, variability and form	• Maps, posters, pictures • Primary written sources	• Pupils using maps and written accounts to locate places in Cowley prior to the car industry. • Working on observing, categorizing and recording the type of transport available.	Geography
The coming of the car – impact on Cowley workforce and housing	• Economic growth • Prosperity • Migration	• The role of the car • The development of Cowley	• Worksheets • Local environment • Audio tape recorder work	• Pupils answering questions verbally and in writing on the development of the car. • Map work and discussion on the workforce. • Study of local homes in the environment.	Geography Art
The impact of World War Two on Cowley/car industry	• Industrial flexibility	• Cowley during the war; changing processes and ideas	• Worksheets	• Pupils using the worksheets to create a picture of dynamic change during the war years. • Importance of facts and figures of production – charting these.	Science Technology

Building the cars – factors of production, design processes	• Streamlining • Production line	• The manner of the productive process from start to finished product	• Worksheets, pictures • Factory visit • Computers	• Pupils develop understanding of needs of car manufacture and answer questions on this. • They see the importance of streamlining through IT work and the production methods through visual analysis of line methods including factory trip.	Science Technology Mathematics Economic and industrial understanding IT
The role of William Morris, Cowley and Oxford	• Individualism	• Information on, and impact of, Morris: his importance in the community	• Library books, newspapers, magazines	• Pupils working to collaboratively collect and collate information to develop a wall display on Morris; timeline use.	English
The impact of cars on the environment	• Mobility • Congestion	• The need to preserve the city • Park & Ride • Environmental concerns	• Statistics, graphs, charts, figures	• Pupils plotting and evaluating the figures on car usage to see the need for more efficient use of the transport system.	Mathematics Environmental awareness Geography Citizenship
The future of the car industry and Cowley	• Development	• People's changing needs • Consumer demands • Long-term planning considerations	• Plans	• Pupils listening to accounts of likely change, study plans for future developments and consider their own views on this.	Geography Art Careers education and guidance

Enquiry Task

Choosing any one of the History Study Units, consider your planning along the following lines:

- Which key issues need to be covered? Which of these key issues are to be given prominence? (Don't forget to ensure that PESC requirements are included when key issues are being formulated.)
- What ideas are you going to highlight and draw out through the content?
- How will your activities support the learning outcomes?
- Choose resources which will support pupil activities and enhance the furthering of the key elements.

lays down the bedrock on which an understanding of a pupil's place in the world is formed. Though there are constraints on what any teacher can do within the confines of the content areas in the National Curriculum there is nothing to stop the argument being put forward for some of the non-National Curriculum time to be devoted to wider historical issues and themes.

History is one of the most fascinating, enlivening and enlightening areas for any child to study, for it deals with the search for understanding, why people acted as they did and the repercussions of that action on the world we live in today.

Acknowledgments

With thanks for the help and support of Miss A Jordan and Mrs R Butler who contributed to the work on Figures 6.2 and 6.3.

References

ANDREETTI, K. (1993) *Teaching History from Primary Evidence*, London: D. Fulton.
BELL, P. (1991) *Practical Topics for the Primary School, Part 2*, History and Geography, Preston, Topical Resources.
BOURDILLON, H. (ed) (1994) *Teaching History*, London: Routledge.
COOPER, H. (1992) *The Teaching of History*, London: D. Fulton.
DES (1991) *History in the National Curriculum*, London: HMSO.
GRIFFIN, J. and EDDERSHAW, D. (1994) *Using Local History Sources*, Hodder and Stoughton Education, London.
KEITH, C. (1991) *A Teacher's Guide to Using Listed Buildings*, London: English Heritage.
MOFFAT, H., *et al.* (1994) *School Museums and Primary History*, London: Historical Association.
NCC (1991) *History Non-Statutory Guidance*, York: NCC.

7   Geography

John Halocha and Maureen Roberts

In this chapter we will look first at the new Order then investigate the changes and implications with a view to forming a sound base for revising school geography planning.

There have been improvements to the quality of geographical education since the introduction of the National Curriculum's requirement for its inclusion across the primary age range (Lloyd, 1994). This chapter aims to see how this progress can be sustained and enhanced. It examines the Order from a practical perspective. The Order, and in particular the changes to the Order, will need to be considered by all primary schools if they are to continue developing an effective geographical understanding in their pupils while recognizing the new requirements and time constraints. Geography offers exciting possibilities for active learning, enquiry-based approaches, and achievement for all children. The challenge for all of us, as we revise our plans, is to ensure that we provide geographical experiences which will prepare children to become informed citizens of the future.

Revision of the Geography Order: Key Stage 1

The three localities specified in the old Order have been replaced by two: the immediate locality of the school; and one other contrasting area (in human or physical terms) in the UK, or beyond.

The framework of specified locational knowledge has been abandoned. The focus is now firmly on children's ability to observe, question, record, and to communicate ideas and information. Within this brief, there are six areas of knowledge to be taught; geographical terms, fieldwork activities, following directions, making maps, using globes and maps including naming constituent countries of the United Kingdom and children must know where they live. Finally, there is a requirement to use secondary sources such as CD-ROM and aerial photographs.

The previous long and complex list of unconnected themes has been replaced by a compact thematic study of an environment in any locality. Pupils will be expected to express views regarding the environment's attractiveness or otherwise, and note any changes occurring so as to form an opinion regarding the quality and sustainability of the selected environment.

Overall, there has been a substantial reduction in content. The arbitrary division imposed by the five Attainment Targets (ATs) have been replaced by a single AT: Geography. The new structure is based instead around the three concepts, Skills, Places (localities) and Thematic study – these all being taught through geographical investigations. The concepts should not be viewed as three isolated aspects of geography to be taught separately, but instead they should be seen as elements to be combined for effective planning. The layout of the Places and Themes section of the new Order perhaps does not make the potential interconnectedness clear. The relevant linking of skills, places and thematic studies will help in effective planning. The contrasting locality investigation should also include these. Incidentally, this may be a good opportunity to use a European Union location.

Although teachers are asked to concentrate on two localities and a thematic environmental study, there is also a clear requirement to ensure that the localities studied are set within a broader geographical context. For example, when looking at local traffic you might identify from the writing on vans, lorries and coaches their places of origin. By doing this, additional geographical knowledge might be developed and young children can be helped to understand that localities can be connected in many different ways. Children will enjoy being introduced to a wide range of skills through fieldwork activities. The use of simple and appropriate information technology fits neatly into this aspect of the whole-school planning process for geography, as well as for other subjects. Going back to our previous example, you might like children to record the types of vehicles and their origins using a simple database.

Revision of the Geography Order: Key Stage 2

The five locality studies have been reduced to three, of which one is a broader study of the school area and will build on one first undertaken in a more limited form in Key Stage 1. One other locality should be within the UK and the other in a country in Africa, Asia (excluding Japan which is studied at Key Stage 3), South America or Central America including the Caribbean. Reference here is to geographic localities and not, as previously, to the nature of their economic development.

In these locality studies, pupils should be taught about the main physical and human features and discuss how the localities may be similar and how they may differ. They also need to understand how the features of the localities have influenced the nature and location of human activities within them. Teachers are encouraged to use any recent or proposed changes in the localities as well as setting the localities within a broader geographical context.

The potential for progression from Key Stage 1 to Key Stage 2 has been enhanced by clearer definitions of the extent of the localities to be studied. However, to ensure progression and continuity and avoid repetition, you will need to liaise with other teachers and define the extent and content within locality studies in both Key Stages.

The content of the thematic studies has been reduced from eleven to four. The

Order encourages more imaginative and flexible choice of the places used to study these themes. You may find it helpful to ascertain which themes are best represented within your school locality, a contrasting locality in the UK or a locality in Latin America, Africa or Asia (excluding Japan). The four geographical themes are Rivers, Weather, Settlement, and Environmental Change. Geographical contexts within the European Union should be used where relevant to the theme being studied. For example, it may be appropriate to study extreme weather patterns in other European countries when developing work on the 'Weather' theme. Themes may either be taught alone or often in combination with each other where this will improve geographical understanding. Linked to our previous example, the themes of 'Weather' and 'Settlement' could be planned together. This would enable children to understand why, for instance, the 1995 floods in northern Europe occurred and their devastating effect on settlements and low lying farmland, particularly in the Netherlands.

The geographical skills to be taught at Key Stage 2 are a more detailed version of those already introduced at Key Stage 1. Through investigations of places and thematic studies, children are given opportunities to observe and ask questions about geographical features and issues, collect, record and interpret evidence to answer the questions, and, most fundamentally, to analyse it in order to draw conclusions and communicate findings. The appropriate use of information technology needs to be enhanced further throughout this Key Stage. An example might be the comparison of teletext weather data with the children's own database of weather statistics. Alternatively, the wealth of interactive data available on CD-ROM may be used where appropriate. Some children will end their geographical studies in school at the end of Key Stage 3 and this places a heavy responsibility on the provision of knowledge, skills and understanding that an effective primary course should provide.

The immediate school locality can often provide many easy to reach, and relatively inexpensive, opportunities for geographical enquiry. If your school has not yet undertaken an audit of its locality, this may be a valuable use of a school development day. This kind of audit helps to identify what is available in the locality. What is not available can help to identify a suitable contrasting locality. It may also be a most effective way for you to become more familiar with the vicinity of your school from a geographical perspective. Viewpoints can be identified; local contacts developed and fieldwork organization clarified. While the local study will provide some obvious opportunities for you to integrate thematic studies, you will find that paragraph 6 in the Key Stage 2 Order also includes the use of a range of scales from local to national, as well as contexts from different parts of the world. It is well worth reading this paragraph to clarify for yourself the importance attached to using a variety of interesting and appropriate geographical locations and topical events like the 1995 Japanese earthquake.

Issues and Implications in the New Order at Key Stages 1 and 2

In our view, the new document should not be viewed as laying out a constricting framework for the study of geography. It might be helpful if you think of it as

Enquiry Task – Locality Audit

- Together with at least one other colleague carry out an audit of your locality from a geographical perspective.
- What would you use at Key Stages 1 and 2?
- The aim is to list what is available and to note what is not. This will help you to select your contrasting locality.
- Examples of things to note:
    streams
    slopes
    types of buildings
    services
    street furniture
    quality of the environment

a minimum entitlement to a range of quality geographical experiences. You should feel confident to grasp local issues and wider topical events so as to provide a relevant and enriched curriculum. By doing this it will be possible to fulfil the requirement for providing wider locational knowledge.

Looking at the new Order, a number of important questions will need to be considered both in terms of whole school planning and the impact of those decisions on children's geographical understanding:

- Are you aware of the access statement for all pupils located at the beginning of the geography Order? If you are, what are the implications for your school?
- Does your planning allow for the use of enquiry-based methods by your pupils?
- Does your planning cycle include quality fieldwork experiences?
- Do you know your locality well enough from a geographical point of view?
- Are you providing a range of experience of the wider world, including images of other countries, avoiding undue stereotypes?
- Are you including, where appropriate, European Union locations and issues?
- Have you looked at the revised maps now embedded within the Order?
- In the light of the points above, have you considered a review of your geography resources in general?
- Do you look for opportunities to discuss values? These might include environmental questions, sustainability and development education.
- Are you integrating the four new themes in your planning in such a way as to provide balance, a variety of scale, and relevance?

The first three items in the list relate to skills and understanding. The rest look at the knowledge of the wider world and our developing perception of it. It is worth noting that this list, and those in National Curriculum documents, are not intended to be hierarchical and need careful integration in order to provide a broad and balanced view of geography. We will now discuss what these questions mean in practice and how they influence planning decisions.

Special Needs

Ensuring access and entitlement to the geography curriculum for all children is essential and the issues deserve detailed attention beyond the scope available in one chapter. Sebba (1995) discusses these in depth and offers practical advice and examples of some creative opportunities available to teachers to involve all children in geographical education.

Geographical Enquiry

The use of enquiry methods is still seen in the new Order as fundamental to geography. HMI as long ago as 1986 explained that:

> Pupils should not be primarily passive recipients of information, but should be given adequate opportunities to carry out practical investigations, to explore and express ideas in their own language. (DES, 1986)

The essence of good enquiry is the posing of questions which can act as a framework for increasing children's geographical understanding. These can range from a single carefully thought out challenge, for example, 'Why was the local out-of-town shopping centre built where it was?', to a selection of related and stepped questions which help children build their knowledge of geographical processes. Good geographical enquiry should have the following stages:

- choice of strong focus;
- ask appropriate questions or pose hypotheses;
- contain opportunities for the collection of data from primary sources and secondary data bases;
- give time to analyse and interpret the data;
- include the presentation of findings and conclusions in a variety of formats.

We have found the description in Foley and Janikoun (1992, p. 4) invaluable. Taking time to think carefully about framing the question or questions to ensure that they are appropriate vehicles for the intended study has proved worthwhile for us. You may find it useful to discuss these during the whole school planning process so as to ensure that children experience a full range of enquiry activities during their time at primary school. Whole school planning should also provide you with the flexibility to make full use of a range of questions from the local to the global as they arise in everyday life.

Enquiry Task – Wider Locational Knowledge

This task relates to Key Stage 2

- Pre-record both a local radio and a national news bulletin.
- Play this to your children and ask them to locate the places mentioned on maps, globes and in an atlas.
- Observe the children using these geographical resources.
- What does this tell you about your children's geographical skills and knowledge?
- List ways you will incorporate what you have found out into your planning.

Quality of Fieldwork

One lesson outdoors is worth seven inside. (Tim Brighouse, CEO Birmingham)

Wherever your school is located, it will provide opportunities to investigate both its immediate environment (Key Stage 1) and the slightly wider locality (Key Stage 2). Although time and money are very limited in primary schools for all types of visits, economies are possible. For example, it may be possible to combine your residential visit (always assuming you have one) with the required study of a contrasting locality. You are likely to find that links with primary schools in other localities also allow savings if resources and knowledge can be shared. Some primary schools already make visits to other European Union countries and these can provide excellent opportunities for thematic studies. Fieldwork activities need to be planned carefully to ensure active experience and a progression of geographical skills. A useful detailed plan is to be found on page 8 of *Fieldwork in Action* by May, Richardson and Banks (1993). Examples of appropriate fieldwork activities might include, field sketching, using a clinometer, relating maps to the physical environment, and collecting, recording and interpreting data.

The Nature of the Locality Study

At Key Stage 1, early fieldwork still involves increased familiarization with the school buildings and grounds. It can then be extended to one or two streets adjacent to the school. Additionally, you will need to develop children's ability to assess the quality of the environment. This will probably involve you planning for the development of basic geographical skills and vocabulary through fieldwork. We have found that frequent small-scale visits enhance children's maturing appreciation of the local environment and the changing seasonal patterns: an example might be the study of a local stream in flood in winter and its dried up bed in summer. Relevant links may be made with science.

At Key Stage 2, the locality of the school extends to an area containing the homes of most of the pupils. This will vary in size depending on the rural or urban location of the school. This gives you considerable flexibility to include local features of relevant special interest. Examples of this might be the local quarry or power station. Again, rather than one or two long locality studies during Key Stage 2, you may like to consider the benefits of more frequent small-scale visits which will provide your pupils with regular experience of the environment and offer them chances to progressively develop their geographical skills in the field.

The Wider World

> . . . children are better informed about places (both near and far) than ever before, particularly as a result of their own widespread travel and increased access to television and video. (Wiegand, 1993, p. 67)

At Key Stage 1, the Order states that pupils should have the opportunity to investigate another area either in or beyond the United Kingdom. This flexibility of wording allows you to select a EU location for the first time at Key Stage 1. A suitable choice will need to take into account your children, the school and your resources. You may find it useful, as whole school planning develops, to keep an inventory of each year group's experiences of places around the world. 'Whole world' is a difficult concept for young children to understand. You may find that children learn better if you consciously thread geographical knowledge across the curriculum and build up pupils' experience of different countries, places and cultures. During Key Stage 2, pupils should continue to develop this understanding of the wider world by looking at a locality in a contrasting part of the UK. The Order does not require this to be the same contrasting locality as studied at Key Stage 1.

The revision of the curriculum provides the opportunity to consider the relative merits of breadth or depth in curriculum planning. You may need to decide how an additional locality in a country in Africa, Asia (excluding Japan – as this is reserved for Key Stage 3), South America or Central America (including the Caribbean) is to be included. The size of the school locality and the size of the contrasting UK locality should be similar to assist children in making comparisons. These enquiries must be based on evidence and include experiences with which the children will be familiar: food, shelter and shared human values, such as friendship, at this scale all help to avoid the problems of stereotyping which may occur in such studies. However, the opportunity to place these localities in a broader context also helps to introduce the breadth of physical and human environments within a country. When you are selecting these localities you will need to consider their potential for providing coverage of the four themes of Rivers, Weather, Settlement and Environmental Change.

Maps

The maps to be studied have been located within the text of the Order. The world map F is a new projection and has been included to raise awareness of how we represent places on maps. It is an equal area map but does distort shape closer to the poles. The north sign on this map has been printed incorrectly in the Order and should follow the curve of the lines of longitude. We recommend that schools have a variety of projections among their resources. Indeed, as you look at your revised plans, you may find it helpful to identify new resource needs and update your current collection.

Values

At Key Stage 1, children have to study 'the quality of the environment in any locality'. This work should lead to a natural progression as children undertake the Environmental Change theme at Key Stage 2. This theme provides you with the opportunity to introduce children to a variety of perspectives on environmental questions. It is important because environmental issues have been reduced significantly from other National Curriculum subjects. Examples of this might include exploring how energy is used around the school or the effects of a power station in a locality being studied. For younger children, value questions arising from this work could include, 'Who needs more warmth: school children or someone in hospital?'; for older children the issue may be, 'Which fuels should we use to retain the quality of the environment?'

Enquiry Task – Values

- You will need a selection of duplicate photographs showing one of the localities or highlighting one of the issues to be studied in your school.
- Work with a colleague and select the three photographs which typify the area or issue.
- Give each other reasons for including or discarding photographs/pictures.
- Discuss the value judgments which have been highlighted by this selection process.

This is an activity you could also use with children – we have found to be effective in discussing values within development education.

Themes

In your whole school planning, the themes of Rivers, Weather, Settlement, and Environmental Change, can be used in a number of ways. In order to maximize the quality of geographical education, it will often be beneficial to link themes. For example, if you link the Settlement theme with aspects from the Rivers theme, you get the opportunity to study the relationships between these in a practical way: 'Did the town grow at a place where the river could be crossed?', 'Was this the furthest inland point on the river for ships to go?' Alternatively, all four themes may be taught within one of the locality studies if appropriate and if done in sufficient depth. This flexibility should be viewed as an advantage. But it does mean that as a staff you may need to look carefully at your overall plans to ensure that all aspects are covered adequately.

> Taken together, the studies should involve work at a range of scales from local to national, and should be set in a range of contexts in different parts of the world. Contexts should include the UK and the EU. (Key Stage 2, paragraph 6)

Geography Planning at Key Stages 1 and 2

The Way Forward

Although the content of the geography Order has changed, you should not feel that all your previous planning and ideas are of little use. The aim of this section is to highlight the key issues in effective planning which will help you to make the most of developments which have already taken place in your school and integrate them within the requirements of the revised Order. You may wish to use these points as part of a framework for planning with colleagues in staff meetings and INSET activities. You might use them as a mirror to reflect on your current practice and the decisions you are having to make in terms of the new legislation. It is not possible in one short chapter to provide full details of all planning models. We deal with one in depth. One of the strengths of the geography Order is that it enables you to plan your curriculum, beginning with the school locality and, hopefully, including resources that you have developed as a staff.

Reviewing and Evaluating – General Advice

You may find that if you look carefully at your current activities, you can retain the most effective and interesting elements and make the most of staff expertise, resources and valuable time already spent in planning. For example, you may have spent time developing schemes of work and links with a contrasting locality in the United Kingdom at Key Stage 2. These may be developed effectively within the *Places* requirements for the revised Key Stage 2 Programme of Study. However, as we have said in the previous section, it is advisable to avoid planning which will create a rigid seven section approach to geography: under *Themes* the Order states that 'thematic work should be set within the context of actual places'. Your contrasting locality may be a very suitable place in which to study a river estuary. This theme may then be planned into your contrasting locality studies. Do not feel forced to include all aspects of river study if they are not appropriate to your locality. If the contrasting locality is far inland, look at other areas of your geography plans to ensure that river tributaries and mouths are included in another appropriate part of your school's overall curriculum plan for geography. An important part of teaching with the new Order is to be able to draw these experiences together for children, in order that, during their work at Key Stages 1 and 2, they are encouraged to think about their various geographical experiences and begin to relate different parts of their spatial awareness to gain a greater understanding of the world.

You might find it helpful to examine your existing planning sheets and grids before you begin your planning for the new Order. Some designs can restrict your ideas and indeed control the way in which you plan. Do not assume that all units of work have to be the same length of time. Not all should last half a term, for example. If your grid includes all subjects, it may be better not to plan all of them into each unit. You will need to consider how to make relevant links which help children to understand the key concepts being taught and the relationships between them.

Whole School Issues

When you examine your whole school plans, check the balance between the time spent on teaching geography as a subject in its own right and the time where it is integrated with other subjects. Both approaches have advantages and disadvantages and, perhaps, the key question to ask is to what extent can integration and individual subject teaching help children understand the work with which they are engaged?

In the past HMI (DES, 1989) had two major criticisms of topic work; one was about the way in which excessive integration of subjects has created ineffective teaching and lack of clarity in understanding the aims of the work both for pupils and teachers. The other criticism related to an overemphasis on skills teaching. Awareness of these concerns may also help you to understand and plan more effectively from the new Order if you begin by thinking in terms of subjects and perhaps revise your plans in the future as confidence and knowledge increases. You may like to use this time to reflect on why some teachers plan from topics and others plan from subjects. Discuss with colleagues the benefits and problems of each approach.

Enquiry Methods

As we have mentioned already, geographical enquiry needs to be planned carefully to ensure that children develop in a progressive and coherent way their skills, knowledge and understanding. As you create your geography curriculum, check that you have a balance of enquiry starting points as described earlier. This will also help to ensure that your children will be learning and extending a range of geographical skills that can be found in the Order. Related to this is the importance of devising areas of study or topics which are the most suitable vehicles through which to plan geographical enquiries. Look at your existing plans in order to include those topics or themes which work well, but also use these opportunities to remove units which may either be inappropriate under the new legislation or which your experience shows to be less effective. For example, an existing topic which is heavily based on transport may need revising to place more emphasis on the environmental impact, like that of road widening schemes.

Fieldwork

As stated previously, you will need to include fieldwork within your planning. This implies that you will need to select sites and activities which will make best use of the time and expense involved. An effective whole school plan may include visits ranging from work in the school grounds to residential experiences. Special needs such as access for a wheelchair must now, by law, be considered.

Balancing and Integrating Skills, Places and Themes

As you plan units of work, you will need to consider how geographical Skills, Places and Themes will be integrated within them. This does not mean that you have to include an equal balance of all three in each unit of work.

We believe that better quality planning will take place when the whole school geography plan is examined to make sure all parts of the revised Order is included and that this integration helps children to understand more clearly the interdependent aspects of geography.

Enquiry Task – Balancing Skills, Places and Themes

- Divide a large sheet of paper into three columns headed, Skills, Places and Themes.
- Choose one of your school's present schemes of work for geography.
- Fill in the columns with the appropriate details you expect to include from this scheme.
- Discuss what the most effective links might be. (For example, if your Key Stage 1 study is Homes, under Places you may have, *investigations on the children's own homes and homes in a contrasting locality*. In the Themes column you may investigate the quality of the environment in and around the children's homes. The Skills column may include making simple plans of homes and maps of both localities, extending vocabulary about homes, early data collecting, sorting (i.e., photographs of pupils' homes) and classifying.
- Does this help you evaluate your plans in terms of Skills, Places and Themes?

This is just one way of looking at the content of your schemes of work: you may like to devise others which fit better the needs of your school. Catling (1994, p. 13) describes another model for looking at the same issues.

Choosing Localities

The geography Order does not specify actual locations, localities or places to be studied in detail. This is one of its strengths, and, as such, enables you to use the flexibility provided to chose locations that are appropriate to your children and which, when seen from a whole curriculum perspective, will provide them with a balanced and coherent experience during their primary years. For those children who do not study geography beyond Key Stage 3, the primary school will be providing the bulk of their geographical knowledge, skills and understanding; it is important that they receive a balanced and varied curriculum.

Current Issues

You may also wish to consider how your plans allow current issues and events to be incorporated into the children's studies. These may well change if your school plans cover a period of two or more years. For example, if a village by-pass is being planned in your locality, it is an excellent opportunity to build geographical enquiry around this development. We have found it helpful to study local developments carefully so as to assess which aspects of Skills, Places and Themes can be used within the children's studies; don't forget to maintain adequate records of these. Check that the studies of current issues do not dominate the curriculum and destroy your overall plans and the direction of your curriculum.

Cross-curricular Themes

The revised legislation and associated documents do not provide new materials for developing work on cross curricular themes. Many useful ideas appropriate for the new National Curriculum are contained within National Curriculum Council (NCC) Curriculum Guidance documents – *Curriculum Guidance 7: Environmental Education* (NCC, 1990) offers many ideas which will be helpful in future planning.

Information Technology

The information technology (IT) Order requires IT capability to *be developed through a range of curriculum activities, including work within National Curriculum subjects*. Geographical enquiry provides many opportunities for using IT in relevant ways. As you modify your plans in the light of the revised Order, examine ways in which appropriate technology and software could be used in your own school geography plans. The Geographical Association (GA) and National Council for Educational Technology (NCET) offer a range of booklets (GA/NCET, 1989) which can help in this process. Indeed, the GA can be a source of many ideas to develop in your geography plans. At the time of writing (February, 1995) we understand that the

School Curriculum and Assessment Authority (SCAA) will publish guidance booklets to cover this area.

Allocating Time

Finally, the revision of the National Curriculum has returned to schools the ability to allocate some of their own curriculum time. The geography Order is a minimum entitlement. Since geography can blend with a variety of other subjects, such as local studies in history, residential experiences, science and mathematics, we would strongly argue that it deserves due time and consideration. It has considerable potential to enhance children's understanding of the world in which they live and help them become informed citizens of the future.

References

CATLING, S. (1994) 'Back to the bare necessities', *Primary Geographer*, 19, pp. 12–13.

DES (1986) *Geography from 5 to 16: Curriculum Matters 7*, London: HMSO.

DES (1989) *Aspects of Primary Education: The Teaching and Learning of History and Geography*, London: HMSO.

FOLEY, M. and JANIKOUN, J. (1992) *The Really Practical Guide to Primary Geography*, Cheltenham: Stanley Thornes.

GA/NCET (1989) *Geography Through Topics in Primary and Middle Schools (including applications of information technology)*, Sheffield: Geographical Association.

LLOYD, K. (1994) 'Place and practice: The current state of geography in the primary curriculum', *Primary Geographer*, 17, pp. 7–9.

MAY, S., RICHARDSON, P. and BANKS, V. (1993) *Fieldwork in Action: Planning Fieldwork*, Sheffield: Geographical Association.

NATIONAL CURRICULUM COUNCIL (1990) *Curriculum Guidance 7: Environmental Education*, York: National Curriculum Council.

SEBBA, J. (1995) *Geography for All*, London: Fulton.

WEIGAND, P. (1993) *Children and Primary Geography*, London: Cassell.

8   Art

David Menday

Many of you are familiar with, and have been working to, the Order for Art published in 1992. The revised Order, 1995, is not substantially different in content but there are changes to the format and language used in the previous version. What we have now is a tighter, clearer and much shortened framework for the art curriculum, allowing you plenty of scope to exercise your professional judgment in the planning and teaching of art. It is an easy document to work with, but the structure and language do require interpretation and understanding for you to make the most of it.

What is 'Art' in the National Curriculum?

At first this may seem an unnecessary question, but it is fundamental, and, because of the brevity of the document, not adequately answered by the National Curriculum Order for Art. Everyone has a concept of art, developed and influenced by experience and culture, but which most often is limited to 'fine art' – gallery art, especially painting and sculpture. Perhaps this is because to some people 'art' is a status word whereas 'music' is not. We ask 'Is it art?', but rarely, 'Is it music?' To draw up a list to the question, 'What do we mean by art?' may seem the easy answer, but it is pointless as any list (except one which is exhaustively and exhaustingly long) is likely to leave much out. We also have to remember that art moves on, artists invent new forms and make use of the current technology; a list of a few years ago would not have included computer-generated images or holography.

It may seem something of a contradiction, but the work of artists in our everyday lives is, to most people, 'invisible'. We (and our pupils) are surrounded by, and affected by, the work of artists: it is a matter of perception, of recognizing the work of the artist in the commonplace as well as in the gallery. One way to make the work of artists 'visible' is to look at it from the perspective of our pupils' lives and of their world. What do they see in school, on the way home, in homes, when they go to the shops, and so on, which has been shaped by artists, crafts people and designers? There are, of course, the clothes they wear, logos, the interior decorations in their homes, the cups from which they drink, the family shopping basket, the quilt made by a relative, cartoons and comics, advertisements on hoarding and television, magazines, and so on. Most of these could be broken down into smaller sub-categories (just think of a magazine, newspaper or picture book – photographs, illustrations, the layout, the style and size of the lettering . . .). All of these could form the subject matter of exploration, making and understanding in the National Curriculum for Art.

This broad definition of art could overwhelm some teachers. It was relatively easy when art was thought of, wrongly, as paintings and sculpture, some textiles and pottery. Art is much broader than many people might imagine.

The Order title, 'Art', is intended to be interpreted as 'art, craft and design'. You may need to consider what these terms mean in order to offer pupils a broad view of what constitutes art, and avoid restricting yourself, as a teacher, in the material and subject matter you could be exploring.

Enquiry Task

- Together with other colleagues, consider what you might include under the heading of 'art, craft and design' to show a broad interpretation of the terms. Does the content of your present art curriculum reflect this?

- With your pupils, make a class picture (a collage using photographs, drawings, etc.) of the art in their, and your, lives.

Visual Literacy

In art, good teaching and learning is more likely to take place if you understand the fundamentals, the intentions and the long-term aims of the requirements. A string of unrelated art activities may appear to satisfy the Programme of Study, but will do no service to your pupils.

The requirements have been made clearer than in previous editions of the Order but you may still be confused by unfamiliar terminology and ideas. A key to understanding for teachers without, or with, a special knowledge of art is through the concept of 'visual literacy'. This term appears in the Order and is central to our understanding of what should be taught and learnt in art. Consider this definition of literacy:

> By literacy I mean the ability to represent or recover meaning in a variety of forms through which it is made public. In our culture, words, numbers, movements, images, and patterns of sound are forms through which meaning is represented. To read those forms requires an understanding of their rules, their contexts and their syntactical structures. (Eisner, 1989)

This definition may look relatively simple but you must consider what it means, in practice, to teach children to represent and recover meaning in images.

Most primary teachers would say they have more of an understanding and skill in teaching English (though they might use the word 'language' instead of 'English') than in teaching art. A useful comparison can be made between the two discipline areas when using the concept of 'literacy'.

When teaching writing and reading you might get your pupils to write a description of a member of their family, a story, a diary, an advertisement, a set of instructions for a practical task. You would want them to understand the different characteristics, forms and conventions of these types of writing. In creating these pieces, they would be given the opportunity to explore new or different uses of vocabulary, draft ideas, shape them up before presenting a final piece. In order to help them to understand the style and form you would read to them, show them what other writers have done, so they had some reference points and inspiration. These tasks and approaches have a parallel in the teaching of visual literacy.

The fundamental questions are the same, for instance: why do we want children to be literate in their use of language? In a world in which the spoken and written word is a major form of communication we know we must provide them with the ability to make full use of language, in Eisner's terms to 'make and recover meaning'. However, increasingly in the contemporary world, visual images and artefacts are being used to convey ideas and meaning, and teachers need to equip future generations with the ability to be visually literate.

Before looking at the Order in more detail, we can construct some parallels with the language examples given above. In art we would want pupils to be able to make visual descriptions of people, places and things, to tell a story through a narrative sequence of images, to record incidents, ideas, and impressions in a notebook (like a diary), to construct a powerful image for a poster, to make a vessel, and so on. In doing these things we may want them to use (and as they get older, to select) an appropriate medium, to consider colour, form, lines (the vocabulary and syntax of art), and to collect resources, experiment and investigate a range of possibilities before settling on a final idea. In order to give some context and inspiration, we would introduce them to, and get them to consider, other examples of similar work by different makers.

Learning in Art

You will find it helpful to have the National Curriculum Order for Art open in front of you when reading this section. It doesn't matter whether you are looking at Key Stage 1 or Key Stage 2. On the left of the pages in sections 1–6 are the general requirements, and on the right the two Attainment Targets (ATs) called 'Investigating and Making' and 'Knowledge and Understanding'.

Keeping with the concept of visual literacy, 'Investigating and Making' corresponds to 'Writing'. 'Investigating' has been included in the title of the Attainment Target in order to stress the importance of the process. Sections 2, 3 and 4 provide a general idea of the breadth of work required for you to teach.

'Knowledge and Understanding' corresponds to 'Reading'. It requires you to introduce your pupils to the work of artists, crafts people and designers, (painting and sculpture, photographs, pottery, furniture, book cover design, buildings, etc.) in the same way you would introduce them to different kinds of writing (stories and novels, advertising copy, letters, instruction, etc.). You should help them to develop the ability to learn from what other artists have done, *not* copy their work, but pursue similar ideas and methods in their own way. The previous version of the National Curriculum for Art had emphasized reference to 'influential' artists, which was rather restrictive, but in section 5 of the new Order you will notice that the work of established artists in the Western European heritage forms only a part of what pupils should know. They should, for example, be made familiar with the work of local artists, pupils' work from a secondary school, artwork in a local museum (5a). It is also important that you introduce pupils to work from other cultures (5c) and times (5b). This may fit in with topics centred on other subjects, such as geography (India) or history (Victorians).

Lastly, through appraising others' work you will need to help pupils to develop the ability to respond critically to their own work. This is the vital link with AT1. The relationship between the two Attainment Targets is very important. The boxed section at the top of the left hand page makes it clear that, wherever possible, the work you devise should bring the two components together.

There is not the space here to investigate the fine detail of the Order, especially as we are looking at both Key Stages 1 and 2, but we can look at some common features in the Programme of Study and introduce examples which will serve all ages, 5–11. A particular feature of art is that it can be seen as a 'spiral' curriculum – elements and subject matter are revisited throughout a pupil's school life. They may make a portrait of themselves at age five, and again many times, in different ways, right up to 'A' level, and maybe beyond.

Section 7 contains six requirements (a–f), common to all Key Stages, which state the opportunities we should provide for pupils:

(a) record responses, including observations of the natural and made environment;
(b) gather resources and materials, using them to stimulate and develop ideas;
(c) explore and use two- and three-dimensional media, working on a variety of scales;
(d) review and modify their work as it progresses;
(e) develop understanding of the work of artists, crafts people and designers, applying knowledge to their own work;
(f) respond to and evaluate art, craft and design, including their own and others' work.

The emphasis is on 'process'. The key here is in the language and the way it can be interpreted. For example, if you look closely at 7a (above) you will get some idea of the work you need to do to expand on the document in order to make it come alive for yourself and your pupils. It says pupils should 'record responses . . .', you need to consider what this means. You may think that it means 'drawing' (what *is* drawing?) – but it also means much more. For example, say your topic is 'Wood and Trees', and you, and your pupils, have brought in a selection of pieces of bark from different trees and you want them to focus on their differences – it's a good starting point for direct observation, and pupils often find it easier to spot differences than similarities. This might lead you to ask a series of questions fundamental to the art curriculum, for instance, *why* do you want pupils to record what they see? There's no point in engaging in art making if you do not know what you want them to learn from it. You may want them to develop their visual perception and explore and record the surface quality of the bark in a way that other means cannot. You may ask them what they see in order to draw their attention to the pieces' shape (contour) and form (3-dimensional roundness), colour, tone, texture, pattern.

You must consider what you want your pupils to record. It would be a difficult task to attempt to record all of these elements in one go. It might be better to select certain aspects, say, texture. Before tackling any task like this, it is useful to explore what you want them to record *in words*: to focus the pupils' minds with questions about the objects. You could ask them to describe the surface quality and make comparisons. You then need to consider how they are going to record the tactile qualities of the bark. It may be, especially with older pupils, that you want them to suggest methods, or you might want them to try a technique you know they have not experienced before. In this case you will need to demonstrate or show them examples of other artists' work. Whatever approach you choose, you will be *teaching* them. Pupils could:

- make rubbings from the surface of the bark;
- cover the surface with ink and make prints from it (but only if you didn't want to use the bark again later);
- use charcoal (itself made from wood) to make big drawings;
- use paper, sand, scraps of anything, glued to a card base, and get them to reconstruct the way it looks and feels – 'Rub your fingers on the bark and try to make the same feeling with your materials';
- use clay, saltdough, Plasticine;
- use an art program on a computer, and using the various textures some provide, combined with some of their own making, save and print their work;
- photocopy the bark (with care, assistance and permission, of course). If the machine has the function they could enlarge the image and then work on it with other materials.

These are some of the many ways 'recording' can be interpreted.

A project of this kind enables you to cover various aspects of the art curriculum. It enables pupils to record their responses and observations (7a), and encourages them to 'explore and use two- and three-dimensional media, working on a variety of scales' (7c). They can 'gather resources and materials, using them to stimulate and develop ideas' (7b), and in your teaching and questioning of their work they may engage in (7d) – 'review and modify their own work as it progresses'.

You may not have shown or referred to the work of other artists (AT2). The Order says that AT1 and AT2 should be brought together 'whenever possible'. Sometimes it is not possible, and there is no need to force the issue. It is a matter of balance; sometimes you will place more emphasis on investigating and making, and at other times you will concentrate on responding to others' artwork.

It would be easy to redress the balance with a topic like the one given in the following example. On another occasion you might show the pupils the work of a local person who uses wood in craftwork, for example, a turner who make bowls, a basketmaker or a dolls' house builder. You might discuss the pieces with them, in order to introduce them to the language of art. You could show them the work of the contemporary artist Andy Goldsworthy who has constructed outdoor sculptures from branches, twigs, leaves and then photographs them so he has a record of the structure when it has collapsed or blown away. Your pupils might try this, gaining inspiration from his work. In this way you would be covering (7e) 'develop understanding of the work of artists, crafts people and designers, applying knowledge to their own work', and (7f) 'respond to and evaluate art, craft and design, including their own and others' work'.

Sections 8 and 9 of the Order for art elaborate upon the six areas in section 7. They are specific to particular Key Stages whereas section 7 remains constant.

Art in Other Subjects

The above demonstrates how work in art can be incorporated into a topic approach. A variety of topic themes can also include learning in art. There are many opportunities for artwork in other areas of the curriculum; some subjects specify it. In history, the 'key elements' require you to look at the culture of different times, and this must include reference to art, including 'paintings, photographs, artefacts, buildings, country houses and their estates . . .'. If at Key Stage 2, you were looking at Study Unit 3b: Britain Since 1930, you could investigate areas of design: interiors, consumer objects (for example, how radio designs have changed), posters (for example, the London Underground, petrol), architecture (for example, the 'prefab' and the Royal Festival Hall).

In geography, pupils are required to be able to record and recognize features: for example, in Key Stage 1, to make a pictorial map of a place featured in a story (this links with art: 8a – 'record what has been . . . imagined'). There is much scope for the use of photographs in geography, both in reading them as evidence ('What can you tell from this photograph of a landscape and these close-ups of the vegetation?'), or for recording (the locality).

For 2000 years, Christians have expressed and celebrated their beliefs through paintings, sculpture, architecture. People from other religions have chosen different images, for example Islamic pattern. These are powerful images and artefacts, and a knowledge and understanding of them serves both the art and RE curriculum. It is worthwhile investigating how Christianity and other religions have celebrated and expressed their beliefs through the visual arts.

Enquiry Task

- When planning your term's topic, or the work in other subjects, investigate, and list, the opportunities for learning *in* and *through* art.

Teaching Art

> Creativity is not a special faculty with which some children are endowed and others not. It is a form of intelligence and as such can be developed and trained like any other mode of thinking. (Calouste Gulbenkian Foundation, 1982)

Sadly, it is still commonly believed that the opposite is true. The School Curriculum and Assessment Authority (SCAA, 1994a) reports that many parents consulted on the new National Curriculum, 'assume(d) that the skills involved in . . . art . . . can be taught only if children have some *natural talent or ability*' (my emphasis). Parents can pass on such beliefs to their children creating a barrier to learning that is hard to shift. To complicate matters further, many teachers hold the view that their own (in)ability in art precludes them from being able to teach the subject. One teacher quoted in Clement (1994) expresses the view of many.

> The expectations of National Curriculum Art are beyond my own experience. You can read up on mathematics, science etc., music and art are talents.

Parental misconceptions, pupil's lack of expectation, and the teacher's perceived inability to teach art can make for problems in the child's art education. You may want to consider how you can change this situation, perhaps through your work with pupils or their parents. Let me take up a few of the issues as they affect teachers.

The Teacher's Ability in Art

All teachers can teach art, but many teachers *believe* they cannot *do* art, and this precludes them, they believe, from being effective teachers. This is not true. This situation arises, generally, because of the way people measure their competence in art. Most people use the criterion of being able *do draw*, ('I can't teach art because I can't draw') and by this they mean the ability to make a 'realistic' copy, normally in pencil, of whatever the subject matter is – a figure, animal, landscape, and so on. This 'theory' of art asserts that the more an image is in proportion, has lifelike form through 'shading', is 'finished', and approximates to a photographic copy, the better the work is. This promotes the dominance of one style of drawing, one way of representing, one medium as being the standard by which all competence is assessed. Such accurate representation is a skill, but it is only one among many, and it should not be seen as the summit of artistic achievement. Nor should we judge pupils' ability in art by these limited criteria. Further, you might like to consider the point of either your pupils or yourself pursuing the goal of this type of photographic reality when we, and they, can make use of the technology and take a photograph.

You may find it useful to refer back to the concept of visual literacy. You are unlikely to say, 'I am no good at writing because I cannot use language like Wordsworth or Bronte or any other great writer', and then abrogate all responsibility for teaching English to your pupils. You have the ability, in the spoken or written form, to describe a person's features, create a story, write in the style of a newspaper report, and all of the other tasks required by the National Curriculum for English for whatever age of pupils. You are able to read and interpret the literature – the stories, poems, plays and help your pupils understand style, form, characterization, mood, etc. You are not likely to consider yourself a 'writer' or 'literary critic'. Similarly, you could do the equivalent in art without worrying about being an 'artist' or 'art historian and critic'.

The discussion about 'what is art' will have alerted you to the art in your own life and those interests and skills you have, which you would not normally associate with art, either in making art or having knowledge and understanding in areas of it. You probably engage in a number of activities which require art or art related skills, for example, designing your garden, interior decoration, choosing clothes, furniture, crockery, taking a photograph, watching films, and so on. These involve you in either art making (making choices of, and using, colour, form, line, shape, different materials and techniques) or as users, or consumers of other people's art (not a satisfactory term but you know what I mean). Whenever you make a choice, for example between three different vases when you need buy only one, you are making artistic and aesthetic judgments which also may call upon cultural and historical knowledge. Your response might be, 'I prefer that one because it's a Victorian style and will suit the decor and the William Morris wallpaper of the room'.

In making such choices you are exhibiting knowledge and understanding related to Attainment Target 2, without necessarily having much knowledge about (gallery) art. In terms of National Curriculum Art, you probably have some interests and expertise which can form starting points – personal points of entry from which further knowledge and experience can develop, including that of our heritage of fine art.

An Attitude of Mind

It is part of your professional responsibility to teach National Curriculum Art. This focuses the mind, but you should not feel threatened by this responsibility. It does not, as some people have suggested, take the pleasure out of engaging in art, but it does require an attitude of mind which looks upon teaching art with the degree of application and rigour in which other subjects are approached. The art curriculum implies learning, not therapy, pastime or the production of pleasing artefacts. Clement and Tarr (1992) point out that

> . . . it is comparatively easy to structure children's learning in such a way that they may be enabled to produce pleasing and attractive images. You can 'programme' children to make well observed drawings and attractive objects to take home to parents. It is much more of a challenge to find ways to enable children to use art and design purposefully and to be educated through the making of art.

As with other subjects you will need to set appropriate challenging tasks and have clear objectives of what you want your pupils to learn, though not necessarily a preconceived notion of the finished product, or a formula, so that all pupils' work is similar.

You have to *teach* art not just provide for it to happen. You should provide time for intervention, for encouragement and advice, sensitive questioning, offering ideas for routes to take, and so on, using all the strategies teachers can call upon and use to facilitate learning.

Learning about Art

The teacher quoted above (Clement, 1994) said that, unlike other subjects, you could not 'read up' on art. In one sense you can but it requires a different interpretation of reading. As far as making art is concerned, it is no different to trying out a science experiment. You will first need to build your confidence by trying out new ideas and techniques yourself, and to achieve results good enough to provide a resource for teaching. If you wish to introduce to the pupils a technique or approach which is also new to you, you might ask another teacher to show you or follow the instructions in the many books which provide guidance. You could experiment with the task you wish to set the pupils, try out the idea, the medium and technique, so you know what they will do. Show the pupils what you have done, tell them your difficulties and achievements, learn together. This may require a change of attitude on your part but it will be worth it in the end.

In another sense, learning about art *is* a matter of reading. Those teaching history at Key Stage 2, will need to know about life in Tudor times including exploring the paintings and architecture of the time. Similarly, in the art curriculum itself you need to find out about symbolism in Tudor portraits before you investigate the paintings with the pupils. For example, you could ask the question, 'Why do you think that man is wearing a sword and standing next to a globe?' Pupils could then make portraits of themselves, members of their family or well known people using contemporary artefacts which contain social, cultural and economic significance. Such a painting project would bring together Attainment Target 1 and Attainment Target 2. You cannot be expected to know everything: when you come upon a difficulty, ask someone who knows or search out the information you require.

Helping Pupils to get Better at Art

It is a fact that pupils do not get better at art simply by getting older. You need to know what you want your pupils to learn, and how your planning and teaching can help them achieve that learning. The intention of National Curriculum Art is for children to gain competence in art which will prepare them for the 'opportunities, responsibilities and experiences of adult life'. That is very wide ranging, you are not trying to produce little 'artists' but develop in young people skills in art, craft and design which have value in their own right and are transferable to other situations. It follows that if you are not sure of what you want them to learn, then you will have a problem identifying progress and strategies for development.

Some writers on children's art have suggested that progress is linear and that all children go through pre-defined stages. Most studies have focused on Western European or North American culture, but the theories collapse with children from other cultures. There is no *natural* universal model of development; it is culturally determined by custom, belief (some cultures place restrictions on *what* can be represented and *how* it can be represented – for example, representation of the human figure is forbidden in Islamic cultures), environment. In short, children are socialized into the artwork of the common culture. However, as I have already noted, there are still underlying assumptions that 'progress' follows a 'scribble to photographic realism' model, but this is *not* the foundation of the model of progression implicit in the National Curriculum for Art.

Before looking at attainment and progression in the Order for Art it might help if we consider in general the ways in which pupils get better in art. The National Curriculum Council's Arts in School Project (NCC, 1990) identified four principles of progression. These principles constitute a good starting point for understanding and assessing attainment with any age of pupil, with any aspect of the art curriculum.

We must ask whether pupils are capable of more *complex* work than they displayed previously: this returns us to the notion of the spiral curriculum, revisiting aspects of the work with a greater command of the issues. They should also be capable of more *control*, for example in the use of different media, materials and techniques. As pupils get older, especially moving towards Key Stage 3, they should begin to work in greater *depth* in certain chosen areas. Finally, as pupils become more confident and experienced it should be expected that they develop and exhibit greater *independence*, to make their own choices and judgments, giving reasons to support their decisions and opinions. This way of looking at attainment and progression is entirely compatible with the National Curriculum for Art.

The work required at each of the Key Stages for Art shows a clear progression but using an approach specific to each element of the Programme of Study. Once again, it will help if you have the Order in front of you. Look at Key Stage (KS)

1, and, by way of an example, focus on section 8b. Then turn the pages and look at the requirements for 8b for Key Stages (KS) 2 and 3. As a sequence they look like this:

KS 1: recognise images and artefacts as sources of ideas for their work;

KS 2: record observations and ideas, and collect visual evidence and information, using a sketchbook;

KS 3: select and record observations and ideas, and research and organize a range of visual evidence and information, using a sketchbook.

There is a clear progression implied in the language of these expectations, and one which embraces the notions, mentioned earlier, of developing depth and independence. The key to making this aspect of the Order workable and practical is to explore the language. For example, look at how each statement begins – 'recognise' (KS 1), 'record' (KS 2) and 'select' (KS 3). You should consider what is meant by these terms and how they can be put into practice.

Enquiry Task

- For the Key Stage you teach, follow through, explore, and list the possible interpretations of the 'language' used to define progression in the Order.
- Consider what this means in practice.

Continuity Through Planning

The National Curriculum states in section 7 that you should provide certain 'opportunities' in art; sections 8 and 9 tell you what you must 'teach'. Progression will only take place if there is continuity of experience and learning, and this should be provided through your planning.

It is part of your professional responsibility to plan *an* art curriculum, and it is 'an' art curriculum rather than 'the' art curriculum, for, as SCAA says:

> . . . schools should use their professional judgment to create schemes of work which are based on the programmes of study and which incorporate plans for teaching and everyday assessment in ways which are appropriate to the school and its pupils. (SCAA, 1994a)

The new Order for Art has been described as a 'permissive' document. It is designed and worded to encourage you to take ownership of what you teach: *good* teaching in art will satisfy the requirements. Much freedom is given to you to respond to local needs and utilize local opportunities. There may be a school plan provided by an art curriculum coordinator, sometimes these are tightly organized but usually they are a framework and you have freedom to choose subject matter and approach as you think fit.

Assessment and Recording

The purpose of assessment in art, like any subject, is to keep track of learning, guide intervention, and to inform strategies for the development of pupils' learning. Some teachers are reluctant to assess work in art, maintaining that it is a matter of personal opinion; again, this is a misguided view. In assessing a pupil's work in art you should not be basing your evaluation on your subjective response, but rather be making objective judgments related to the criteria outlined in the National Curriculum for Art. Two questions arise from this.

1   *What informs those judgments?*
    The Programme of Study provides a framework for making judgments. Looking at each element of the Attainment Targets (sections 7, 8 and 9) you can ask two simple questions: 'Can they . . .', and then, 'How well can they . . .' do what is required? It is not quite as straightforward as that, because you have seen already how each element in the Attainment Targets needs to be interpreted and defined into clear tasks. For example, look at 8b for Key Stage 2, and the requirement to use a sketchbook. This gives you an outline of what you should provide opportunities for, and teach pupils to do, but obviously you will set the content and standards of the work (what the sketchbook should contain) and make judgments based on those expectations.

    Look now at the End of Key Stage Descriptions at the end of the Order. They are your long-term guide, specifically related assessment to be made *at the end* of Key Stages, but also useful throughout. Art does not have level descriptions. It is for the school to decide and agree upon criteria which will promote consistent judgments. (More guidance on this can be found in the Dearing Report, SCAA, 1994b, especially Appendix 6.)

2   *What counts as evidence?*

Obviously, the artwork your pupils produce constitutes the major part of the evidence for the judgments you make. You must be careful though and not put too much emphasis on finished pieces of work. National Curriculum Art particularly stresses the processes of making and understanding in art. Note how the elements of the Attainment Targets concentrate on exploration and investigation. You must look at the way pupils approach this exploration and not concentrate too much on finished product. 'Evidence' is also what the teacher 'observes'. For example, how good are your pupils at producing and exploring ideas? How well do they use materials and practice the techniques they have acquired? How well do they incorporate the ideas of others in their own work? Do they exhibit a knowledge of art? This last point shows another major form of evidence, through what they say: you will see that 9e is concerned with the development of the language of art.

Enquiry Task

• Choose two or three pupils in your class and write a few concise sentences describing their ability to create ideas, their technical expertise, their ability to critically engage with the work of others, and their knowledge of art. (If you are unsure of what these mean look at the attainment targets for your age group.)

• What variety of evidence did you use to make those judgments?

• Get together with other teachers, bring some examples of pupils' work (choose specific areas and provide a range of ability) and in a collective way attempt to construct broad descriptions of attainment using the End of Key Stage Descriptions. What other knowledge of the pupils do you need to bring to this task?

Record Keeping

Record keeping is something quite different from assessment and therefore not to be confused with it. As a teacher you are assessing pupils' work every time you look at it and make a comment, you only need to record your observations to aid your memory in order for you to plan the curriculum and fulfil your duty to report the pupil's attainment to others. Dearing says that, 'Much of it (*the information*) will, necessarily, remain in the teacher's mind', (SCAA 1994b, Appendix 6, para. 8), but it is useful to note the significant progress of each child. This does not mean tick lists against each of the elements of the attainment targets. It is helpful if you retain a selection of the pupils' work as a reference. If the work is large or you do not have much space, or they want to take it home, then take photographs – they are much easier to store. (Again, Appendix 6 of the Dearing Report clarifies many of these issues.)

Enquiry task

• How can significant progress of each pupil be recorded in a form which is useful, manageable and easy to interpret?

• What do you need to record and what can be retained in your memory?

• What evidence will you keep?

Summary

This chapter has attempted to fulfil two main objectives; to explore the format and interpret the language of the new National Curriculum Order for Art, and to give all teachers confidence to teach art. The main focus has been upon the notion, central to the Order, of 'visual literacy'. Teachers should develop pupils' visual awareness by providing a programme of work which engages them in investigating and making art, and in relation to this, give them opportunities to respond to the artwork of others. Ways in which pupils can be helped to progress in art have been considered, as have methods for assessing and recording that progress.

References

CLEMENT, R. (1994) 'The readiness of primary schools to teach the National Curriculum in art and design,' *Journal of Art and Design Education*, Corsham: NSEAD.
CLEMENT, R. and TARR, E. (1992) *A Year in the Art of a Primary School*, Corsham: NSEAD.
EISNER, E. (1989) 'Structure and magic in discipline-based art education', in D. THISTLEWOOD, *Critical Studies in Art and Design Education*, Harlow: Longman.
NCC (1990) *The Arts 5–16: A Curriculum Framework*, London: Oliver and Boyd.
SCAA (1994a) *The Review of the National Curriculum: A Report on the 1994 Consultation*, London: SCAA.
SCAA (1994b) *The National Curriculum and its Assessment*, London: SCAA.

Suggested reading

BARNES, R. (1987) *Teaching Art to Young Children 4–9*, London: Unwyn Human.
CLEMENT, R. and PAGE, S. (1992) *Principles and Practice in Art*, London: Oliver and Boyd.

David Menday

DURBIN, G., MORRIS, S. and WILKINSON, S. (1990) *Learning from Objects*, London: English Heritage.

ISHERWOOD, S. and STANLEY, N. (1994) *Creating Vision*, London: Arts Council/ Cornerhouse.

MORGAN, M. (1988) *Art 4–11: Art in the Early Years of Schooling*, Oxford: Blackwell.

MORRIS, S. (1992) *Using Portraits*, London: English Heritage.

MEAGER, N. (1993) *Teaching Art at Key Stage 1*, Corsham: NSEAD.

PEPPIN, A., SMITH, R. and TURNER, A. (1992) *Approaches to Art*, London: Ginn.

9 Music

Patricia Thompson

Introduction

Did you enjoy music at school? Do you enjoy music nowadays, long after school memories have faded? You may have been one of the fortunate few to have received a rich and varied diet of music; or you may remember, with some embarrassment, being told that you couldn't sing, or were not able to keep time. You may have remained untouched by the 'school music experience', your time being spent responding to a narrow range of music, often concerned with peripheral aspects, with underlying perceptions of high and low brow, and of the potency of cheap music. All kinds of musics are found in the new National Curriculum. Every child is entitled to receive minimum musical experiences. These are outlined below.

Best primary music practice may be characterized by children responding to music physically: giving the body rhythm; creating music, from first doodlings using raw sounds, to producing more sophisticated compositions as musical understanding, knowledge and skills grow. Children develop through having direct, firsthand experience of making music, individually and in large- and small-scale ensemble. Thus, a balance between skill acquisition, creativity and aesthetic response comes through ensuring that each child's needs are catered for, in an ambience of encouraging, non-threatening, non-judgmental behaviour. The vital underpinning element is the element of fun. The word 'enjoyment' has been used for the first time in the statutory Orders for music. I remember when Key Stages were modulations (changes of key in a piece of music).

Teaching music is a great leveller. It requires clearly delineated mixed-ability teaching across a wide ranging spectrum. Your primary class may contain a child who has had instrumental lessons from an early age, and who has acquired already a high degree of competence in performance. This may contrast with another child who has yet to discover music or to experience it firsthand. You, the professional practitioner, will want to involve every child in this essentially practical subject, in the very stuff of music, ensuring that progress is made at whatever level of experience and achievement a child brings. One of the most liberating characteristics of musical involvement is that there are no right or wrong answers when using your musical imagination. Beauty is in the eye of the beholder – or more appropriately the ear – and the act of creativity involves decision making, choice, independence of thought and mind: all vital, transferable skills for life.

Everyone can participate in music at whatever level, with activities finely honed to cater for all abilities. Experienced musicians can be encouraged to bring instruments to every music activity, parts being created or recreated by the players themselves. The act of *valuing* extra-curricular music making, bears positively on curricular music, enhancing every child's experience along the way. Similarly, starting with an individual's own musical experiences, children from various ethnic backgrounds can be encouraged to share their music with the rest of the class, either by bringing along instruments, recordings – even a musically proficient family member. I once observed a teacher rehearsing with children an arrangement she had made of a current pop song. Through one of the children, she had invited into school a local Scottish piper to add the vital missing element of timbre. From this direct experience, the children were able to witness the practicalities of playing the bagpipes: a piper needs to fill the reservoir of air before he can be prepared to play with everyone else after the usual introductory rhythmic count of 'Three, Four'. All these are examples of the teacher *valuing* children's previous musical experiences, and using those experiences as raw, sonic material through which to weave musical tapestries.

Every child has the right to learn to play a musical instrument, as a creative means of self-expression and to perform re-creatively and interpret other people's music. The problem is how to achieve this in an age of economic stringency? Cheap and cheerful, and most portable of instruments is the descant recorder. This old technology *can* sound horrendous, and be horribly ear-splitting! As a stimulus, play a brief extract from the slow second movement of J S Bach's *Brandenburg Concerto No 2 in F major*. The children may be able to recognize some of the solo instruments in the small group: violin, maybe oboe, but they will probably say 'flute' rather than 'recorder', as they might not recognize the recorder played so beautifully. (Practical note: choose a recording featuring authentic instruments, i.e., descant recorder *not* flute.) If children are taught to play with good breath control and clear articulation from an early age, benefits are clearly seen and heard – a sweet, attractive tone encouraging healthy breathing habits and physical posture as important by-products.

Enquiry Task

- Consider the scope of your children's previous musical experiences.
- Assess individually each child's existing skills, knowledge and understanding of music.
- List home/community cultural influences which might enhance your class music?
- How might these be incorporated?

Summary of Main Changes between Old and New Music National Curricula

Compared to the old version, the new music National Curriculum appears infinitely more attractive and approachable, slimmer and trimmer with its minimal use of non-statutory examples. Sir Ron Dearing's conclusions appear slightly contradictory, although they do attempt to offer maximum support to the classroom teacher. The dichotomy lies in the fact that reduction in volume of material taught will certainly make it less daunting to non-specialists, whilst reduction in overall prescription so as to give more scope for professional judgment may overawe even the most professional teacher, *albeit* non-specialist musician.

The layout of new statutory Orders makes them seem more user-friendly. Reduction from four pages for each Key Stage to two pages emphasizes a reduction in content. The two Attainment Targets (ATs) have been retained – AT1 *Performing and Composing*; AT2 *Listening and Appraising* – with those for each Key Stage fitting conveniently, on one page. The facing page has the Programme of Study clearly set out with the two Attainment Targets interlinked throughout. This is headed by an outlined statement emphasizing activities which *bring together* requirements from both *Performing and Composing* and *Listening and Appraising*. Previously this integrated approach with constant intertwining of the two Attainment Targets in all music lessons was only really made clear in non-statutory guidance.

The detailed list of non-statutory examples, which illuminated the End of Key Stage Statement and Programme of Study for each Key Stage of old Orders, has been abandoned. Instead we have no naming of names: not a single composer nor performer (past or present) is mentioned anywhere in the document, leaving scope to choose within guidelines suggested. Interculturalism is taken seriously. By Key Stage 3, guidelines have been gradually extended from the old Order:

> The repertoire chosen . . . should include examples of works taken from:
> **a**   the European 'classical' tradition, from its earliest roots to the present day;
> **b**   folk and popular music;
> **c**   the countries and regions of the British Isles;

but with addition in the new Order of

> music in a variety of styles:
> **d**   from cultures across the world;
> **e**   by well known composers and performers, past and present.

Thus what has been suggested as examples at Key Stage 2, is itemized individually at Key Stage 3, highlighting the wide range of musics available for you to choose from. The curriculum at Key Stages 1 and 2 includes musical activities, definitions of musical terms and clarification of musical concepts.

Further, the content of Programmes of Study for each Key Stage has been restructured into three parts. First, the introductory statements define a range of musical activities and a breadth of repertoire for performing and listening. The introductory statements derive from General Requirements for Programmes of Study in the old Order. They have been placed on the page which faces the other requirements in order to emphasize their importance. The facing page has general programmes of study written down the left-hand column. These define opportunities given in all Key Stages. As they are common to all, continuity of musical experience from ages 5 to 14 is provided. Opportunities have been grouped into six areas, providing a simple framework for planning, teaching and assessing. The division of four for *Performing and Composing* and two for *Listening and Appraising* reflects weighting for Attainment Targets of two-to-one in favour of the first, originally indicated in non-statutory guidance.

These six areas are directly related to statements on the right of the same page, so enabling you to plan from general to specific, moving naturally from left to right. These programmes of study define essential skills, knowledge and understanding which children should be taught in each Key Stage. The total number of statements in each has been reduced, noticeably in AT1, to thirteen by removing unnecessary overlap. Again, there is two-to-one weighting, eight statements for *Performing and Composing* and five for *Listening and Appraising*.

Enquiry Task

- Choose two from the thirteen statements in the Key Stage-specific programme of study, one from *Performing and Composing*, and the other from *Listening and Appraising*.
- Outline a scheme of work to develop both of these simultaneously across one Key Stage.
- Develop ways to observe and record children's progress in both of these two areas.

As with art and physical education, End of Key Stage Statements have been retained but revised, rewritten as prose in line with changes made to the ten-level scale in other subjects. These appear in new Orders as End of Key Stage Descriptions, clarified by including qualitative words (like 'attentively') to help define levels of attainment. Statements are matched to broadly equivalent level descriptions in other subjects.

There is helpful repositioning of musical elements. Moving the first statement in the Programme of Study for AT2 *Listening and Appraising* to introductory statements in each Key Stage emphasizes their central role. They also serve as a really useful music planning tool, a checklist to ensure that all musical elements have been covered, not just once, but constantly revisited. The order of musical elements has changed slightly. *Dynamics* has risen from number 6 to number 3. The musical term *Tempo* has replaced *Pace* – *Speed* has been discarded from the draft new Order. *Silence* has been relegated from being a musical element in its own right to being listed under *Dynamics*.

Enquiry Task

- Choose one of your favourite music activities.
- Compare with that of a colleague.
- Make a note of the musical elements covered.
- Consider how you might extend the activities.
- How many more musical elements can you add?

The last few bars of *Sibelius Symphony No 5* underscore the dramatic import-ance of silence in a musical composition. It might be used as an exemplar to your class's own composing. Sound takes on far more import if juxtaposed with silence. Key Stage 1 seems a symbolic place to begin understanding of this important con-cept, when children are experimenting freely with sounds, individually and in com-bination, using pattern, repetition, question and answer.

Some subtle changes have ensured that, within musical elements listed in the introductory statements for each Key Stage, some requirements have been placed into more appropriate Key Stages. For example, *Phrase* (a musical sentence) and *Polyphony* (several melodies simultaneously) have been moved on a Key Stage from 1 to 2, and from Key Stage 2 to 3 respectively. Whereas *Ostinato* (a persistently repeated melodic or rhythmic pattern) has been moved from Key Stage 3 to 2.

Ways Forward

The benefits of taking part in music making activities are widely acknowledged. They include: developing skills, co-ordination, perception, intellect, aesthetic response, expressiveness, social skills, language acquisition to specify but a few. The problem is how to fit this in, during days and weeks already crammed with activities. One of the most heartening and reassuring thoughts is that musical skills, knowledge and understanding are acquired *little but often*.

If any of you have ever tried to learn to play a musical instrument, you will know that it is not very helpful to progress if you 'forget' to practise every day and suddenly try to put in all the week's accumulated practice time the night before your lesson. The way to acquire any skill is to spend a brief time daily on correct repetition of tasks in hand. Your practice may be divided into:

- 'warming up' – both yourself and the instrument;
- revisiting yesterday's newly-learnt skill
- practice of new skills; and
- playing something already known and liked.

Many parents assume that arts' skills can be taught only if children have some natural talent or ability. It is not so much innate talent that makes a musician as opportunity, motivation and sheer hard work. You have to put in at least 5,000 hours of good practice to learn to play an instrument well.[1]

To overcome feelings of boredom and low motivation, you have to make the lessons fun and enjoyable with lots of praise for achievement. Assisted by supportive parents, children will develop a strong sense of their own musical capabilities, a powerful motivator on the road to musical success. The new Orders for music are based on the assumption that every child is capable of acquiring instrumental competence by the age of 14. No previous music curriculum has ever made such an assumption. As a primary class teacher, you are a vital element in that developing sequence. In the early stages of skill acquisition, you are the best placed person to make full use of those precious moments in the daily round. Routine tasks can be used to practise and reinforce understanding of most, if not all, musical elements. Shy children can clap a response to your singing their name:

Teacher: Kate Ashcroft?   *Child*: Yes, Mrs Thompson.

More musically confident children can repeat the little phrase you have just made up to sing their name:

Teacher: Kate Ashcroft? Child: Yes, Mrs Thompson.

Further development can be seen if the child responds with an answering musical phrase to balance your musical question:

Teacher: Da-vid Pa-la-ci-o? Child: Yes, Mrs Thomp-son.

Here, the key is confidence, in just letting it happen naturally. Remember, there are no right nor wrong answers. We will rarely improvise naturally without a sense of musical line and phrase. It is only when our mind becomes distracted by actually thinking about it, rather than just doing it off the top of our head, that we feel less than satisfied with the end results. So just go ahead and sing! Lose your inhibitions: children will love you for it. They are very forgiving of even the most corncrake voice, and will appreciate opportunities to participate themselves.

Other windows of opportunity include hijacking class management techniques for musical gain. If you want to attract children's attention when they are all working in groups, gently clap a simple rhythm for children to copy. Continue for a little while, in question and answer fashion, until you are the focus of all attention. This can be a tremendous boon for a tired voice, whilst providing serendipitous practice in 'performing short musical patterns by ear'. For example:

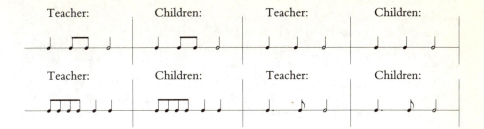

Firm Foundations

A rich and varied musical diet of well known songs – nursery rhymes, rounds, action songs, partner songs – rhythm games, responding to music physically, learning to play instruments, creative and re-creative music making will provide firm foundations and an enjoyable and productive ambience across the whole school environment. Performing fits especially well into the primary school ethos as it is, in essence, *sharing* music with others. Some children will already know many nursery rhymes and action songs from early childhood experiences. It is therefore easy to build on these, adding on rounds, partner songs ('matching' songs sung simultaneously) and the children's own instrumental accompaniments, to particularly assist their understanding of texture and structure through direct practical experience. Do not worry if you feel less than confident about teaching children the melody of a song. Many songbooks have accompanying cassette tapes. Some cassette tapes have songs recorded in stereo with melody and accompaniment on different tracks. So, by using the balance control, the accompaniment only (or singing only) can be heard. This highlights a way of teaching melody first. Then, when the children are able to sing the melody unaided, they can sing along with accompaniment. Being able to perform a part independently is an important developmental goal.

Rhythm games and activities are useful ways into music, not least because children often find rhythm infectious, more immediately accessible than pitch. Choose music with either a strong pulse or beat, or music that has an instantly appealing rhythm for them to catch on to, and even use in their own creative music making. There are various kinds of listening to music. Children will often hear music as they are walking in to or out of school assemblies, which is a very useful familiarizing activity akin to having first heard well known compositions in media advertising. To achieve a more concentrated kind of listening, where children will really focus on music being played, ask them to either answer a question or to respond physically to music. For example, the opening of *African Sanctus* by David Fanshawe has eight loud drum beats before the main music begins. The children could be asked how many pulses or beats are there before the music really begins; or they could be asked to move slowly and heavily round the room keeping their foot stomps in time with pulse. With practice this can be developed into a *stomp clap stomp clap* repeated pattern (ostinato) with claps on and off beats. (A note of caution: time your listening extract fairly carefully as children tend to lose concentration after about forty seconds of listening to previously unheard music.)

Whilst these activities may appear brief contributions to the 5,000 hours' target to achieve a high level of musical competence, they provide clearly attainable progressive steps. It is very helpful to include a longer time, at least once a week, for creative activities. The organization and classroom management of thirty children with a similar number of musical instruments requires setting out and clearing away times before the hands-on activity is even considered. If instruments are kept centrally some distance away from classroom or hall where the activity is booked to take place, then success of the session is almost wholly dependent on how well prepared you are, as a class teacher/manager/organizer. I have found that the best way of approaching composing with children, is to have them working in small groups of four to six in number. But before they can do so successfully, you need to introduce them to some preliminary activities, so they understand clearly what is expected of them in this kind of music making.

A good way in, is to take the topic in hand (for example, Science, Key Stage 1, Materials and their Properties – Metal). Brainstorm with the children lots of nice-sounding words associated with this topic. Shape some well-chosen words into two contrasting rhythmic phrases.

Split the class into two equal groups. Rehearse each group chanting the phrases rhythmically. Discuss appropriate hand gestures for simple instructions (for example, start, stop, louder, softer). Compose and perform a group composition with you as director/conductor. Remember to start the tape recorder to record improvised class composition, as children will listen far more intently to their own music making than to anybody else. Finally, let children have a turn at being director/conductor.

Further Practical Options

A dramatic change in music teaching and planning was brought about by the advent of GCSE Music. It is therefore gratifying to see that the basic philosophy of an integrated approach to the teaching of the two Attainment Targets has been retained and indeed reinforced in the new Orders. This can be understood by three interlinking circles of musical activities, with the emphasis always on the practical aspects of the subject, that provide a useful planning tool, ensuring coverage of appropriate skills, knowledge and understanding.

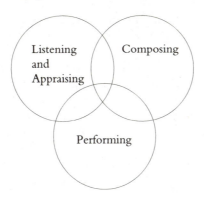

Links with Other Areas of the Curriculum

Music can create links across the curriculum in the same way as other subjects. Below I outline a topic approach I observed being used with children at Key Stage 2. The teacher began by asking children to listen to a brief piece of music ('Introduction and Courante' from *Terpsichore* by Michael Praetorius). She asked them to focus on certain questions during the listening:

- When was this music written?
- For what occasion?
- Which instruments can you hear?

The ensuing discussion covered some of the musical elements; for example, tempo, structure, texture, timbre, as well as mood.

Using basic skills, knowledge and understanding of playing recorder, the children began to compose in small groups a dance, using notes G, A and B on descant recorder, a drone bass on notes G and D played on low pitched tuned percussion, and adding suitable untuned percussion accompaniment. Later a second recorder part was added, three or six notes higher than the composed tune. The teacher suggested that the children started and ended on G (the key note), and finally came to rest on a long note to make the piece sound finished.

After much experimentation, with intermittent sharing of ideas so far with the rest of the children, and their subsequent support and suggestions for improvement, each group performed and recorded their compositions, initially on to cassette but eventually using appropriate notation.

Through these planned activities, the children constantly revisited the two attainment targets, *Performing and Composing* and *Listening and Appraising*, with recommended emphasis on practical activities.

Here are some brief suggestions for practical ways to link with other subjects:

English – adding sound effects to the telling of a favourite story.
Mathematics – practising and performing counting songs.
Science – investigating the science of sound.
Design & Technology – designing and making musical instruments.
Information Technology – using electronic resouces and synthetic sound to compose and notate music.
History – developing a sense of musical period.
Geography – learning and performing songs from around the world.
Art – using visual art to stimulate creative music making.
Physical Education – responding to music physically.
Religious Education – understanding and performing music for religious festivals around the world.
Drama – creating incidental music.

Enquiry Task

- Consider your whole school planning.
- List any cross-curricular links with music.
- Divide into those activities specifically supporting development of music skills, knowledge and understanding, and those supporting learning in other curriculum areas.
- Remember to include any whole school extra-curricular activities.

Summary

The new National Curriculum music is less prescriptive. It allows you to challenge and choose activities and materials which enhance every child's experience of practical music making, which enthuse you, the classteacher, and widen your experience so that you can widen the experiences of others.

Note

1 First Results from a Biographical Study of 255 Instrumental Learners. Jane Davidson, John Sloboda (Keele University) and Michael Howe (Exeter University) cited in *Proceedings of the Society for Research in Psychology of Music and Music Education*, 1994, 22, pp. 85–90.

References

DEPARTMENT OF EDUCATION and SCIENCE (1992) *Music in the National Curriculum (England)*, London: HMSO.

DEPARTMENT FOR EDUCATION (1995) *Key Stages 1 and 2 of the National Curriculum*, London: HMSO.
DEPARTMENT FOR EDUCATION (1995) *Music in the National Curriculum (England)*, London: HMSO.

Annotated List of Suggested Reading

ELLIS, S. (1993) *101 Hints for the Non-Specialist Primary Music Teacher*, Halifax: Educational Guidance Organisation.
(A concise booklet giving practical tips for teachers in the classroom.)
GLOVER, J. and WARD, S. (1993) *Teaching Music in the Primary School*, London: Cassell.
(A comprehensive book covering the introduction of the National Curriculum for music into the primary classroom.)
HARROP, B., FRIEND, L. and GADSBY, D. (1995) *Okki-tokki-unga*, London: A and C Black.
(A new edition of this popular book of action songs for children with accompanying cassettes.)
LASLETT, S. (1993) *Sound Activity Book*, Leatherhead: Letterland Direct.
(A science activity book with games, puzzles and experiments linked to music.)
MILLS, J. (1991) *Music in the Primary School*, Cambridge: Cambridge University Press.
(A wide-ranging source book covering all aspects of music in the primary curriculum.)
ODAM, G. (1989) *Silver Burdett and Ginn Music*, Morristown, New Jersey: Silver Burdett & Ginn.
(A comprehensive music programme consisting of Teacher's Editions, Cassette Tapes, Teacher's Resource Books, Language Skills Handbooks, Multicultural Awareness Handbooks, and Scope and Sequence Charts.)
PAYNTER, J. (1992) *Sound and Structure*, Cambridge: Cambridge University Press.
(The definitive book on organizing and managing composing in the classroom.)
SWANWICK, K. (1979) *A Basis for Music Education*, Windsor, Berkshire: NFER.
(Sound philosophy to underpin classroom practice.)

10 Physical Education

Jennifer Gray

Introduction

Physical education was one of the last subject areas in the phased implementation of the National Curriculum. It was not until August 1992 that the Order was introduced in respect of pupils in the first year of the Key Stage and 1 August 1993 in respect of all other pupils. There has, therefore, been little time for teachers to experience teaching the curriculum before the new changes were introduced.

Physical education has historically developed from a games tradition where it was thought that moral qualities were trained. It was through games that boys were taught the qualities of self-control, vigour and decision of character. Gymnastics, which was not introduced until the late 19th century, was seen as remedial. Gymnastic drill was only seen as of value to the elementary schools where games were not seen to be suitable for the age range or where lack of space dictated that games could not be played. It was not until after the Education Act of 1870, when physical education was introduced into training courses for new and already qualified teachers, that girls were considered. It still took further reports by HMI before girls were allowed to participate in games.

It is from this historical background that physical education has developed and the new curriculum is not without its historical influence. However, in this chapter, I will concentrate on the practical application of the Order rather than the political or historical background. My aim is therefore to help the non-specialist teacher translate the Order into a practical application.

National Curriculum – Old and New

The most significant changes in the National Curriculum for physical education are the reduction, from five to three, of areas of activity at Key Stage 1, and the transfer of emphasis from planning, performing and evaluating to performing. The general requirements still state that planning, performing and evaluating should be a continuous process, but that greater emphasis should be placed on performing.

The general requirements of the Order have been simplified with an emphasis on the promotion of physical activity, positive attitudes and safe practice. Reference to the development of the pupil as an independent learner has been removed. However, development of the individual is inherent in good primary teaching and, for this reason, should not be ignored in physical education.

The Order at each Key Stage has been simplified. The End of Key Stage Statements and Programmes of Study (general) have disappeared and have been replaced by areas of activity and End of Key Stage Descriptions. These layout changes have led to easier access to information.

Key Stage 1

The areas of activity at Key Stage 1 have been slimmed down. Athletic activity, games, gymnastic activities, have been removed as separate areas. Games, gymnastic activities and dance with the same option of swimming, if facilities allow, remain. The general statements stress that these activities should make use of indoor and outdoor environments as appropriate. Throughout the Key Stage, the emphasis is on pupils emphasizing the changes that affect their body during exercise, and the recognition of short-term effects of exercise.

In the games element of the Order, there is still major emphasis on the skills required in games activities, building to small-sided, simple, competitive games. The relatively 'new' concept of *games making*, where the children are placed in a problem-solving situation and asked to evolve their own games, has disappeared, although advocates of this teaching method could still include this concept in 'simple competitive games'.

Gymnastics has been slimmed down by excluding the necessity to teach lifting and carrying of equipment, and also to practise, adapt and improve the children's individual actions. On the other hand, it would be impossible to teach effective progressive lessons without adapting and controlling the children's action. The End of Key Stage Description states '*They improve their performance through practising their skills*' (p. 118).

Dance has moved from a totally creative perspective to one which includes set patterns of movement from traditional dance. The creative element has been simplified, with an emphasis on *participation* rather than *evaluation* by the children of what they have been performing. There is still emphasis on allowing children the freedom to interpret moods and feeling through the basic actions of travelling, jumping, turning, gesture and stillness.

Swimming, if facilities allow, may be taught at this Key Stage, although I will confine discussion to Key Stage 2.

Outdoor education has been removed from the syllabus for physical education, although the orienteering section has, to a degree, been retained in the Order for geography, where children are required to follow directions and use maps and plans.

Concern has been expressed that athletic ability has been excluded at this Key Stage, but many of the elements of running and throwing are included in the games activities.

Enquiry Task

Consider the physical skills the children in your class have acquired. Plan a scheme of work covering part of the National Curriculum.

- Which activity area will you concentrate on?
- How are you going to deliver the programme?
- Do you have the expertise necessary to deliver the programme?
- Where can you access the expertise?

Discuss what you have written with an experienced colleague. Add to your plan in the light of this conversation.

Key Stage 2

Key Stage 2 has retained its six areas of activity and, although the layout has been simplified, the content, with a few exceptions, remains similar. The activities have been prioritized with games, gymnastic activity and dance being taught in all years of the Key Stage, and athletic activities, outdoor and adventurous activity and swimming being taught at some time during the Key Stage. As in Key Stage 1, an implicit priority of the activities appears in the Programme of Study. Previously, activities were listed alphabetically, but now games is listed first, followed by gymnastic activity and finally dance. As in Key Stage 1, the concept of games making has been removed and there is an emphasis on building towards an understanding of mini-games and the progression of skill training. In my view there is no place in curriculum time for the large-sided game. We have all seen the games where children follow the ball like bees round a honey pot. Team games require an understanding of space and the role of the individual performer within the game. These skills can be developed during Key Stage 2.

Gymnastic activities concentrate on the refinement of movement and the development of increasingly complex sequencing. Dance continues to emphasize body control and aesthetic awareness though responses to varying stimuli, but now includes dances of different times and places including traditional dances of the British Isles. Folk/country dances which have historically played an important role in primary education, are therefore, now included in the National Curriculum.

Athletic activities include the development of the basic skills of running, throwing and jumping, and include measuring and comparing children's own performance, but the Order has eliminated *competition*. Outdoor and adventurous activities continue to make use of the local facilities, as well as providing challenging and problem-solving activities.

Swimming has, on paper, been slimmed down considerably, but there seems to be little effect on the actual curriculum to be taught. The new syllabus demands that the teacher researches the subject more thoroughly. The syllabus is less prescript-ive, and it could be translated into less or even different content.

Cross-curricular Links

As with the previous Order, there is the opportunity for teaching other areas of the curriculum through physical education. For example, in science, pupils are required to understand forces. Gymnastics and ball skills offer opportunity for the practical application of changes of speed and pushing and pulling. Sections on humans as organisms in the science curriculum, and, in particular, the naming of external body parts and the effects of exercise on health, provide other excellent opportunities for science to be taught through physical education. Mathematical language of size and comparatives, as well as geometrical shape and angles, can also be experienced through gymnastics. The necessity to include traditional dance with set patterns can enrich the teaching of history at Key Stage 2. Music from different cultures and times must be experienced so, through a dance programme, three areas of the curriculum can be simultaneously covered in a practical and stimulating manner. For example, one teacher I know combined Tudor dance and music together with film clips to create the period.

Implementing the New Order

For many primary teachers, the new Order is as daunting as the previous one. With the legally binding introduction of the National Curriculum in 1992, some teachers felt that they had lost their autonomy to teach what they believed was import-ant, and also what they felt capable of teaching. Previously the physical education experienced by the children was,

> a matter of chance, dependent on the teacher's personal persuasions and capacities. This never guaranteed consistent breadth, relevance, progression or coherence.

Do you think the situation described above has changed?

The new Order requires, considerable change to what you teach currently. Physical education has often been seen by some teachers as a low priority subject area. Furthermore, its very position in the phased introduction of the National Curriculum placed it at a disadvantage, with teachers having to 'get to grips' with the considerable changes in other subject areas. In some schools, physical education has not yet been considered to the extent required.

There is a recommendation, but not a statutory requirement, that two hours per week should be allocated to physical education. However, if the National Curriculum for PE is to be implemented fully, then this time is needed and must not be lost through other uses of the physical education facilities such as using the hall for dinners, assemblies, displays, educational visits, etc. Furthermore, excluding children from physical education can no longer be used as a disciplinary measure. If the demands set by the new Order are to be realized then PE must be seen as a priority.

Teachers' Concerns

Utilizing teacher expertise

As with the previous Order, the concerns of teachers are numerous, and depend on previous experience and expertise. There are few teachers who are specialists in all areas of the curriculum.

Physical education is an area where you may feel you have inadequate knowledge to build or deliver programmes of work which are progressive and valid. For the curriculum to be taught effectively, your expertise must be utilized effectively. You may be able to get help from within your school or through the sharing of staff from within your school cluster or partnership group. This sharing could be on a teaching basis, or it could be used to develop a programme of teacher development. A good starting point may be to identify your knowledge strengths and weaknesses and then to identify strategies to overcome your specific weaknesses. This might be met by individual research, attendance at local or county inservice training, the sharing of staff as an advisory mentor, or attendance at a specific sport teaching course organized by the relevant National Governing Body (NGB). Sport-specific governing bodies have seen the need for teaching rather than the traditional coaching courses and many NGBs have introduced teaching certificate courses to meet the demands of practicing teachers. For example, the Amateur Swimming Association has, traditionally, fulfilled this role, and the NGB for gymnastics has introduced recently a teachers' qualification. The governing bodies of all of major games have a programme of skills based courses which can be adapted to meet the needs of practicing teachers.

Enquiry Task

With reference to the new curriculum:

- identify the areas of knowledge strength that you could offer to other teachers.
- list your areas of knowledge weakness.
- list the strategies that you could use to overcome these weaknesses.

Time

Time is also a major problem in the effective implementation of the curriculum. A philosophy needs to be established in every school whereby physical education is seen as a unique experience and one which is contributing fully to the overall education of the pupils; no school should have a philosophy which allows physical education to be cancelled at the slightest opportunity. However great the priority, time is still very short. It takes time to organize pupils and equipment, time to change clothing, and, if necessary, time to transport the children to the facility, e.g., the swimming pool or the games field. All this means that the time available for participation time is far less than the time allocated on the timetable. You must ensure, through effective planning, that the time is fully utilized.

Financing the equipment

The introduction of Local Management of Schools (LMS) has seen not only greater competition *between* schools for scarce resources, but also greater competition *within* schools. Competition between subject areas is, therefore, high, and funding often reflects the hierarchical status afforded to each subject. As stated earlier, physical education was one of the last areas to implement a National Curriculum and so in many schools finance was already allocated to the core subjects.

Resources are a major factor in the ability to implement the curriculum, and the teaching of games skills requires sufficient equipment for every pupil to participate. Whilst the Order no longer states that a variety of games equipment must be experienced, sufficient compatible equipment must be available for effective teaching. This is not always the case. 'How am I expected to teach soccer skills to a group of 30 pupils with only one ball?', is a plea heard quite frequently from teachers. The answer is that you cannot.

Equipment must also be user friendly. This means that your school must cater for not only the difference in age range, but also ability level. Research has shown an increase in the average height of children in primary school, and this means that your school must ensure that equipment is safe for the size of pupils in your present class. You will need short tennis or badminton equipment to teach net and wall games. Whilst your pupils can be grouped, so that they do not all require the same equipment at the same time, you will need to provide for an increase in both variety and number of items of equipment.

Enquiry Task

Examine the new Order for PE.

- List the resources required to teach the curriculum to your class. Remember to take into account how you will group the children and how many teachers are available.
- Identify the resources currently available in your PE stock. Audit the condition of the equipment.
- Find out if any missing resources are available within other curriculum areas.
- List the equipment which still needs to be acquired or replaced.

Swimming

Providing for swimming has always been a problem. Maintaining a swimming pool is expensive and transport to local facilities is both expensive and time consuming. Provision of specialist teachers has also been cut. With increased awareness of health and safety, teachers are either required to have current life-saving awards or there must be qualified life savers in attendance. For this reason, before the implementation of the National Curriculum, many schools opted out of swimming; those schools that retained swimming often asked parents for voluntary contributions to pay for expenses.

Although swimming is a requirement of the curriculum, the requirements are minimal. Because of this, a pupil should not be judged *competent* to swim 25 metres just because they have struggled the 25 metres to achieve a distance award. This distance is rather misleading and many teachers are concerned that this distance will be taken as a maximum rather than a minimum, and that only the non-swimmers will receive tuition. Local research has shown that this is already happening. Some pupils are even being excluded from swimming when they have passed their 25 metres award, even though they have shown minimal water confidence. You need to be aware of the water safety and survival elements within the syllabus and also the requirement to develop in your children effective and efficient swimming strokes, both on the front and on the back. Many teachers are aware that they require inservice training to up-date not only their life saving, but their knowledge of 'modern' swimming strokes. Many teachers are unaware that strokes have been streamlined to be more efficient and many teachers are still teaching very wide wedge kicks in breaststroke and trying to eliminate efficient bent arm pulls in back crawl.

Equal Opportunity Issues

You will need to make special provision to cater for pupils with special needs. The Order states, on page 1, that:

> appropriate provision should be made for those pupils who need activities
> to be adapted in order to participate in physical education.

You may have to adapt equipment, purchase specially adapted equipment, and/or arrange practical help to allow the pupil to participate. The cost of providing whatever is required may be high.

Traditionally, although not current practice in most primary schools, games were organized according to gender. Boys played football and girls netball. It was not considered correct for girls to participate in football skills, let alone rugby! Provision is now usually made for all pupils to participate in all games activities, but equal access is not the same as equal opportunity. You will need to consider, for example, whether girls do obtain equal opportunity by playing football or netball with the boys. It may be that the boys become dominant and the girls are made to feel inferior. You may need to consider whether either mixed ability or ability grouping facilitates greater learning opportunity. Provision must also be made for the variety of cultural and religious beliefs. Schools must consider changing and shower facilities for the pupils with due regard paid to privacy as well as hygiene.

Enquiry Task

Examine your school's policy for 'equal opportunity'.

- What provision has been made for any children with special needs?
- In what ways have you involved children in previously 'sex inappropriate' games? Have any problems arisen from integration?
- List the ways that your school is making provision in PE for children from differing religious backgrounds.

Assessment

Concern has also been expressed with regard to assessment. End of Key Stage Descriptions are general and have been written to be more qualitative in nature. For example,

> Key Stage 1; Pupils plan and perform simple skills safely, and show control linking actions together. They improve their performance through practising their skills, working alone and with a partner. They talk about what they and others have done, and are able to make simple judgments. They recognise and describe the changes that happen to their bodies during exercise. (p. 118)

Descriptions have been redrafted in an attempt to differentiate better between pupils' attainment, but the guidance notes state that teachers have requested further guidance on assessment, recording and reporting.

Enquiry Task

Using one of the activity areas:

- Decide whether you are going to plan differentiated work or whether differentiation by outcome may be more suitable.
- Discuss with a colleague which areas could be assessed.
- Decide how you are going to make these assessments through practical work.
- Design a recording mechanism for your assessment.

The Future

Despite the gains in provision since the National Curriculum was introduced it is possible still to see pupils engaged in large-sided games where the most able dominate and the least able never see the ball. Equipment is often either too large or unsuitable for the needs of the individual pupils. Gymnastics is sometimes organized so that pupils queue to use equipment. Apparatus is too large or small for safe usage, clothing inadequate for the work undertaken, and children not given the opportunity to experiment and discuss and evaluate each other's work. Outside facilities are often inadequate for the numbers and size of the children and changing facilities do not allow for adequate hygiene. Occasionally, teachers can be seen teaching PE in their classroom clothing and adopting outdated practice; what messages does this way of working convey to children concerning the role and status of PE?

If the new Order is to bring a change in the teaching, and therefore the learning, of physical education, then the planning must offer an effective and relevant curriculum which motivates all and allows children to progress. Curriculum provision must reflect the needs of the individual, including giving opportunity to those pupils who need to work outside their current Key Stage. It must allow pupils to develop their skills to provide a quality of movement in all spheres. It is not sufficient for children to have 'had a go'. They need the satisfaction that comes through practise, refinement, time for improvement and the development of personal expertise. Experiencing a broad and balanced curriculum does not mean that children should not hone the skills they possess. To enable this development, you may need to develop your physical education specific knowledge beyond the basic statutory requirements. You will seek to facilitate opportunities for your pupils to experience the broad range of the curriculum and also to develop their individual talents.

You should not be afraid to find unconventional ways of meeting the requirements of the new Order. Partnership or cluster schools may have the expertise to develop inservice sessions. You may require help from the specialist in the secondary school or the national governing bodies of sports. Community schemes may also offer expertise in specific area. Local sporting clubs may organize youth coaching schemes or coach development. Through such sporting bodies it is often possible to organize skill-based inservice programmes. Such bodies, although not always possessing the same teaching skills as you, have a wealth of sport-specific knowledge, which may be necessary for effective teaching. Sports coaches should not be seen as a threat. They can offer valuable experience.

So far, I have concentrated on the development of games skills, but don't forget that dance groups, especially folk groups, are often keen to pass on their knowledge, through demonstration, workshops and teacher training. Again, such people not only have a wealth of knowledge, but a love and enthusiasm for their work which is difficult to emulate.

You may need to explore new ways to fund opportunities and equipment. Equipment sharing, where schools timetable so that the same equipment can be used in two schools, could be considered. You may be able to use senior school outdoor facilities or local recreation ground facilities. You may explore local sporting or community ventures and industry either for direct or indirect funding. You may find it is possible to use enterprise/training schemes to make or mend equipment, such as goal posts and storage facilities. Games and play equipment for the swimming pool is expensive, but technology projects may be able to produce safe equipment at a fraction of the cost – e.g., weighted hoops which can be used as underwater slalom courses can be designed and made. Sinkable objects which can be retrieved from the pool bottom are ideal subjects from design projects.

As mentioned previously, physical education is often given a low status in school. Therefore, to ensure that the status of physical education in your school is enhanced you will need to be aware of, and monitor the implementation of, your school's policies and practices. This is unlikely to be achieved through showcase activities, such as public displays and competitive sports results, but through a more general raising of awareness of the subject's value.

Enquiry Task

- List opportunities that are available to raise the profile of PE in your school and in the wider community, e.g., parents meetings, governors meetings.
- How might you go about realizing some of these opportunities?

Planning Strategies for Implementing the Syllabus

The reduction in areas of activity may be welcomed by some teachers, but I am sure that the new Order still presents the dilemma of, 'What shall I teach and when?' You may decide to plan in units of work. These units of work may be linked to topic based work, or it may be subject based. You might ask yourself:

- What your aims are in teaching this unit?
- What you are trying to achieve?
- What you hope the children will to learn?
- How you are going to facilitate this learning?
- What resources will be required to facilitate this learning?
- How you are going to assess this unit of work?
- Are there cross-curricular links which can be examined?

For all subjects it is important for you to have clear learning objectives. It is essential that you know the previous experience and attainments of individual pupils so that work can be based on progression. Under the previous regime teachers may have made a subjective statement of attainment, but it would be unusual to find reference to any testing. Records would usually have been of class participation rather than attainment of individual pupils. In the context of the new curriculum you will have to find additional ways of assessing and recording progress. Although there are no formal, nationally set exercises, you will need to continually assess individual

---

Enquiry Task

Select one activity area from the new Order.

* List your aims and objectives when teaching this area.
* List the teaching strategies you are going to use to achieve these learning objectives.
* List the resources you will require to deliver this unit. Remember to include your research as well as the equipment. Also remember to include other teachers, where appropriate.
* Plan the method(s) of assessment.

---

children's progress to evaluate the effectiveness of your teaching and the children's learning. You may need to continually ask yourself, what are the children learning? Could another task be more effective in the teaching of that skill?

Conclusions

There can be no doubt that schools have come far since the advent of the National Curriculum. Even so, there is still a visible difference between the written policy statements of schools and what pupils experience each week. Unless headteachers consciously lend an ear and understand fully the rationale supporting a strong PE curriculum in their schools, under the effects of poor resources and reduced financial and time restrictions, this very necessary subject will disappear due to the weighty influences of the core subjects.

It will be important that the PE coordinator in your school, understands fully what unique experiences can be attained through physical education and what PE is contributing to in the overall education of your pupils. Subject coordinators need to articulate the strength and importance of the subject not only to colleagues, but also to their headteachers, governors and parents.

Achieving change needs patience and persistence. This may be difficult in some small schools where one teacher may be coordinator for two or three curriculum areas. The PE coordinator may have responsibility for an area in which they are not a specialist so therefore may have difficulty in articulating the strengths and unique potential of the subject. But, teachers in primary schools:

> take their duty to educate their pupils very seriously and they are understandably reluctant to introduce/deliver content/methods in subject areas which they are unsure about. (Larr, 1994)

Greater links must be made with sports coaches and governing bodies to build relationships which will help the inservice development of subject knowledge and allow teachers like you to deliver the curriculum in a progressive and confident manner.

Enquiry Task

Which of the following resources are available in your school?
Find out which are available locally e.g., in your local teacher centre/library/university.
Examine those that are available.
Order others from your local library.
Draw up a prioritized list of equipment to be purchased by your school.

Dance

• Movement and Dance in the Primary School	Violet Bruce	Open University, 1988.
• Inspirations for Dance and Movement	Judy Evans & Hazel Powell	Scolastic, 1994.
• Let's Dance	Kate Harrison	Hodder and Stoughton, 1993.
• Children Dancing	Rosamund Shreeves	Ward Lock, 1992.
• Creative Dance in the Primary School	Joan Russell	Northcote House.
• Dance Lesson Ideas		Staffordshire County Education.

Games

• Games in the Primary School	R M Lenel. Revised by Alison L. Parratt	Hodder and Stoughton, 1984.
• Teaching Children to Play Games	Brenda Read Phyl Edwards	National Coaching Foundation, 1992.
• Rugby Football Union Cross		RFU, Twickenham, TW1 1DZ.
• Curricular Project for Primary Schools		

Gymnastics

Gymnastics 7–11

A session by session Approach	Carroll, M.E., and Manners, H.K.	Falmer Press.
• Educational Gymnastics Step by Step	Bruce Long	Hodder and Stoughton
• Movement Education		
• Gymnastics 4–7: A session by session approach	H.K. Manners & M.E. Carroll	Falmer Press
• Persil Funfit Reward scheme 1994 (3–5) and (5–11)		BAGA
• Curriculum Gymnastics	Anne Williams	Hodder and Stoughton 1987

Swimming

• National Curriculum Pack		ASA Loughborough
• Swimming Teaching and Coaching Level 1	Edited by Rick Cross	ASA
• An Illustrated Guide to Teaching Early Practices	Anne Eakin	ASA
• The Competent Swimmer An illustrated guide to teaching further practices	Anne Eakin	ASA

Outdoor Education

• Start Orienteering books		Adventure Ed 39 Brunswick Sq. Penrith Cumbria CA11 7LS

Safety

Safe Practice in Physical Education

11   Design and Technology

John Siraj-Blatchford and David Coates

Introduction

The National Curriculum for Technology has, since its introduction in 1990, transformed the practice of design and technology in most primary schools. While many schools have always taught some elements of design and technology – they have taught cooking, the use of textiles, construction kits, and various crafts, for example – the underlying assessment framework will have been quite new. Some of the materials and activities have also been introduced for the first time into many schools. For example, few will have previously provided structured curricula concerned with design, mechanisms, structures or control. It's not perhaps surprising, given the relative youth of this area of the curriculum, that it has been surrounded by controversy, and that it was one of the first subjects of the National Curriculum to be subjected to major revision.

Concern has been expressed already regarding many of the changes that have been introduced in these revisions of the subject. Teachers and educationalists have complained about the lack of any specific references to 'fitness for the purpose', to 'human needs', and to products as 'expressions of values' in new definitions of the technology Order. As John Eggleston (1993) has argued, these new definitions may not have provided so much a simplification as a *new alignment* of the subject. While the National Curriculum Council (NCC, 1993) claimed that 'good quality products' were of necessity 'fit for their intended purposes' (p. 5), the point was missed that much of the professional concern has focused on the sociocultural dimensions that might easily be neglected. Products that are perceived to be of 'good quality' are only *necessarily* 'fit' for the purposes of the group evaluating them as such, and this may not always be either the final consumer or those most affected by them. We can only hope that the statement that has now been included in the new Order (SCAA, 1995) will clarify the point:

Pupils should be taught:
h to distinguish between how well a product has been made and how well it has been designed;
i to consider the effectiveness of a product, including the extent to

which it meets a clear need, is fit for purpose, and uses resources appropriately (p. 5).

Manufactured products may be evaluated according to the degree to which they comply with their design specifications. Designs, on the other hand, must be evaluated according to the degree to which the product satisfies the needs identified initially. To be adequate, the children in your class will need to consider the consequences of actually implementing designs. In deciding what constitutes an appropriate technological solution value considerations are often involved. While the explicit references to value decisions and to the technology of other times and cultures that were emphasized in the 1990 National Curriculum Order (DES, 1990) have now been removed in the process of 'slimming down', they are still relevant. The introduction into the Programmes of Study (PoS) of 'Knowledge and Understanding: Products and Applications' has been broadly welcomed by teachers and may provide you with an alternative context for much of this work. The Nuffield Design and Technology Project has published recently a range of evaluation techniques that may be used to take children from a user-centred viewpoint through to one which considers the appropriateness of a design and its impacts on a wider audience (Barlex, 1994).

The reduction in Attainment Targets has been generally welcomed and you may find the more balanced assessment weighting of designing and making helpful. It is important, however, to recognize that the novel structure of the assessment model provided in the 1990 Order has not changed substantially. The emphasis is still upon the assessment of 'capability' within the design and technology process, which, while no longer reflected in the four Attainment Targets (figure 11.1), still defines very similar strands within the Programmes of Study (figure 11.2).

Programmes of Study

The Programmes of Study detail what you need to teach and have been split into five parts. The first two parts concern the nature of the tasks, activities and assignments to be provided, and the range of materials, skills and understandings to be applied. The third part is *designing* and the fourth *making*, and these are supported at each Key Stage by additional programmes covering *knowledge and understanding* (fifth part). Given the need for brevity, the Order does not show progression in skills or knowledge in any meaningful way, but simply indicates the areas to be covered at each Key Stage. (In the bibliography we provide some useful sources for additional guidance that you may find useful.) The Key Stage Programmes of Study thus indicate the broad range of activities that your children are entitled to; the making and designing, planning and evaluating skills to be taught, the knowledge of materials, mechanisms, structures and products to be covered. The Programmes of Study will help you to plan across the Key Stage and they include guidance on quality and on health and safety. The Programmes of Study for 'making' and for 'designing' are intimately linked, and you should not attempt to teach one without the other.

Figure 11.1: *The Attainment Targets provided in profile component 1, National Curriculum Technology (1989)*

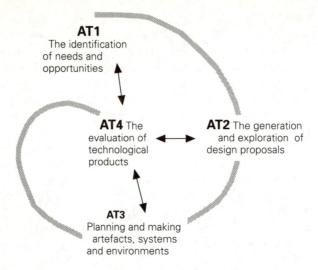

. . . in technology, where the processes of designing and making lie at the heart of childrens' work . . . pupils should be taught the relevant know-ledge to support their designing and making, rather than being taught facts merely because they are specified for a particular level of attainment. (NCC, 1993, p. 15)

Our task as teachers is to help children acquire the appropriate knowledge, skills and concepts. In design and technology we must often employ group work, but *each* child needs to learn the specific skills, knowledge and concepts. Technological activities should also give children the opportunity to use their knowledge and skills gained in other areas of the curriculum. Increasingly, you may find that you are able to encourage your pupils to select resources, and materials for themselves. They must be taught to work safely and hygienically.

You will need to consider carefully your classroom organization in order to maximize the pupil's experience of technology. You are likely to need to employ a variety of teaching styles (e.g., group activities, whole class activities) and approaches (e.g., thematic, focused). The classroom environment you provide is very important as this also is a part of the learning provision. You will need to plan your classroom environment rationally so that displays provide both inspiration and encouragement. As Williams (1990) has put it:

. . . if designing is concerned with aesthetic considerations and an under-standing of the rightness or fitness for purpose of man made objects, then children cannot relate these aspects of their work unless their environment is in line with their needs. (p. 117)

Figure 11.2: The strands identified in the two Attainment Targets of Key Stage 2 of the new National Curriculum for Design and Technology (1995)

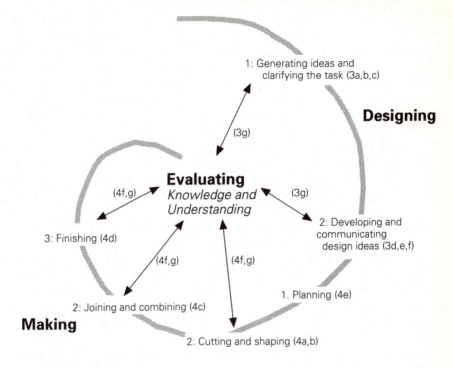

These aspects really are crucial so it is well worth spending a little time considering them further. There is no time like the present!

Enquiry Task

Review your classroom environment. In what ways does it provide inspiration and encouragement for design and technology? Make a list of all the opportunities you can think of for achieving this.

Developing Capability

Pupils are required to develop their design and technology capability through three types of activities, focused practical tasks; investigating, disassembling and evaluating tasks; and designing and making assignments. The designing and making assignments are at the heart of the technological process and should involve contexts that are familiar to the children. At Key Stage 1, for example, children might design and make gingerbread people after listening to the story of the *Gingerbread Man* (Hunia,

1994). Many schools will choose to carry out at least one designing and making assignment each term.

There is a real need to give children the opportunity to develop and practise skills, and to develop their understanding of technological concepts, both before and during designing and making assignments. These assignments allow children to apply what they have learnt and understood in focused practical tasks to unfamiliar situations. Cross-curricula focused practical tasks should involve the development of drawing and modelling skills; the investigations of the properties of materials, structures or mechanisms; and the examination, disassembly and evaluation of products.

Focused practical tasks can thus be used to develop and practise particular designing and making skills. It is here that children will gain a wider knowledge of materials, of control, and of a range of practical skills, strategies and techniques. It will be during focused practical tasks that children will be instructed in the safe use and care of tools (see, for example, NAAIDT; 1992). Children at Key Stage 1 need to work with a range of materials, such as reclaimed materials, paper, card, textiles, food and construction kits. This work may then be extended so that at Key Stage 2 children include wood for frameworks, and mouldable and stiff sheet materials. At Key Stage 2 children should also be using electrical and mechanical components. These choices of material cannot be left completely to chance, and in most schools it will be the subject coordinator's responsibility to ensure that pupils work with the full range of materials. This will often be achieved through whole school planning of topic schemes of work.

Control at Key Stage 1 is linked with work dealing with structures and involves simple mechanisms. This work can be built upon to include gears and pulleys, and may be developed further through electrical control to the use of sequenced instructions using computers in some schools. The investigation of simple structures may be extended to the study of frames and shells and methods for reinforcing structures. Much of this could be taught using LEGO or STEP materials; other alternatives are included in the bibliography.

When investigating, disassembling and evaluating, children will be looking at existing products and applications to find out how they work. This work is very important because by looking at, and evaluating, products children are better able to make products themselves. Key Stage 1 children can examine, for example, familiar products to see how they are used and discuss the purposes for which they were intended. This can be developed further at Key Stage 2 to look at case studies of famous textile designers, cooks, engineers and technologists, and at the historical developments of products. One may take the view that such hagiographic approaches are undesirable, and in this context 'Intermediate' and 'Appropriate Technology' materials may be used to good effect. These case studies provide many accounts and examples of technological products designed by ordinary, if often remarkable, people for quite unremarkably common, yet essential, human needs. The bibliography provides details of some valuable sources. The Channel 4 television series 'Small Objects of Desire' has recently provided yet another valuable source of information.

An Integrated 'Holistic' Approach

Much of the best practice in primary schools has been where design and technology has taken a central role in the topic planning. A great deal is also to be gained by endeavouring, as far as possible, to provide both the 'focused practical tasks' and the 'investigation', 'disassembly' and 'evaluative' tasks, within projects that involve the children in holistic 'designing and making' assignments. A fully integrated approach is thus desirable.

We have found that the investigation and evaluation of products has often provided a powerful stimulus for launching designing and making assignments. Where the teacher's, or a published, design of some product is introduced to provide a focused practical task we have also found that its subsequent evaluation has provided an equally useful starting point for 'designing and making'. In such cases, the children may often be involved more in the adaptation or modification of designs than in invention. We would argue that these actually provide a more realistic basis for design and technology education than pure 'invention'. In compiling your policies and schemes of work, such issues will, of course, need to be considered carefully by your school. Figure 11.3 provides a representation of the form of design and technology curriculum that we propose. As the new Order emphasizes:

> Pupils should be taught to develop their design and technology capability
> through combining their Designing and Making skills (Paragraphs 3 and 4)
> with Knowledge and Understanding (Paragraph 5) in order to design and
> make products. (SCAA, 1995, p. 2).

In the next section we provide a few concrete examples that may help illustrate the general approach to design and technology that we are advocating. But before you go on to these we suggest that you spend some time studying figure 11.3 and identifying a range of focused tasks that you could employ in your own classroom to support a designing and making assignment.

Enquiry Task

* Using the form of representation provided in figure 11.3, for a chosen topic area, identify a range of focused support tasks that you could use in your classroom to support a designing and making assignment.

Playground Apparatus: A Reception/Year 1 (Key Stage 1) Activity

In the early years, as at other ages, children need to be given positive designing and making experiences. This activity was developed within a topic concerned with

Figure 11.3: A representation of a design and technology curriculum

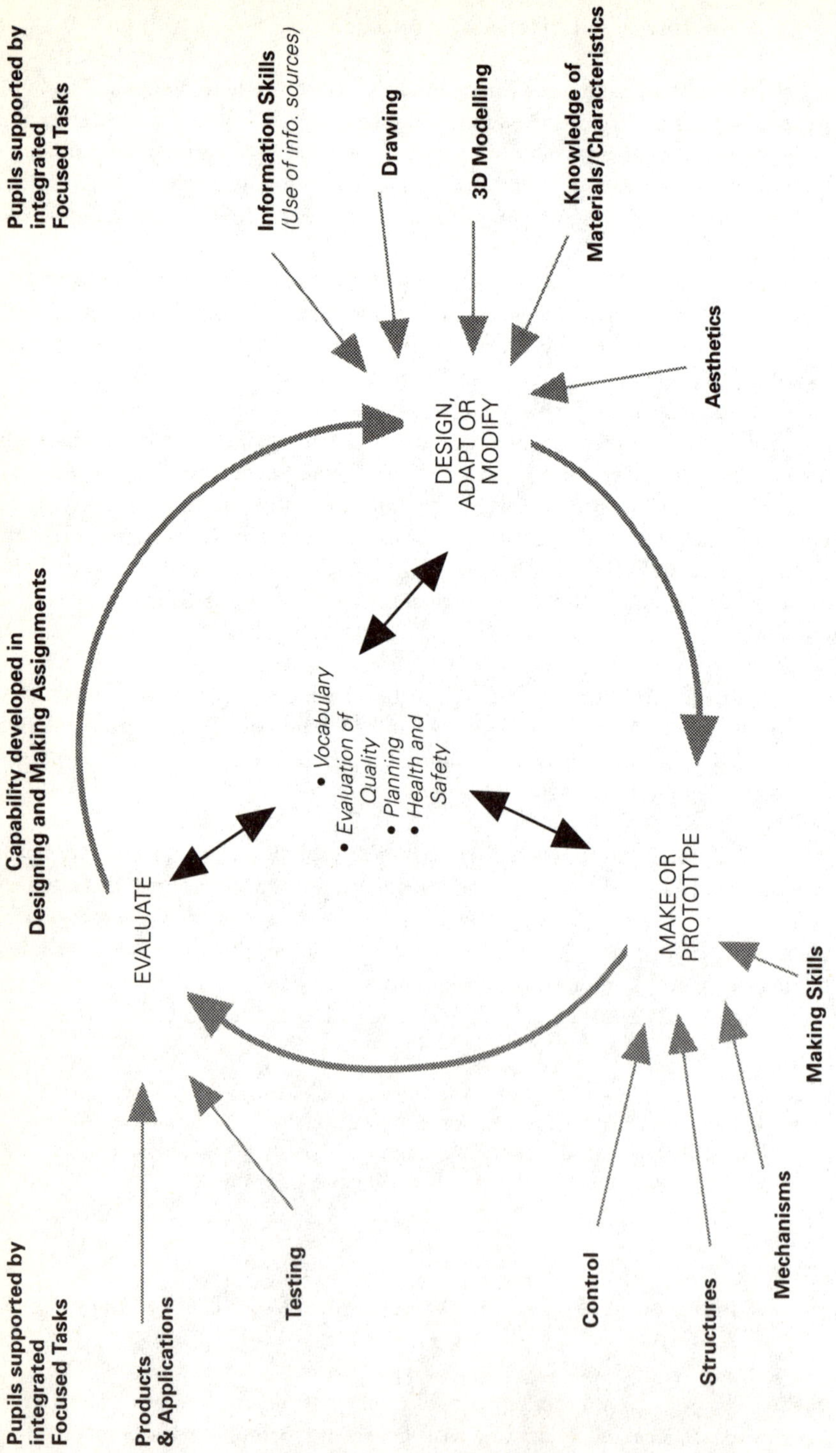

Pupils supported by integrated Focused Tasks

Information Skills
(Use of info. sources)

Drawing

3D Modelling

Knowledge of Materials/Characteristics

Aesthetics

DESIGN, ADAPT OR MODIFY

Capability developed in Designing and Making Assignments

• Vocabulary
• Evaluation of Quality
• Planning
• Health and Safety

EVALUATE

MAKE OR PROTOTYPE

Making Skills

Control

Structures

Mechanisms

Testing

Products & Applications

Pupils supported by integrated Focused Tasks

safety on playground and park apparatus. It provided an introduction to structures and an early experience of designing and making. A project was chosen that related closely to the children's own experiences.

Following a visit to a park, the teacher had introduced the idea of making a playground diorama for the children to play on in the classroom, small scale (mobilo) people were to be used. In order to encourage and support their development, children were provided with a series of linked assignments that offered early and guaranteed success. Opportunities were provided for them to work in groups and, when available, with close parent, teacher assistant and teacher, support and encouragement. Some very effective projects had been developed in the school at other times when the infants were grouped with older Key Stage 2 children for assignments.

The assignment was planned with an associated science topic involved testing the effects of dropping things onto different surfaces. The children were first invited to decide, on the carpet, which groups were to make which playground apparatus. At this stage the simple designs were taken from construction kit resource packs but these could also have been supplemented with the teacher's own designs. Designs might have been presented in photographs and drawings or even as 3D constructions for the children to copy.

Given the inevitable shortage of materials, these activities were carried out by groups at different times over the period of a week. Differentiation was achieved through the use of alternative, simpler, or more sophisticated, mechanisms and construction kits (DUPLO and LEGO DACTA), and through encouraging children to attempt progressively more complex designs. Lego provide a range of support materials that provide guidance but schools may also develop their own. Ross and Browne (1993) demonstrate how children can be given an equal opportunity to develop their capability in this area. They explain how this requires more than an equal access to the materials. On completion of the activity the class discussed, again on the carpet, the various technical merits of their designs. The language focused upon by the teacher included; 'under', 'over', 'high', 'low', 'around', 'stable' and 'corners'. These terms were used by the children as they described how their model had been made and how the apparatus would be used. All of this led into the introduction of a designing and making activity concerned with producing a climbing frame.

The teacher first demonstrated how art straws and pipe cleaners could be used to make frame structures. Each of the children was then given the opportunity to prototype a climbing frame as a whole class activity. Again differentiation was achieved through providing the most able children with straws while a few of the less mature members of the class were encouraged to use a construction kit (REO CLICK). Measurement activities were also introduced by the teacher as she went around the class helping each group in turn. The completion of this activity led to further discussion and a collective evaluation the next day. Those aspects that gave the models strength and stability were identified. The final phase of the activity involved the children, in groups, improving upon their designs, trying out alternative materials, and in testing their models in play on the diorama.

Tea-cup Cosies: A Year 2 (Key Stage 1) Activity

By the end of Key Stage 1 children might be expected to attempt more sophistic-ated assignments. This activity was launched following the class teacher's expression of dismay regarding a cold cup of tea. He had only just found time to make it in the staffroom during breaktime and it had then been neglected until it was too cold to drink. This was a regular occurrence. His pupils were quick to suggest some solutions to the problem and the opportunity was taken to introduce a science investigation of heat loss. The following week the teacher brought in a number of very simple cylindrically shaped teapot cosies for the children to study. These were commercially made felt jackets with holes made for both the spout and for the handle. The teacher suggested that what he needed for his tea was a 'cup cosy' and that the children might enjoy making their own as a present for one of their parents. First of all, following a demonstration, groups were given the task of unpicking the stitching from one of the tea cosies, drawing the pattern to make a copy, and restitching both. During the two weeks that this work was being carried out during 'design and technology time' the children were also carrying out various mathemat-ics assignments involving the manufacture of 'nets'.

The children were finally given the task of designing their own tea-cup cosy for home. The children discussed the difference between the mugs they had brought in from home and the teapots that they had been working with. Drawing on the earlier science work, some identified the need to provide a hinged lid. Before beginning the 'making' activity they were first instructed to identify who the cosy was to be presented to. What was this person's hobbies and favourite things? The children had to draw their designs to show how they would be decorated. They were also required to justify in writing to the school subject co-ordinator the specific materials required. Many of these 'justifications' included references to the scientific investigations carried out; all the children made aesthetic cases. While waiting for the materials to be obtained (begged, stolen, bought and borrowed), the children were required to produce a 'mock-up' in paper to '*avoid any wastage of materials*'. This provided an opportunity for them to prototype their designs and, on evaluation, many of the children chose to modify their designs significantly. In some cases further 'bids' for resources were required.

Making Yoghurt: A Lower Junior (Key Stage 2) Activity

Yoghurt is a very good material for children to use in their designing and making. It is easily accessible in a variety of plain types, set, runny, Greek etc. It is also possible for children to make their own yoghurt from milk, and thus to explore the associated science of yoghurt (Science: Life Processes and Living Things; Pro-gramme of Study 5 and Materials and their Properties; Programme of Study 3). Yoghurt is eaten in a number of situations and these can be used as starting points for an assignment. In this case the celebration of Divali introduced Indian food and yoghurt dips. The project was set in an Economic and Industrial Understanding (EIU) context. The children designed and made a flavoured yoghurt after carrying out some market research. They then designed and made a carton for the yoghurt and an advertising poster.

The children first carried out a survey to find information about the consumption of yoghurt in their class. This meant looking at favourite flavours, the types and the shops where it was purchased. Blind tastings of different types with the same flavour were carried out; children used tally charts and drew graphs of this information. This was a focused task in which the children evaluated a simple familiar product. After the initial research the children were placed in groups or 'companies' to research and market their chosen product. The children were required to decide on a name for their product, and then work in their company to make their flavoured yoghurt. This was then tested on the whole class in a market research exercise. The children were told that this was the way that food companies actually worked to refine and develop their products. They were encouraged to see this as an effective means to achieve quality in their products and they were instructed to make a careful note of ingredients so that they could repeat and refine their recipe. The children were also taught about working in hygienic conditions and to wash and clean their equipment carefully after use. All of the work surfaces were cleaned with Detox before the children started to work and the washing up was done in a bowl specially reserved for this purpose. A science activity was introduced to look at conditions for food decay and at the effects of 'good' (in yoghurt making) and 'bad' bacteria (Science: Life Processes and Living Things; Programme of Study 5).

Many of the children used fresh fruit or vegetables in their yoghurt. They therefore needed to be taught how to use knives carefully, how to use graters, and how to measure quantities with care. After completing their market research the children then designed a carton for their yoghurt and developed a design for the top and/or sides. They needed to find out the type of information found on carton lids and repeated this on their own. They thus studied, and compared, prices, contents and joules. The children then made paper nets of their carton designs before selecting their final one. This then led into their advertising campaign with posters, jingles and so on.

Through this assignment it was possible to cover a very wide range of the Designing and Making Programmes of Study and to assess the children's attainment. The children were generating their own ideas and clarifying the task by firstly investigating bought flavoured yoghurts and then developing their own types. They were developing and communicating design ideas when they made their cartons for the yoghurt. Knowledge of the materials involved, as well as a number of planning, designing and making skills were essential in order to make a product that was 'marketable'. Some children required, and received, appropriate focused tasks in preparation for the assignment. The project was then extended as the children carried out further market research to try and improve their yoghurt and take further cycles in the *evaluating – designing – making* process.

A Model Conveyor Belt System: Upper Junior (Key Stage 2) Activity

Many modern factories have production lines that use conveyor belt systems to move things around. Car assembly plants, for example, often have conveyors in the press shop, welding shop, and in final assembly. This assignment was introduced after a visit to a factory where conveyor belts were used. A video might have provided an alternative source of stimulus. An historical approach was also employed in introducing the project (Coates & Taylor, 1995). The children were taught how motor companies had moved away from a system where each car was being made by one group of employees to a modern system of 'just in time' where parts are delivered to the plant only when they are needed, and where each employee does just one specific job. 'Just in time' saves the company the cost, and trouble, of keeping large quantities of expensive stock in the factory.

The class first simulated these production systems. They were divided into two groups to manufacture envelopes. In one group the children had to make the envelope themselves, from cutting out to gluing, with limited resources. The second group were each given a different task, they simulated a production line with the same resources. The groups were then compared to see which had completed twenty quality envelopes in the shortest time.

The children were then given the challenge of making a model conveyor belt system for some part of the production process. The conveyor had to be controlled using an electric motor and which should be capable of turning on and off, and, perhaps, even reversed. They needed to have the belt speed controlled, and so needed to first investigate gears to decrease the turning speed and increase the turning force. The children were thus given focused practical tasks to increase their knowledge of mechanisms and to help them in the designing of their own systems. The LEGO Control System provided a very useful resource and the children investigated mechanisms using the LEGO 1030 kit. An alternative approach might have involved the use of a construction kit, such as TEKO, or improvised mechanisms. Some children were able to link their systems to a computer to control the movement of their conveyor belt. The children needed to have an understanding of suitable materials, and to gain the appropriate 'making skills' to manufacture the framework for their system. Construction kits and 3D 'Jinks' type frames (wood frame held together with cardboard triangles) were employed. Designs were prepared on paper first, although use of a simple computer assisted design (CAD) program, like Flexicad, would have been even better. Use of construction kits allowed the children to develop their 2D designs into 3D prototype designs before they started to make their final models. There were several links with science in this work as the children were also investigating forces and electrical circuits. The project also provided a good opportunity for the children to refine their craft skills using woodworking tools. The conveyor belt had to be well built for the belt and gear systems to work effectively, and therefore the quality of manufacture needed to be stressed at all stages.

Again the assignment covered nearly all the aspects of the Designing and

Making Programmes of Study. The children generated their own ideas and clarified the task after their visit to the factory. They designed their conveyor belt using various techniques taking into account the properties of the materials selected and ensuring that the belt moved as it was intended to do. Clearly, the children needed to plan how they would make the conveyor belt, and to work carefully with tools and the materials selected. They were also required to evaluate the effectiveness of their systems by developing tests to check and improve on them. At this stage the teacher's role in terms of safety was largely monitorial, the instruction had come in earlier projects and the children had been taught to predict and plan ahead for potential hazards (NAAIDT, 1992).

Enquiry Task

- For the project that you chose for the previous task, or for one of the projects described in the examples above, list the ways in which you would differentiate the activities to provide for the specific needs of your children.
- Discuss these with a colleague.
- Add to your list in the light of this discussion.

Summary

This chapter has attempted to introduce the subject of design and technology, and to summarize the changes that have been made to the National Curriculum requirements. A new curriculum development model has been introduced and teachers recommended to develop their practice within an integrated holistic framework. The exemplar activities described illustrate progression across the two Key Stages. In the early years children often discuss and work together as a whole class while older children are increasingly able to work in small groups, or individually, to work out their own design strategies (Siraj-Blatchford, 1995). A number of differentiation strategies have also been illustrated. Children may be given alternative focused support tasks, their designing may be supported by providing exemplars, they may be given alternative materials to work with, or instructed to use alternative techniques in the process of their making. The importance of evaluation and of a consideration of 'values' has been stressed throughout.

The National Curriculum for design and technology provides teachers with a supporting framework or 'constructive scaffolding' (Siraj-Blatchford, 1993) which may be used to provide children with the maximum freedom and autonomy while securely developing their practical capability in designing and making. The 1990 National Curriculum Order for Technology was introduced first into primary schools and it is primary teachers who have gained the most experience and expertise in applying this Order. It is to be hoped that the views and opinions of primary practitioners will therefore be taken into account fully in the next review of the curriculum, which is predicted for the year 2000. We can begin this review process right now by making every effort to share, in the teacher press, in subject journals, and in other publications, whatever good practice we are involved in or witness.

References

BARLEX, D. (1994) 'Winners and losers', *Design and Technology Times*, Technology Education Developmental Unit; Cheltenham.

COATES, D. and TAYLOR, P. (1995) 'The Rover Project,' (unpublished), Oxford: Westminster College.

DEPARTMENT OF EDUCATION and SCIENCE (1990) *Technology in the National Curriculum*, London: HMSO.

EGGLESTON, J. (1993) *Teaching Design and Technology*, Milton Keynes: Open University Press.

HUNIA, F. (1994) *Gingerbread Man*, Loughborough: Ladybird Books.

NATIONAL CURRICULUM COUNCIL (1993) *Technology Programmes of Study and Attainment Targets: Recommendations of the National Curriculum Council*, York: NCC.

NAAIDT (The National Association of Advisors and Inspectors in Design and Technology) (1992) *Make it Safe*, Eastleigh: NAAIDT Publications.

ROSS, C. and BROWNE, N. (1993) *Girls as Constructors in the Early Years*, Stoke on Trent: Trentham Books.

SCHOOL CURRICULUM ASSESSMENT AUTHORITY (1995) *Design and Technology in the National Curriculum*, London: HMSO.

SIRAJ-BLATCHFORD, J. (1993) 'Constructing Design and Technology: An Early Years Perspective,' *International Journal of Technology and Design Education*, Vol. 3, No. 3.

SIRAJ-BLATCHFORD, J. (1995) *From Collective Designer to Design Collective: Teaching the New National Curriculum for Design and Technology in Primary Schools*, Stoke on Trent: Trentham Books.

WILLIAMS, P. (1990) *Teaching Craft, Design and Technology*, London: Routledge.

Annotated List of Suggested Reading and Resources

BAGSHAW, H. (1992) *STEP: Design and Technology 5–16*, Cambridge: Cambridge University Press.
(This contains Teacher's Resource files for KS1 and 2, a Story Book Pack and Flip Book for KS1 and Information Books for KS2. There is a particularly useful Datafile for KS2 that contains photocopiable sheets covering all aspects of D&T.)

BUDGETT-MEAKIN, C. (1992) *Make the Future Work*, London: Longman.
(This is an important book that puts technology into a world-wide perspective. Contributors provide a range of perspectives in examining values and appropriate technology.)

LEGO (1994) *DUPLO® TOOLO*, Wrexham: Lego.
(There are 20 design-and-make tasks linked with the resource kit. This is particularly useful when introducing mechanisms to KS1 children.)

LEGO DACTA *Technology Activities Workcards*, Wrexham: Lego.
(These work cards are to be used with the TECHNIC 1 construction kit. There is a

teacher's guide and information booklet. There are different work cards that allow children to develop their own knowledge and understanding and then use this in design-and-make assignments. Subjects covered are forces, levers, pulleys, gears, wheels and axles and energy.)

NATIONAL CURRICULUM COUNCIL (1992) *Technology for Ages 5 to 16*, London: HMSO. (The first proposed changes to the original Orders. The Programmes of Study provide valuable details of progression in skills, knowledge and understanding. These proposals were welcomed by teachers because they were much easier to understand but they were flawed because they tried to put levels to aspects that were not easily justified.)

12   Information Technology

Chris Higgins

The Philosophy

The use of Information Technology (IT) in the primary school has two aspects for the teacher: first the development of each child's personal IT capability and skills; and second, the possibilities for IT to enhance children's learning in other areas of the curriculum. The first aspect is widely felt to be important, as can be seen in the report (SCAA, 1994) of the consultation on the review of the National Curriculum.

> Parents and employers think children of all ages should be taught IT. They
> feel they primarily should learn how to use computers, and the main types
> of software (word processing, databases and spreadsheets).

The two different aspects of IT use in the primary school are emphasized by how IT is treated in the National Curriculum. It appears in two distinct ways, first as a subject in its own right with an Attainment Target and associated Programmes of Study for all Key Stages, and second, within the Programmes of Study in other curriculum areas.

The philosophy inherent in the National Curriculum for the development of a child's IT capability and skills is that generally this development should take place in context in other areas of the curriculum and not in specific IT time or sessions. As an obvious example, rather than talking about databases in the abstract, you would wait until you were collecting some suitable information together in class. You could then explain about databases in context, get the children to enter the information into a database to investigate it, and so develop or practise their database skills as well as answer the questions you started with.

When drawing up the curriculum Order a nominal total of hours was assumed to be required to carry out the IT activities. It was felt that twenty-seven hours would be needed at Key Stage 1 and thirty-six hours at Key Stage 2. To emphasize the approach that both the teaching about, and the use of, IT skills would take place wholly within other areas of the curriculum, all other curriculum subjects (except PE) have a statement within their Programmes of Study saying:

> Pupils should be given opportunities, where appropriate, to develop and
> apply their information technology capability in their study of . . .

Some subjects go on to have explicit references to particular opportunities for IT use within the subject. English and mathematics have a number of places where specific possibilities for IT use are mentioned, but science, geography and music have some explicit references as well. We will come back to this later in an enquiry task.

What Has Changed?

The previous version of the National Curriculum created some confusion about the relative status of information technology and design and technology. The National Curriculum documents included the Order for 'Technology in the National Curriculum' (DES, 1990) which contained Attainment Targets (ATs) and Programmes of Study for both design and technology, and IT. To make things worse the design and technology Targets were labelled as AT1 to AT4, and the IT Target was labelled AT5. This created the wrong impression that IT and design and technology were somehow part of a single entity, whereas in reality IT was viewed as a cross-curricular activity and was supposed to be dealt with separately. This problem has been corrected in the revision of the National Curriculum, and IT is now treated as a subject in its own right. The content, though, is still effectively the same as it was for AT5 in the old National Curriculum.

The revision of the National Curriculum has also simplified and clarified the IT Attainment Target and Programmes of Study. Originally 40 Statements of Attainment were defined for ten levels from Key Stages 1 to 4. There is now a single overarching statement of IT capability:

Information technology capability is characterised by an ability to use effectively IT tools and information sources to analyse, process and present information, and to model, measure and control external events. This involves:

- using information sources and IT tools to solve problems;
- using IT tools and information sources, such as computer systems and software packages, to support learning in a variety of contexts;
- understanding the implications of IT for working life and society.

This is combined with Level Descriptions for Key Stages 1 to 3 to describe the types and range of performance that pupils working at a particular level should characteristically demonstrate.

The Programmes of Study were originally also presented in detail together with what should be taught at the different levels and examples of suitable activities. To begin to make some sense of the mass of detail five strands of IT capability were identified – communicating information, handling information, modelling, measurement and control, and applications and effects. The Programmes of Study too have been simplified in the revision and the process of grouping elements of the IT capability together has been continued. In the revised National Curriculum an overarching statement for each Key Stage is given first, which provides a focus for the activities at that stage and helps to highlight progression. These are:

> KS1   Pupils should be taught to use IT equipment and software confidently and purposefully to communicate and handle information and to support their problem solving, recording and expressive work.

and

> KS2   Pupils should be taught to extend the range of IT tools which they use for communication, investigation and control, to become discerning in their use of IT, and to select sources and media for their suitability for purpose.

Hence, in Key Stage 1 pupils are essentially gaining experience of a variety of IT applications in a range of contexts, whilst in Key Stage 2 they are essentially extending their experience of using IT, and becoming more sophisticated in their choice of IT to use.

Then the substance of the Programme of Study is set out in more general terms in just three sections – what opportunities should be given to pupils, what should be taught about communicating and handling information, what should be taught about controlling and modelling.

The National Curriculum Order sets out the essential knowledge and skills of IT capability. It is the statutory definition of the legal curriculum and must stand unchanged for a length of time so it is phrased in terms of the processes involved and is independent of current software, hardware or curriculum practice. It requires the expertise of an experienced teacher to put the flesh of classroom activities onto the bones of the legal framework. There is a danger that as a result of the simpli-fication, the specific requirements for IT activity would seem to be less. However, if you keep in mind the aspect of IT as a tool for enhancing teaching and learning in other subjects the opportunities are still there.

The original version was accompanied by packs of non-statutory guidance (National Curriculum Council, 1990) for each subject containing ideas on planning, exemplars of activities etc., which were intended to assist and support teachers as they implemented the curriculum. IT is one of only two subjects (design and technology being the other) which is to retain the concept of non-statutory guid-ance and a booklet of support material is to be issued for primary teachers. This will have three sections – an introduction to the nature of IT capability and the struc-ture of the Order; illustrations of the depth and range implied in the Programmes of Study with descriptions of classroom activities; and identification of issues for planning. It is intended that the features of progression within each Key Stage will form part of the support material. This guidance can be easily updated as software, hard-ware or curriculum practice develops. The intention is that if the exemplar activities are carried out successfully the requirements of the Programmes of Study will be met. Obviously, more experienced teachers can just use the guidance exemplars as

starting points for their planning. The non-statutory guidance issued originally remains a useful source of ideas and approaches.

Incorporating IT Activities into the Curriculum

When considering an IT activity for your children you have to be careful to see
it as an integral part of the curriculum and not as something to be added on. IT
activities should be embedded in the rest of the curriculum as a natural part of what
is going on, so the IT activities should be there for a reason. It might be that this
is an opportunity to develop a particular aspect of the child's IT capability. It might
be that the computer will manage an activity in an interesting way, so allowing you
to step into the background and observe what is going on, or even to be part of
the team carrying out the activity, as with a Newsroom simulation where information arrives at intervals triggering the next stage. Perhaps the IT will enhance the
children's learning by presenting an activity in a different and possibly better way,
as with a program to create a key or binary tree to classify objects. The program
will take over the structuring of the information that the children put into the tree,
while freeing them to concentrate on the observation of the objects being classified
and the language to use to describe their observations. Sometimes an IT activity can
extend their learning by adding something that could not be attempted before, as
in some simulations or in a data handling exercise with large quantities of data.

Another way to approach it is to consider the outcomes of the IT activity
that you might be hoping for. Outcomes that have been frequently reported from
observations of good IT practice include the following. Focused discussion and
interaction takes place when a small group of children carry out an IT task. The
important word here is 'focused' as the discussion does tend to stay on the job in
hand. High levels of motivation are reported and children will work hard for long
periods on a problem or task. The thought processes involved may be exposed both
to the child and to the teacher, for example when using a text disclosing program,
making it easier to offer help and advice. Many IT activities lead to problem-solving
strategies being developed, either when specific pieces of software are used which
encourage that kind of activity, such as an adventure program where the children
encounter logical problems, or when a task involving a software tool requires a
solution to be found to some intermediate problem, such as when using desk top
publishing to prepare a display. Last, but not least, the children tend to take more
control of the learning process. So you can see there are many reasons for introducing IT activities.

As an example of incorporating IT use into another area of the curriculum, let
us look at writing activities in the English curriculum. First let us look at the basic
writing process and the teaching of writing skills. At both Key Stage 1 and 2 we
see explicit references to IT use.

KS1   Pupils should have opportunities to plan and review their writing,
assembling and developing their ideas on paper and on screen.

KS2 Pupils should be given opportunities to plan, draft and improve their work on paper and on screen.

Also at Key Stage 2, the stages of the writing process are described in greater detail as follows:

To develop their writing, pupils should be taught to: plan – note and develop initial ideas; draft – develop ideas from the plan into structured written text; revise – alter and improve the draft; proofread – check the draft for spelling and punctuation errors, omissions or repetitions; present – prepare a neat, correct and clear final text.

The relationship between the use of computers and the teaching of writing skills is very complex. Using a word processor for this writing process does give a different character to the various stages. It implicitly practises and develops word processing skills, but it also enhances the language work. So sometimes when children are writing you should get them to use the word processor.

The following style of enquiry task can be carried out whenever you are considering IT use. Try to make explicit why you are going to use IT and what the benefits are of using an IT approach rather than any other.

Enquiry Task

Consider the writing process as described above and write down what you think are the advantages and disadvantages of using IT rather than pen and paper at each stage.

	Advantages	Disadvantages
Planning		
Drafting		
Revision		
Proofreading		
Presentation		

There are also many other language activities that you can organize with a word processor which, again, implicitly practise and develop word processing skills but which are worthwhile in their own right. For example, you can give the children a piece of writing on the screen with the punctuation removed and then get them to put it back so that the text makes sense. You can present a poem on screen with the lines mixed up and get the children to use the cut and paste facilities of the word processor to put them into the correct order. You can use this re-sequencing activity with many other texts as well for different purposes, e.g., a recipe, an experiment, the dialogue in a play, a sequence of logical deductions, etc. In this way you will be enhancing other areas of the curriculum and also be carrying out in a meaningful way the requirements of developing the children's IT capability with a word processor.

A less common example of using IT to enhance an area of the curriculum would be that of using a concept keyboard for organizing information that the class has collected. Concept keyboards have tended to be thought of as mainly suitable for young children or special needs applications, where input is required other than by typing at a keyboard. However, there can be a benefit for children of any age when the physical layout of the overlays used mirrors some aspect of the information being presented. For example, suppose a topic has been carried out collecting information about the local village, its buildings and the people who live in them. The top overlay could be a simple map of the village with an initial amount of information about particular buildings and places of interest presented on the screen when the symbols representing them are pressed on the keyboard. However, passing to the next layer of overlay, architectural details about the houses could be presented. At the final level a discussion of the people who currently lived in the house could be found. The fact that all the information about the village is being presented in a layout similar to the original positions gives a powerful impetus to the children's attempts to get to grips with organizing the mass of information.

A history project about an area or topic could be presented in a similar way. The top overlay could be a present day discussion, the other overlays could represent earlier periods of interest, and going down through the overlays would have echoes of an archeological dig through layers of earth. Again you would be introducing, practising and developing skills of communicating and handling information at the same time as adding something to the geographical or historical activity from which the information came.

Planning for IT Activities

There are a range of points which need to be borne in mind when planning to involve the children in using IT as part of some activity.

First are the considerations about what needs to take place before, during and after the activity. The IT activity should fit naturally into the progression of ideas the children are developing. You should consider what activities need to be carried out before the IT activity takes place. For example, some time before using a data handling package that drew graphs of the information collected, it would be best for the children to have drawn by hand count frequency graphs and pie charts of small simple collections of data. This would ensure that the concepts and techniques were firmly understood before using the power of the software package.

On a shorter time scale you have to decide if the instructions on how to use a program, CD-ROM, etc., are easy to understand, or if the children will require some explanation before they will be able to use it. You may need to decide whether or not a set of written instructions beside the computer would help.

When considering the outcomes you are hoping for from the IT activity, you might want the children to employ a range of recording techniques while carrying it out. They might draw a sketch of where they went, or keep a log of what happened and the decisions they took during a simulation or adventure program. They could keep a record of their attempts at spellings or calculations or attempts to solve problems.

There are a range of possibilities for follow–up work after the activity. The children could interpret the output of the graphs, etc., of the data handling package, and report on the results obtained. They could write a log or story of their experiences when using the simulation package or adventure, or draw a map of the route they followed. The record of their spellings etc. would provide some concrete evidence of what they were trying to do and what their problems were so that when you talk about the activity afterwards you have something on which to base your comments and discussion.

All of these considerations require you to become familiar with the IT software and CD-ROMs that you are going to get the children to use, so that you can think through the before – during – after aspects of the activity.

Enquiry Task

- Choose a piece of software that you might use with your children.

- List the prior knowledge that they would require so as to make the best use of the program.

- Evaluate how easy it is to understand the instructions for its use, and how you would prepare the children to use it.

- Decide what you would want them to do during the IT activity, and any recording you would want them to carry out.

- Think of a list of follow up tasks that you could get them to carry out.

Allied with any IT activity you wish to carry out is the question of how you will organize it in the classroom. Computer time is still a scarce resource in most classrooms and quickly used up by individual and small group work. One way to cope with this is to have a rolling programme of IT use, so that every child doesn't have to carry out the same IT activities during the same task or topic but that there are opportunities over a period of a term or a year for that particular activity to be carried out during a variety of other tasks. For example, for a child to really benefit from writing using a word processor they should be able to go through all the stages of the writing process mentioned before. This takes time. However, planning could ensure enough opportunities during a given period for each child to have the chance to carry out this extended writing activity on one piece of work.

This approach implies some recording of your children's work in terms of IT capability so that you can keep track of who has done what and who still needs opportunities for various tasks. The benefit of the revised National Curriculum is that as it is less prescriptive in terms of detailed requirements, you have more flexibility in terms of giving children different opportunities which will practise or develop the same IT skills.

Allied to this is the effect of the decision to express Attainment Targets in terms of Level Descriptions. These bring together the key indications of IT capability at each Level. Each Level gives an overview of IT capability at that Level. This approach allows a holistic assessment of a child's IT capability in the context of their learning across the curriculum, rather than in terms of their response to specific IT tasks. This is much more in tune with the philosophy of IT as a tool for learning in every other subject.

Issues

One problem for a cross-curricular subject, such as IT is intended to be, is that it may fall down the cracks between the other elements of the curriculum. For a child's IT capability to develop to the full, and for the benefits of IT to be used to enhance their learning, careful coordination of the IT activities across their whole school career is needed. This is the only way to ensure that each child is exposed to a variety of IT activities at the right stage for them and that there is a progression in the activities over time. The first stage in ensuring this coordination is to create a map of the IT curriculum for a child in the school (see Enquiry Task p. 176). This audit and mapping process will itself raise two issues. First is the question of resources. IT is a fast developing area with new ideas and technology appearing at an ever increasing rate. For example, laptop computers are now available that could enhance the learning process by making it possible to use IT during fieldwork, in museums and at home, and thus take the IT tools to the activity rather than having to carry out some recording and return to a static base to use the IT tools. Similarly, a wide range of CD-ROM information sources are becoming available that could enhance work in the classroom in a variety of areas. Ideally you would be able to take advantage of each new development as it occurred but the purchase of such new resources is costly. We can console ourselves with the thought that a great deal of the IT curriculum will be able to be carried out with the standard IT equipment available in schools.

The second issue is the recognition of the need for time and resources for the training of teachers who will want to improve their expertise and knowledge so that they can recognize the opportunities for IT use in the curriculum and exploit them. The simplification of the IT curriculum makes it look less intimidating but requires a great deal of knowledge and experience on the part of the teacher to make the most of it. This is why support materials will be so important, and why it is necessary for you to build up a bulk of personal knowledge of IT software and applications that you feel confident in using. The recent national research project on the impact of IT on children's learning (Watson, 1993) shows that the quality and indeed quantity of current IT use in schools is still very patchy.

Enquiry Task

* List the explicit references to IT use in other subjects, e.g.,
  English KS1: Reading 1b
  > '. . . read information . . . including IT-based reference materials . . .'
  Mathematics KS2: Shape, Space and Measure 1c
  > '. . . use computers to create and transform shapes.'
  Geography KS2: Geographical Skills 3f
  > '. . . use IT to gain access to additional information sources and to assist in hadling, classifying and presenting evidence.'

* Decide which of these references would fall within the work in your class and then draw up a diagram of your class's year showing where they would occur, which part of the curriculum they would be in, and what part of the IT capability they address, if any.

* Add to this IT map any other IT activities you already carry out, or would like to include in future.

* Together with colleagues fit your map into an overall IT map for the whole school, thus placing all the explicit references and all the other IT activities you want to carry out in one coherent format.

* You can now see the IT curriculum you are offering. Check to see that you cover the statutory requirements, include all the opportunities for enhancing the curriculum that you can, and have ensured progression and no duplication.

* Audit your existing software, hardware, etc. to see what additional resources are required.

Summary

* There are two aspects to IT use in the primary school: first, the development of each child's personal IT capability and skills; and second, the possibilities for IT to enhance children's learning in other areas of the curriculum.

* The philosophy in the National Curriculum is that the development of a child's IT capability should take place in the context of other areas of the curriculum.

* The new curriculum is appreciably simpler than the old one in terms of the detailed requirements stated for IT use. However, this means that you will

need experience of IT activities to spot the opportunities for IT use to enhance the children's learning.

- You should incorporate IT activities into the curriculum for a reason, so try to decide why you are going to use IT, and what the benefits are of using an IT approach rather than any other.

- IT is a cross-curricular activity and needs to be coordinated. You need to construct a map of IT activities for the year for your class and place it in the context of a map for the whole school's IT curriculum. Then you will be able to ensure that each child is exposed to the full range of IT activities, at the right stage for them, and that there is a progression in the activities over time.

References

DEPARTMENT OF EDUCATION and SCIENCE (1990) *Technology in the National Curriculum – Attainment Targets and Programmes of Study in Technology*, London: HMSO.

NATIONAL CURRICULUM COUNCIL (1990) *Non-Statutory Guidance – Information Technology*, York: NCC.

SCHOOL CURRICULUM and ASSESSMENT AUTHORITY (1994) *The Review of the National Curriculum – A Report on the 1994 Consultation*, London: SCAA.

WATSON, D. (ed) (1993) *The Impact Report*, London: Kings College.

Annotated List of Suggested Reading

DEPARTMENT OF EDUCATION and SCIENCE (1989) *Curriculum Matters 15: Information Technology from 5 to 16*, London: HMSO.
(The original discussion in the HMI series about the place of IT in the curriculum.)

NATIONAL COUNCIL FOR EDUCATIONAL TECHNOLOGY (1994) *Information Technology Works*, Coventry: NCET.
(A useful summary of the research evidence on the value of IT for teaching and learning.)

NATIONAL COUNCIL FOR EDUCATIONAL TECHNOLOGY/NATIONAL ASSOCIATION OF ADVISERS FOR COMPUTERS IN EDUCATION (1994) *Reviewing IT*, Coventry: NCET.
(A pack to help schools assess their IT provision, with particular reference to preparing for a school inspection.)

STRAKER, A. (1990) *Children Using Computers*, Oxford: Blackwell.
(A useful practical discussion of using IT in the classroom. Things have moved on very quickly in four years, though, so some of the comments are dated.)

UNDERWOOD, J. (ed) (1994) *Computer Based Learning: Potential into Practice*, London: David
     Fulton.
(A discussion of the extent to which theoretical ideas about IT use have been able to
be put into practice.)

WATSON, D. (ed) (1993) *The Impact Summary*, London: Kings College.
(A short summary of the findings of the research project commissioned by the DES on
the impact of IT on children's learning.)

Section 3

Beyond the National Curriculum

13   Religious Education

Gwyneth Little and Carrie Mercier

The New Context for Development

July 1994 saw the launch of the new National Model Syllabuses for Religious Education (RE). They provided models for education authorities to draw on in constructing their local agreed syllabus for RE.

Unlike National Curriculum subjects, the syllabus for RE, which is the additional subject making up the basic curriculum, is decided locally. This has been the case as far back as the first agreed syllabus in 1923. Having looked at the good practice which had developed, the government in 1944 decided that every education authority should have a syllabus, determined locally, reflecting the needs and views of local people. Religious instruction was to be the only compulsory subject in schools. In the political and religious climate of the time it was assumed, but not stated, that the teaching would be Christianity in order to nurture an active belief in, and response to that religion. It is interesting to note that, until the 1988 Education Reform Act, Christianity was not actually mentioned. This new Act stated that all new syllabuses shall reflect the fact that religious traditions in Great Britain are in the main Christian, while taking account of the teaching and practices of the other principal religions represented in Great Britain.

The National Curriculum Council's (NCC) review of the local agreed syllabuses in existence found that they varied considerably in content and aims. One purpose of the national models was to bring some coherence and commonality to a very widely diverse subject.

In some local authorities there is a relatively new syllabus for RE already in place, and the government circular 1/94 states that each LEA is required to update their agreed syllabus every five years. The first point of reference when seeking guidance concerning RE is therefore your local agreed syllabus.

The social composition of many local authorities has resulted in syllabuses which, quite rightly, reflect the cultural mix of the area, but, without a core of approved material and common aims, the educational opportunities for children in RE have been patchy to say the least! In compiling the model syllabuses the School Curriculum and Assessment Authority (SCAA) was able to draw on the resources of the Working Groups, set up by SCAA, from the religious faiths in Britain. With this expertise, there is now the confidence resulting from having the knowledge and understanding of each religion, as agreed, at a national level, by the members of each faith. There is still the opportunity for the local agreed syllabus to reflect the cultural and religious diversity in schools.

Enquiry Task

- Find out when your local agreed syllabus was written and whether there is any intention to revise it in the light of the new national models.

- Look through the syllabus and establish whether the content reflects the fact that religious traditions in Britain are, in the main, Christian, while taking account of the other principal religions.

Implications for Teachers

The new model syllabuses for RE are not intended for the classroom practitioner but in many ways they are of considerable significance for teachers. Their appearance has heightened awareness among headteachers, governors and parents of the need to fulfil the law which requires that RE be taught to all pupils. As a result, many teachers who once ignored RE are now having to include it in their planning.

The launch of the model syllabuses has helped to focus attention on the requirement for schools to allocate sufficient time to religious education. The models are based on the expectation that pupils at Key Stage 1 will receive a minimum of thirty-six hours of RE a year, and forty-five hours at Key Stage 2. It has also drawn attention to the desperate need for teacher training and resources in religious education. New local agreed syllabuses that have been written in response to the recent government initiative have strengthened the case for INSET in this area of the curriculum; courses in RE, funded jointly by the government and the local education authorities, are now available to teachers.

Further, and this too is very important, the model syllabuses stress the educational rationale and purpose of RE. This includes helping pupils to acquire and develop knowledge and understanding of Christianity and the other principal religions represented in Great Britain. Understanding the influence of religion on lives and cultures and developing positive attitudes towards other people are further aims. Importantly, there is also a recognition of the role RE can play in enhancing children's spiritual, moral, cultural and social development.

Some groups have had a clear notion of the contribution that the subject can make to the whole development of the child. But these have been minority voices, imperfectly heard. Now, with commonly held aims and Attainment Targets, we hope that a more purposeful attitude to the teaching of RE will result. Local authorities, and, more importantly, you as teachers, will be enabled to approach RE from a sound, rational, educational base and grow in confidence in delivering it. We believe that more teachers will be willing to 'have a go' as the aims and material suggested in the documents become more widely disseminated through the agreed syllabuses.

Enquiry Task

- Identify the needs and concerns of colleagues in your school regarding religious education.

- Sort these concerns under headings such as resources, background knowledge, and religious commitments.

- With a colleague, list resources available for addressing each concern, or appropriate strategies for taking remedial action.

Attainment Targets for RE

There are two attainment targets (ATs) within the new model syllabuses: Learning about Religion; and, Learning from Religion. These translate into the religious education of the pupil in the primary school. For example, in a lesson on Muhammad, pupils may hear a story about Muhammad and understand that his life is an example for Muslims today. They may also reflect on whose example they might follow and consider the value of having a role model in life. This latter part of the RE lesson fulfils the second Attainment Target of learning from religion.

The two attainment targets are common to all areas and Key Stages and are complementary to each other — two strands to be woven into the fabric of RE for the enrichment of the child. The first is necessary to the second. Informed responses to religious and moral issues can only be useful if made with as much knowledge and understanding of the relevant religious points of view as possible. Accurate information is vital if children are to be made aware of religious beliefs and practices.

Enquiry Task

Take three of the following topics for RE. Set learning objectives for your class based either on those from your local agreed syllabus or from the two-fold model given here:

- The local church
- Jesus as teacher
- Hannukah

For example,
The Bible as a special book

Learning objective 1 • To know that the Bible is a special book for Christians.
         • To understand why the Bible is a special book for Christians.
         • To know how Christians use the Bible.
Learning objective 2 • To reflect on why certain books are special to us.
         • To consider where we may turn for help and guidance in everyday life.

Identifying progression through what pupils are expected to learn is important in RE, as in any other subject. Your local agreed syllabus may not have Attainment Targets set down. It may be that the syllabus has an accompanying handbook that will help you to set appropriate learning objectives. If there is no guidance at all it is likely that the syllabus was drawn up prior to the 1988 Education Reform Act and the introduction of the National Curriculum when Attainment Targets were laid down in other areas of the curriculum. It may be helpful to take the two ATs *learning about* and *learning from* from the national model syllabuses to help you in your planning.

The Model Syllabuses as a Resource

The national model syllabuses not only establish a context in which new initiatives in RE can gain momentum and find support, they can also provide a resource for discussion and thereby a starting point for change in schools where RE has previously been left out of curriculum planning and debate.

Firstly, these models for RE establish once and for all that the starting point is religious *education* and not religious *instruction*, or religious *nurture*, which are the responsibility of the faith community. From reading the press coverage on the new national model syllabuses you might think that we were in the business of Christian nurture. However, on reading the guidelines in the national model syllabuses you would be hard pressed to find evidence to support such a view. It is clear that the national model syllabuses are intended to secure a place for RE in the curriculum on educational grounds and there is no room for a confessional approach. Religious education does not seek to convert children, or make them practitioners of a particular religion: it seeks to explore the phenomenon of religious thought and practice in order to understand more fully what it is to be human in all its variety and potential.

Secondly, it is important to note that, although the new syllabuses reaffirm the requirement of the 1988 Education Reform Act that any new syllabus must *reflect the fact that the religious traditions in Great Britain are in the main Christian while taking into account the other principal religions* (a point made earlier), there is no precise ruling on the percentage of time to be given to any one religious tradition. A local agreed syllabus can, therefore, establish the kind of balance in the religions studied that best suits the needs of the children in the area. There may be room in some cases for the school to define that balance.

Thirdly, the new model syllabuses affirm what is already good practice in RE in many schools. This is not surprising, as the research that went into the national model syllabuses took into account the best of existing local agreed syllabuses and handbooks for religious education. As this good practice is more widely disseminated, and teachers become aware of the value and interest in the classroom, the provision for our children will be better.

Enquiry Task

- Imagine yourself walking into an unfamiliar school.
- Look and listen in a classroom where RE is taking place.
- What would you hope to observe if the subject was being taught well?

You may have anticipated any or all of the following, and more:

- Children interested in and learning from the material because it is colourful, well produced, accurate, and intellectually challenging.
- Children being given the opportunity to question and discuss.
- Children being given the opportunity to reflect on human questions and express, in a variety of ways, their own responses to them.
- Children beginning to appreciate the variety of religious expression, and valuing the distinctiveness of each.
- Children recognizing the considerable influence of religion on peoples' lives and actions.

In such a classroom we see the fulfilment of the Attainment Targets of the model syllabus; learning about religion, and learning from religion.

Questions and Issues

There is much in the new model syllabuses that will help to promote positive developments in religious education. Nevertheless, concerns have been expressed.

One major concern is the apparent exclusion of a thematic approach. In many primary schools religious education, like other areas of the curriculum, is explored through cross-curricular themes and topics. However, neither of the two model syllabuses allow for such an approach. Indeed it was stated at the launch of the national model syllabuses that 'What we do not recommend is planning RE from themes to which religions are "fitted in". . . .'. On the other hand, some local agreed syllabuses advocate a thematic approach, especially for pupils in the early years. No doubt many of these syllabuses will change in future revision so as to fall in line with the 'one faith at a time' approach recommended in the national models. However, it must be remembered that the models are simply that – suggested ways of creating a syllabus. Local authority agreed syllabus conferences may draw on them to create a syllabus appropriate for their area, and relevant to the needs of their children. Some may also draw on alternative models, such as that produced by a group of university lecturers in RE which offers a thematic approach for syllabus construction, (Details obtainable from Catherine Bowness, School of Education, University of Exeter, EX1 2LU).

Another objection has been that the new model syllabuses are too prescriptive and put too much emphasis on content. One of the reasons why there was said to be a need for national model syllabuses was the view that many local agreed syllabuses did not give sufficiently detailed guidance for teachers. In order to remedy this situation the model syllabuses set out in detail the areas of knowledge and understanding that might be covered at each Key Stage. Local agreed syllabuses appearing in the future will, no doubt, be expected to follow this pattern.

The faith communities working group reports, published alongside the model syllabuses, give very clear guidance on what each faith regards as the essential areas of study, whilst retaining a recognition of the range of perspectives within a religion. This is an important aspect of the models. Now at least you have the opportunity to use material which the faith itself regards as important and appropriate. Some teachers may find it helpful to have such detailed guidelines in an area of the curriculum in which they feel less than confident; others will feel burdened by so much emphasis on content. Always remember, however, that you, as the teacher, choose from the syllabus the religions and areas of study you wish to use. So look carefully and consider your strengths and interests.

Enquiry Task

* Look at the Programmes of Study available to you in the local agreed syllabus.
* Make a note of the content you feel most confident with.
* Start your planning there.

Possible Approaches and Methods

Themes and Topics?

The majority of teachers working with early years children will want to continue with a thematic approach. Families, food, festivals, special people and special places are the kinds of themes and topics given in local agreed syllabuses which can be usefully explored. There is sometimes a problem when the theme or topic planned does not readily translate into a meaningful opening for RE. Water is a popular topic in primary schools and it lends itself well to a cross-curricular approach. In terms of RE, the topic can lead into a valuable exploration of the meaning of water in Baptism, and water as a religious symbol. However, it is important, when trying to find a RE link, to avoid meaningless and tenuous connections. For example, many teachers think of Noah's Ark as suitable for the RE input in the topic of water, and yet the story of Noah is not about water, it is about broken promises, judgment, punishment and renewal. One way to avoid such misunderstanding is to keep in touch with your local agreed syllabus. If the RE link with your topic cannot fulfil any of the aims given in your syllabus, then it is only going to be cosmetic and will not make a valuable contribution to either the topic or the religious education of your pupils.

Something else to avoid with topic work in RE is the problem of trying to cover too much. It is better for pupils to understand that water has an important place in a believer's Baptism, or a Christening service, and that they should remember its meaning as a religious symbol, than to encounter every instance of water used in religious ritual. Quality, rather than quantity, is important when exploring religious beliefs and practices through themes and topics: in this way you will be able to preserve and respect the distinctiveness of each religious tradition.

RE as a Discrete Subject

Popular umbrella titles at Key Stage 2 are ideas such as Light or Journeys. Giving children a focus for their learning in this way offers you the potential for exploring cross-curricular links. RE can be one element of a theme involving several areas of the curriculum.

Whilst the model syllabuses produced by SCAA are not intended as schemes of work for schools, the examples suggested in them are most appropriate for teachers to work with. One of the joys of RE is that the body of material is so vast that one can choose to work with that part of it you find particularly appealing or interesting, and which best suits your personal interests and the educational opportunities you wish to give your children. The world around you, your locality and community, and the media are full of religion in many ways. Make the most of your opportunities!

In the current 'specialist subject' climate in primary schools, however, the RE requirement at Key Stage 2 may be fulfilled more appropriately in a separate time allocation and through Programmes of Study prepared from material in the agreed syllabus. This allows for specific RE topics to be used. Examples may be taken from two or more religions and cover such areas as Pilgrimage, Holy Books or Birth Ceremonies. Alternatively you may choose to concentrate on one religion and study Festivals through the year in Judaism, family life and worship in Hinduism or Stories Jesus told. Whichever pattern is adopted, the requirement is the same. Christianity and two other religions should be studied in depth through the Key Stage. You will need to consider the religions followed by children in the school. Children should be encouraged to understand the distinctiveness of each individual religion, as well as develop an awareness of the similarities among religions, i.e., 'Learning about'.

The Experiential Approach in RE

The knowledge and understanding suggested within the content needs to be intellectually demanding as well as interesting at each Key Stage. However, consideration

---

Enquiry Task

Key Stage 1

Find out if your local agreed syllabus suggests themes and topics for RE in the early years. If it does, choose a topic you might follow in your class. Draw up a topic web with the subject in the centre and brainstorm ideas for cross curricular links.

Key Stage 2

Choose a topic from your local agreed syllabus which is suitable for your year group. An example might be Places of Worship. Draw up a topic web with the subject in the centre. Brainstorm ideas of aspects of the topic you feel would be appropriate for the class. You may, for example, look at symbols or ceremonies, prayer or worship activities. There are many possibilities.

---

should be given also to the opportunity to be offered for spiritual and moral development by allowing for reflection on the personal experience of each child. This may be where the greatest learning takes place – the 'learning from religion'. For some time now RE, perhaps more than any other subject, has recognized the importance of child-centred learning. Here we start from the child's experiences and interests and offer them the opportunity to explore in depth their own feelings, thoughts and ideas. By doing so they become more aware of the same qualities in other people, and see themselves in relation to others and the world they inhabit. So people following rituals and practices, which are initially strange to them, can be understood to have similar instincts, hopes, fears, delights and aspirations as themselves.

Children do not come as empty vessels into religious education. Those pupils who are not from a religious background still bring thoughts, feelings and experiences from their own lives that can offer bridges into the land of RE.

It is not necessary, and often not helpful, to begin with what is explicitly religious, but rather with what is implicit RE. Implicit RE begins with the thoughts, feelings, interests and experiences of the pupils. It may be through the implicit dimension of RE that the subject can make the most valuable contribution to pupils' moral and spiritual development. The new model syllabuses acknowledge, and promote, this aspect of RE as do most local agreed syllabuses.

Before looking at the importance of 'remembering' in Pesach (Passover), or the theme of remembrance in the Breaking of Bread, discuss with your class their memories of holidays, special moments, times of happiness or, indeed, sadness. As an introduction to the topic of Pilgrimage, pupils could look at the feelings associated with journeys and special places in their own experience. Pupils in a Year 2 class joined in an imaginary journey to a special place. They thought about what they might like to take with them, drew their special belongings inside the outline of an empty suitcase, and discussed their feelings of anticipation.

Enquiry Task

List the implicit RE, or the starting points, that might be appropriate for the following topics. For example, starting points for the topic of Sacred Scriptures, may be the children's special books, favourite stories or diaries. Topics:

- Icons
- Prophets and leaders
- Religious festivals
- Harvest Thanksgiving
- The Ten Commandments

Skills and Attitudes

Some skills, such as reading, talking purposefully or researching, apply across the curriculum. Can you think of others which are particularly relevant to RE? You may have suggested the skills of *empathy* and *reflection*. The attitudes you hope to promote might include *openness* and *respect for others*.

In planning a programme of religious education it is important to incorporate the skills and attitudes to be developed. This means planning for a variety of activities and learning experiences. Young children need to have opportunities to look at, and handle, artefacts, visit places of worship, hear believers talking about their faith, and listen to stories from the traditions they are studying. If you are concerned with skills and attitudes as well as knowledge and understanding in RE, you will need to draw on such resources. Children learn through doing and from example. You might encourage observation skills, and the attitudes of respect for the beliefs and practices of others through the handling of religious artefacts, through learning to listen to others, and through actions such as taking off their shoes as they enter a place of worship. Through creative work, and using story, dance, music, drama and art, pupils can develop skills in expressing ideas important in religion; through exploring symbolic meaning they will begin to develop skills in interpretation.

Enquiry Task

- List the skills and attitudes that are recommended in the aims of your local agreed syllabus.
- Do you agree with the recommendations?
- Would you change, (or add) any skills and attitudes mentioned?
- With a colleague draw up your own list of skills and attitudes you would want your pupils to acquire through religious education.

Planning for Religious Education

You have the agreed syllabus, you have made time to plan, and have acquired the money and opportunity to acquire resources. How do you make a start on the planning? Here are a few questions you will need to answer before you begin.

- Do you plan individually, in year groups, across years, in subject areas or thematically?
- Is your school development plan readily available?
- Does your school plan for the year or a term at a time?
- Are there coordinators responsible for each curriculum area?
- In what group or groups is the planning of RE to take place?

In an ideal world your school will have a RE subject coordinator with expertise in the subject and a brief to form the school's policy on RE, coordinate the planning through the school, and advise staff about subject matter and resources. They are likely to be responsible also for keeping up-to-date with local and national INSET, and receiving government publications and publishers' catalogues. The coordinator should keep all staff informed about available support. Normally the coordinator will be the first point of contact for the non-specialist teacher.

Enquiry Task

- How closely does your school's RE policy refer to, and work with, the local agreed syllabus?
- Talk to the other teachers about how the policy is implemented in your school.
- If there is no document, then try to initiate discussion in a staff meeting about the teaching of RE.

First, take a look at the school's policy document for RE. The policy should provide you with a clear idea of the way in which the school approaches the subject, the aims it follows, the content and methods used.

At this point it may be useful to consider the help and advice available to you from outside the school. The LEA advisory service is committed to enabling teachers to provide quality RE in its schools. Assuming your school to be maintained by a LEA, members of the advisory team will, almost certainly, be prepared to visit your school, talk to individuals, address a staff meeting, and help with policy making and planning. They are also very good at getting groups of teachers to do their planning in cooperation with each other. If there is such a service in your area, then make every effort to use it; it can be a worthwhile, even an inspiring experience.

The advisory team in the LEA may run INSET courses in curriculum areas. Such courses may be on, for example, 'RE at Key Stage 1', 'Using Story in RE', 'Planning a Programme of Study'. Some courses may increase your personal knowledge and understanding of the content of RE – Hinduism, Places of Worship or Festivals;

others may allow you to experience and discuss different teaching methods and strategies.

Some LEAs are still fortunate enough to have an RE resources centre where teachers are welcome to view the collection of books, artefacts, videos and other classroom resources. Browsing here, often with the help of experienced and knowledgable staff, can support the busy teacher, particularly those lacking confidence in the subject matter, and can provide up-to-date information on the changing requirements of the subject. Often, there is a charge, or a school subscription scheme, for such a facility, but it can be well worth the investment.

Visits and visitors provide a good way for children to experience the reality of religion. They can also enhance your own knowledge and appreciation of the subject. For example, you may find it helpful to contact local clergy if you are not too sure of how to teach about church colours and vestments, or the order of Baptism. Many clergy are willing to be involved, to welcome children to the local church or chapel, talk to them appropriately, demonstrate ritual, and allow exploration. Members of many faith communities are very pleased to answer queries, visit schools, and conduct children on a visit to their place of worship or local shops. Such encounters need approaching with sensitivity and a very clear idea of the educational outcome expected. Asking around your locality about availability and suitability, can often produce fruitful encounters. Sometimes simply taking a deep breath and initiating the contact yourself can produce fascinating results. Names and addresses of communities willing to engage in this way with schools are frequently published in agreed syllabus documents, or held by the local RE self-help group or advisor. Such experiences will repay the initial effort made to establish the links in terms of children's interest and involvement, as well as the breaking down of assumptions and prejudices all too often held.

Groups offering support nationally, (for example Westhill RE Centre, Birmingham; the National RE Centres in London and York; and the Centre for Development in RE at Westminster College, Oxford), run courses and distance learning programmes which can be exciting and interesting, and contribute substantially to your knowledge and expertise. Good sources of information about such inservice training are the educational press such as *The Times Educational Supplement*, and *Child Education*. *Resource* is a quarterly publication which deals, in particular, with special needs issues in RE. The most informative and up-to-date, publication is undoubtedly the Christian Education Movement's (CEM) publication, *RE today*. As a result of the changing RE scene in recent years there are several up-to-date and good books on planning and delivering RE. For more information see the reading list at the end of this chapter.

Conclusion

The model syllabuses have raised awareness of the possibilities within the teaching of RE. There is much to discuss, and many developments to come, but in the meantime these syllabuses provide a stimulus for improving the provision and quality of RE in schools.

Suggested Reading

Books

Bastide, D. (ed) (1991) *Good Practice in Primary RE*, London: Falmer Press.

Hulmes, E. (1994) *World Religions*, London: Sainsbury Publications.

Cole, W. and Evans-Lowndes, J. (1991) *Religious Education in the Primary Curriculum*, Norwich: RMEP.

Erricker, C. (ed) (1993) Teaching World Religions, Oxford: Heinemann.

Gateshill, P. and Thompson, J. (1993) *Religious Artefacts in the Classroom*, London: Hodder & Stoughton.

Grimmett, M., Grove, J., Hull, J. and Spencer, L. (1991) *A Gift to the Child: Religious Education in the Primary School*, London: Simon & Schuster.

Hammond, J., *et al.* (1990) *New Methods in RE Teaching*, Harlow: Oliver & Boyd.

Jackson, R. and Starkings, D. (1990) *The Junior Handbook of RE*, Cheltenham: Stanley Thornes.

Palmer, S. and Brevilly, E. (1992) *Religion, Education and Life: Infant Teacher's Handbook*, London: Collins Educational.

Rankin, J., Brown, A. and Hayward, M. (1989) *Religious Education Topics for the Primary School*, London: Longman.

Journals

RE Today, CEM

British Journal of Religious Education, CEM

Royal Buildings, Victoria Street, Derby, DE1 1GW.

Religious Education Centres

BFSS National RE Centre, West London Institute of Higher Education, Lancaster House, Borough Road, Isleworth, Middx., TW7 5DU.

The National Society's RE Centre, 23 Kensington Square, London, W8 5HN.

The Regional RE Centre (Midlands), Westhill College, Weoley Park Road, Selly Oak, Birmingham B29 6LL.

The RE Centre, Westminster College, Oxford OX2 9AT.

The Welsh National Centre for RE, School of Education, University College of North Wales, Deiniol Road, Bangor, Gwynedd LL57 2UW.

York RE Centre, University College of Ripon and York, St. John, Lord Mayor's Walk, York YO3 7EX.

14   Drama

David Tilley

Drama is an art, a practical activity and an intellectual discipline. It involves the creation of imagined characters and situations which are enacted within a designated space. A drama education which begins with play may eventually include all the elements of theatre. Like all the arts, drama helps us make sense of the world. (ACGB, 1992)

Drama has a pivotal place in the new National Curriculum, not only as a learning tool for other subjects, but as a practical artistic subject in its own right. Through its inclusion in English, drama has a significant part to play in the statutory requirement of the primary curriculum, and gives drama a central role in developing all major aspects of English. In addition, the 1988 Education Reform Act requires school curricula to be 'balanced and broadly based' (DES, 1989). The National Curriculum is not the whole curriculum. Dividing the National Curriculum into subjects is a way of describing the curriculum, not teaching it. Subject Orders are only the prescribed part of the curriculum and there is a need to address a number of key issues related to drama in the *whole* curriculum.

Primary teachers are being challenged to review, redefine and understand more fully the nature of drama-in-education (O'Toole, 1992) and to exploit fully the potential for learning that the subject can open up. The argument for drama in the primary school presented in this chapter supports the view that, while recognizing the value of all other subject areas, using drama methodology in the teaching of the National Curriculum this must be seen as a supplement to, not as a replacement for, drama as a subject and art form in its own right.

The Nature of the Drama in Education Experience

Drama helps pupils make sense of human behaviour through a physical, emotional and intellectual identification with *fictitious* situations created in order to make meaning and provoke opportunities for reflection. It relies on the human ability to pretend. This active pretence and identification with fictitious situations *as if* you were involved, is crucial and characterizes all drama teaching. Through this act of imagination, pupils can explore how people in particular circumstances might behave now, at different times, and in different societies. Through drama, we re-create and examine peoples' actions, including our own, and see both how they might have come about, and where they might lead. Though imaginary, the exploration can be experienced, examined and shared as if it were real.

Drama in education works towards creating a *fusion* of thought and feeling, creating an affective relationship to the work, and giving dramatic shape to significant ideas and tensions. This is a distinctive type of learning. No medium other than drama offers such direct access to it.

Drama and Another Way of Knowing

Drama draws on the knowledge your pupils derive from their own experience, both in and outside of school. This includes an awareness of people, places and events encountered in fiction, as well as in real life. Drama draws most usefully upon pupils' immediate experience to start with and is a means of interpreting and extending it through the use of the imagination.

Another rich source of knowledge that drama draws on is the knowledge which pupils are given, or need to find out, in order to have sufficient information for a particular piece of drama work. This utilizes, and enlarges, developing research skills, harnessing and extending knowledge from any area of the curriculum. How-ever, the most potent drama work is likely to centre upon social relationships, social issues or moral dilemmas.

Enquiry Task

- Look through the new National Curriculum documents.
- List aspects/areas where you think learning through drama might occur.
- Discuss your list with an experienced colleague.

The Importance of 'Distance'

Pupils are encouraged in drama to discover and examine the consequences and implications of human behaviour, safe in the knowledge that it is clearly fictional, *one-step-removed* from reality, literally, *only playing*. Through the protection of be-ing *in role*, drama provides pupils with the opportunity to encapsulate significant moments of experience but, in recognition of it being a *make-believe* activity, gives you, and your pupils, the opportunity to stop the action, stand outside, reflect on, and evaluate the experience at a safe distance. It is in the fusing of these two pro-cesses – the action and reflection upon it – that the value of dramatic experience lies, and through which learning takes place.

The Importance of Reflection

Pupils should be encouraged to look back periodically on their drama to consider the knowledge they have gained. Dorothy Heathcote puts the case powerfully.

> If you cannot increase the reflective power in people, you might as well not teach, because reflection is the only thing in the long run that changes anybody . . . Reflection is what makes the knowing something that can be touched on and assimilated for later use. (Wagner, 1979)

Such knowledge can usefully be expressed in forms other than that of drama itself; for example, through various modes of writing and speaking, and visual and aural means, such as photographs or video recordings made by the pupils themselves. Sometimes, the most suitable way of conveying the knowledge pupils gain through drama is by showing it to others. A feature of performed drama is that it conveys meanings to an audience in a deliberate and condensed way.

Once pupils are playing freely within the make-believe, adopting and sustaining roles, as if they were a different person in a different place, handling choices and decisions as a group within the safety and pretence of drama, in effect *making drama meanings*, then they are ready to have their *play* challenged by your skilled intervention taking the essence of dramatic playing into a more conscious learning mode across the curriculum. At the same time you are leading your pupils to become *dramawise*, understanding the *bones* of drama, (O'Toole and Haseman, 1987).

Enquiry Task

Discuss with colleagues what important aspects of children's learning are not covered by the new National Curriculum. For example,

- particular aspects of Personal and Social Education;
- skills in reflection and empathy;
- particular aspects of moral and spiritual education.

Which of these might be covered through drama?

The Language of Drama

Primary school pupils need to be given opportunities to acquire proficiency in a range of languages, including the language of drama, and to use these as a medium through which to learn. This entails the deliberate introduction, and development, of an understanding and deployment of the elements of drama – leading throughout the Key Stages towards drama literacy. The language of drama is eclectic, it uses: speech, movement, sound and rhythm, space and object, and draws on the language of other art forms – music, dance and the visual arts. Understanding the possibilities (and limitations) of the drama form, operating greater control over the medium, and understanding its personal, social and political uses should be key aims when working with your pupils.

The Primary Drama Teacher's Dual Aim

As a primary teacher using drama you clearly have a duel aim, using drama as a double-edged learning tool. Firstly, you need to identify potential areas of learning across the curriculum. Once identified these areas of learning can be explored: using *drama as learning medium*. Secondly, you must consciously aim for your pupils to gain knowledge, skills, and understanding of *drama as art form* and satisfaction from developing control of the medium.

Your task, is to guide and help your pupils to make their work in drama significant for themselves within the context of the whole curriculum and the wider community. The quality of a learning experience in classroom drama can only be as good as the the teacher facilitates or enables it to be. This inevitably puts responsibility on the development of practice, and, in particular, the ability to structure learning in, and through, drama.

Drama, English and Language Development

The National Curriculum firmly places drama within the English domain. Drama within English can be seen as a means towards the attainment of *all* English Attainment Targets, and, if you do not employ drama you are placing unnecessary restrictions on the range of teaching and learning approaches open to you, and ultimately denying your pupils access to an exciting and rewarding mode of learning.

Primary school pupils can develop through drama an extensive range of language uses, including the majority of those referred to in the English National Curriculum Order. Reading, research and observation, which give substance to their drama work, provide opportunities for children to weigh alternatives and debate possibilities. Work in drama which stems from shared material and discussion makes demands on children's capacities for alert listening and questioning. The essential social nature of drama places your pupils in situations within which appropriate patterns of language have to be devised.

Drama may be the most potent and appropriate means of providing the types of speaking and listening situations that the National Curriculum demands of teachers. It can facilitate a wide variety of language uses in contexts that require full participation within an affective/cognitive/physical frame, promoting types of talk important to encouraging deep-level thoughts, such as explanation, negotiation, clarification, explanation, persuasion and prediction. This is further endorsed by consideration given to drama in the OFSTED framework for the inspection of schools. Specifically, *speaking and listening*, which extends across all curriculum areas, is a key factor by which inspection teams judge standards of achievement in all subjects.

Enquiry Task

Look at your planning for the next half term. Identify what you want the children to learn in English. Plan at least one drama lesson that will facilitate the children's learning. Observe the lesson carefully (videotape the lesson, if you can).

- Did the children learn what you expected?
- Did they learn things you did not expect? If so, what were these?
- Could their learning have been greater if the session had been better planned?

What did you learn from this exercise?

Drama and the Whole Curriculum

Potential links between drama and other subjects are numerous (NCC, 1990). References to the use of drama in the new National Curriculum subject documents give considerable endorsement within the Attainment Targets, Programmes of Study and non-statutory guidance and suggest clearly that there are many opportunities for drama to flourish as a discrete subject, and to be used with integrity as a learning medium across the primary curriculum. In the substance, concepts and content of what it explores, drama principally shares a close rapport with history, geography, politics, economics and religion.

In primary schools it is potentially easier for drama to act as an *integrating agent* in the curriculum, and for you to draw on different subject areas to create a wide range of learning contexts and outcomes from drama. Drama revolves around human dilemmas, problems, questions and issues of understanding. All it requires is for you to put your pupils in the *as if* mental-set so that they can engage with any kind of subject-matter in this special way.

Enquiry Task

List your objectives in teaching drama.

Discuss this list with an experienced colleague.

For each objective identify:

- how you would know if the objective has been achieved?
- what records you would keep on progress towards its achievement.

Drama and Learning Opportunities

If drama is to be used effectively as a medium for learning, it is important to be clear about the kinds of learning that pupils are expected to achieve. Like learning itself, drama is essentially a social and interactive process. Including drama in the primary curriculum recognizes the need for pupils to be able to find a variety of ways to challenge, enlarge and interpret their experiences. Pupils should be encouraged to use drama as a means of expressing what they find important and relevant. Working on these important ideas they may use their own words, symbols and actions, or they may use those of dramatists. Either way, they will experiment, and include or reject a large number of ideas often until they have arrived at a form which they feel best connects and communicates itself to themselves and then to others. There are specific kinds of knowledge and understanding which pupils acquire or extend through drama work.

Drama and Learning about Content Across the Curriculum

Drama activities at all Key Stages may cover attainment in a range of National Curriculum subjects. For example, a series of drama lessons in which pupils at Key Stage 2 devise a play about the Great Plague of London is likely to involve them in research leading to readily identifiable attainment in science, history and English. Drama's place in the whole curriculum can be strengthened by systematic incorporation of it into your schemes of work in all curriculum areas:

Cross-curricular dimensions, skills and themes that comprise a wider *whole curriculum* beyond *core and foundation* subjects incorporate many aspects of personal and social education, such as problem solving, education for citizenship, equal opportunities and multicultural education. Traditionally, such issues have provided significant content for drama-in-education, where drama is used as a learning medium to deepen understanding and bring about a change in insight, (Bolton, 1979).

The content or *theme* of drama is what the teacher wants pupils to understand. A simple example would be an infant teacher teaching road safety through drama. At a more complex level at Key Stage 2, a teacher might deal with problems of bullying or prejudice by making these concepts a central focus of drama work. This use of drama might be called a *cognitive* approach, where learning objectives are primarily concerned with understanding concepts: Ambition, Jealousy, Friendship, etc. Accompanying such concepts are various kinds of intellectual skills to do with pupils abilities to think clearly and objectively, to see implications, and to articulate feelings and values.

Whatever subject or subject matter is approached through drama, the learning that may arise will not derive particularly from teacher inputs of new information. Pupils will have to make their own relationships with themes, issues, ideas, the *content* of topics, and articulate their own personal response within an engagement with drama. The kinds of knowledge and understanding about content that pupils may acquire from drama will not always be easy to predict or specify. It may be impossible for teachers to set this out as a set of propositional outcomes.

It is important to realize that when drama is used in teaching other subjects it is not necessarily only in a supporting role. There will be two-way process taking place. Other subjects will provide drama with serious and worthwhile content, and in many cases also provide a powerful context for exploration, while drama strategies will enliven and illuminate these diverse curriculum areas. Injection of drama into these areas will add significance, strengthen commitment and belief of pupils, and increase their willingness to work seriously and constructively in drama.

Drama and Personal and Social Development

An emphasis on personal development as a general aim, considering and nurturing aspects of maturation such as sensitivity, commitment, confidence, self-assertion, eagerness to learn, developing positive thinking and acquiring wisdom, are seen as a natural outcome of drama activity over a long period. Drama, because of its *ensemble* characteristic, provides opportunity to promote group awareness. Personal and social development should be a by-product of all good teaching, no matter what subject area. You should certainly not ignore these areas but might justifiably see them at times as being secondary to facilitating your pupils' development as producers and receivers of drama.

Learning about Dramatic Art Form

While potential opportunities for cognitive and social learning through drama have quite fittingly been recognized, developed and woven into the fabric of the National Curriculum, opportunities to learn how to use drama as art form have tended to have been diluted or neglected. There has been a temptation towards over specialization in using drama as a method of teaching, rather than as a valuable experience and art form in its own right. There has, unwittingly perhaps, been also a tendency to train teachers without giving them knowledge, skills and understanding of drama or skills in the basic elements of the medium. Knowledge, skill and understanding of dramatic art form is what is fundamental to effectively harnessing drama to clear educational aims.

Although subject matter or content is central to learning through drama, i.e., *what* a particular drama is about, while teaching drama you need to be teaching simultaneously *how* drama works. There are, rightfully, times when understanding *how* drama works and learning *about* drama are important (Kempe, 1990). You will want your children to be educated in such a way that they become aesthetically aware, conscious of the nature and uses of drama as art form.

Your pupils' experience in drama cannot afford to be merely functional; they should, during their primary school years, acquire basic drama and theatre skills. Drama and theatre are essentially the same dramatic art form. Gavin Bolton puts the case clearly,

> . . . structurally, drama and theatre are indistinguishable. The basic elements of both are focus, tension, contrast and symbolisation. It seems to me that just as a playwright working for theatre is concerned with using these elements to convey his meaning, so a teacher working in creative drama is concerned with helping students to explore meaning through the use of the same elements. (Davis and Lawrence, 1986)

This involves pupils in three central activities which constitute corner stones of a drama curriculum: *making, performing* and *responding.*

Making Drama

Essentially, making drama involves learning how to utilize drama to explore issues, ideas, thoughts and feelings, alongside rigorous reflection on both meaning and execution. Making drama involves you and your pupils learning how to contribute, and develop, ideas in drama within groups, extending pupils' ability to adopt and sustain a variety of roles with imagination and invention. In realizing the dramatic significance of a chosen context, pupils need to learn how to order experience through drama by recalling, recognizing and finding form for thought, ideas, feelings and emotions. Making drama also demands developing auditory, visual and spatial awareness, heightening abilities to communicate through an imaginative and inventive use of space, movement and language.

Primary school pupils making drama are learning to speak and move with confidence and purpose. Physical projection is achieved through posture, gesture, and a sense of timing or an expressive stillness. Dance and mime can be powerful ways of engaging pupils in drama and are a very effective way of introducing pupils to non-verbal theatre. Children's voices, their vocal range and flexibility are developed as they contribute to creating and sustaining dramatic impact. This comes about through variation in speed, tone and dynamic control, and their growing ability to articulate with clarity and vitality.

Performing Drama

Primary pupils should know how to create their own presentations and gain practical understanding of a variety of drama forms which may be employed to communicate to an audience. An awareness of the *totality* of elements that go towards the effect achieved by a dramatic presentation, and how to use some of them, is also important. Pupils need to begin to appreciate texts in a *practical* working context. Play scripts and other materials – poems, original scripts, and other written sources – may be used. Consideration of plays should include their social/historical context where this genuinely illuminates the text.

Performance work in drama gives opportunities for pupils to manage time, space, physical and human resources. Pupils should be encouraged in performance to present roles that are integrated fully, and use spoken language most appropriate to roles, situations and relationships created. Attention needs to be paid in performance to vocal quality, and the rhythms and patterns of pupils' language used to reveal the roles they adopt. In performance, pupils should be encouraged to use space and movement imaginatively, with purpose and coherence this can often effectively engage your less vocally extrovert pupils to play significant parts.

Often pupils of primary age need little encouragement to take advantage of opportunities to improvise and act out plays. Even by the age of seven most children have developed an understanding of dramatic narrative and can render quite sophisticated dramatized accounts of stories they know or have invented. Clothes and properties, well-chosen stories and poems, puppets and musical instruments, are invaluable additional stimuli in drama for younger children. Successful performance work demands from pupils a sustained contribution to the preparation, development and presentation of work. In your performance work, develop *ensemble* qualities, including the ability to be fully supportive of the work of others, and encourage, and give opportunities for, pupils to demonstrate their ability to engage and communicate with a variety of audiences.

Opportunities for performance are usually plentiful in primary schools. Christian and non-Christian religious calendar events, for example, are often times when groups of pupils can prepare plays for assembly or for visiting parents, often involving small groups of pupils improvising scenes and using a range of dramatic techniques – *masks, mime, music* and *dance* to tell a story.

You should not be afraid to consider introducing pupils at Key Stage 2 to scripts, particularly short extracts. Where these relate to themes already improvised they can help to refine and consolidate pupils' dramatic experience and lead to a more precise use of language. In English, pupils of eight or nine are expected to be able to read aloud fluently from familiar stories and poems, and with appropriate expression. Pupils of this age should also be reading scripts and conventions which distinguish play scripts from other literary forms. They should understand how the words on the page notate live action, how scripts become performances and how dramatic productions are rehearsed and presented.

At eleven, most pupils in drama should be able to expand scenarios into simple dramatic scripts (in English, play scripts are mentioned specifically as an example of an appropriate activity for Key Stage 2 pupils). By the time they leave primary school, all pupils, ideally, should know how to polish their work for presentation and should have become accustomed to disciplines of redrafting, rehearsal and refining their plays in response to audience reaction. Whole classes will sometimes take it in turn to perform dramatic work. These occasions are a vital part of the communal life of the school, and a valuable element of a broad and balanced curriculum.

Responding to, and Appraising, Drama

There is a need to give your pupils frequent opportunities for reflection and analysis of their drama in progress, encouraging personal judgments supported by sound argument; developing pupils' abilities to assess objectively their own work and that of others; demonstrating clear insight, and an understanding, of both process and product. Development of the ability to reflect on meanings created during, and after, experience in drama is also crucial, as is development of the ability to discuss drama work, its meaning and shaping, with relevance and discrimination. Pupils should be encouraged constantly to approach drama with open critical minds, able to perceive its strengths and weaknesses.

Academic Learning about Drama

There is a place for academic learning about drama in the primary curriculum. Fundamental knowledge about drama and theatre as a cultural and historic phenomenon includes: knowledge of the place and purpose of drama in society; of the beginnings of drama and its links with religion; of a range of forms in drama and theatre, and their conventions; of theatre as a place of work and cultural influence; of the contribution of the arts to the wealth of a country; of the educational uses of drama and theatre. Visiting a local theatre, or having a visit from a 'theatre in education team', can help children of any age to understand how these forms of drama are part of the fabric of everyday life and of their culture.

Drama in education does not simply intersect with *theatre* in interesting ways; it is itself a potentially radical branch of theatre, a form of theatre practice with the ability to continue to challenge directly dominant perceptions of theatre practice in schools. In essence, drama in education is a search for a relevant and vital theatre form for learning. A theatre of challenge, celebration and exploration. A theatre where all central aspects of theatrical form and content are subject to negotiation and debate, demanding not mere imitation, but innovation, opening up and giving a voice to new lines of development in the primary classroom.

As has been stressed earlier, from the onset of primary education pupils should realize that there is a language of dramatic convention. Throughout their primary years pupils should be given plenty of opportunity to acquire progressively a dramatic vocabulary. Infants should be able to recognize differences between telling a story and acting it, and between reality and dramatized versions of it. By the end of Key Stage 1, pupils should be able to identify essential features which distinguish drama from other forms of human expression and able to realize that there is a link between dramas they make in the classroom and those they watch on television/theatre, or when theatre companies visit schools.

On completion of their primary education in drama, pupils might be expected to be familiar with the basic ingredients of dramatic narrative – tension, conflict, surprise, plot development, and resolution. Furthermore, they should have been introduced to basic dramatic forms, such as comedy, tragedy and farce, as well as to a variety of European and non-European theatre styles, and have the ability to recognize a range of drama forms when confronted by them. Finally, pupils should be expected to have a fair idea of drama's historical and cultural diversity, be able to offer (and receive) criticism constructively, and to place their judgments in the context of a growing framework of dramatic reference. By the end of Key Stage

2 pupils should be able to '*recognize good work in drama through a detailed and critical observation of the characters created, the issues involved and the processes employed*' (DES, 1989).

Drama and Design and Technology

By the end of Key Stage 2, pupils should have grasped the principles which govern the creation of a dramatic *environment* and the potential use of design and technology in drama. They should be able to deploy physical materials, colour, light and sound, and to create a space for drama. Pupils need to appreciate the significance of how things look in performance, and how to use design to make meanings. This applies not only to costumes and scenery of a formal production, but, more fundamentally, to realizing the essential relationship between performers and their environment. Shape colour and texture, for example, are powerful communicators of mood and ideas.

Working in drama encourages the use of any available resources to enable dramatic communication. These resources might include dressing-up clothes, different lengths and texture of fabric, boxes, electric torches and classroom percussion instruments, as well as more formal theatrical resources, such as stage sets, properties, costume, make-up, stage lighting and live or recorded music. Lighting a play, for example, or designing and making costumes, sets and properties, are artistic contexts for solving technological problems. Marketing and publicity involve learning specific skills, while an introduction to box office computerization can engage pupils in problem solving using information technology.

Drama and Other Art Forms

Drama should not be considered in isolation from the other arts (NCC, 1990). Fundamentally, drama like all art forms helps us understand ourselves, and the world in which we live. Indeed, drama may be said to be the most inclusive of all the arts, and has a central role to play in a *broad* and *balanced* arts curriculum entitlement. Plays will often incorporate dance and music, while design is an important feature of all productions. Meanwhile, film and television are, increasingly, forming a firm foundation for pupils' understanding of drama. From an early age, your pupils' dramatic vocabulary is being informed by television. Cartoons, films, stories, soap operas, mini series and plays all contribute to a sophisticated dramatic language reflected in, and informing, all aspects of classroom drama. Many pupils' access to live theatre is restricted, and video-recorded dramas are often the only exposure children get to a variety of dramatic form and experience.

Assessment and Recording Achievement in Drama

When recording achievement in drama, you may not wish to distinguish too rigidly between attainment in drama and other learning outcomes, particularly, those coming under English in the National Curriculum. However, in primary classrooms, foundations are being laid for drama in subsequent years, and it is important that increasing attention is paid to an understanding of the dramatic form in which pupils express their ideas, as well as to the ideas themselves. By using a range of dramatic conventions for structuring drama work, pupils are helped to extend their understanding of dramatic art form beyond simple naturalism and melodrama.

Any approach to assessment needs to be realistic about what it is actually 'capturing'. You will probably be aware of difficulties and constraints that frequently beset classroom drama — pressure of numbers, ephemerality of the medium, the power *context* has over behaviour, the confidence and overall involvement of participants, and how these factors can further alter the context. In one sense, all we can hope for is a system of assessment which recognizes the need to give all pupils a fair chance to reveal, and to develop, their drama potential. In other words, a system of evaluation which gathers evidence over time, and over as wide a range of authentic contexts as possible, of your pupils' ability at *making*, *performing*, and *responding* to drama.

By the end of the primary school your children should be keeping a drama *working notebook*. In this notebook might be kept a record of ideas, simple scenarios, lists of scenes, writing in role, scripted dialogue, music tapes and photographs, and a range of reflections on, and evaluations of, their own work, and that of others. Because of drama's ephemeral nature, records of this kind will be useful *aide-memoires* for pupils, as well as providing important back-up evidence for your assessment.

Recording achievement in drama needs to be seen as an active partnership with your pupils, gathering, interpreting, learning from, and summarizing, any information that either you or your pupils are able to contribute. Assessments to be wary of are those that seek only artificial, and exclusively summative, situations to 'measure' something that is, in the case of drama, often a current activity that, anyway, needs to be assessed continuously as it flows throughout the primary curriculum.

Summary

The new National Curriculum reaffirms that core and foundation subjects are not a complete curriculum, and this gives schools flexibility to include drama as a discrete subject, in addition to fulfilling statutory legal requirements in English, and of a broad and balanced curriculum.

Drama is now clearly acknowledged as a practical artistic subject, and as a unique teaching and learning medium across the whole curriculum. Acknowledgement of the potency of drama as a vital element in English, a springboard for language development, and as an invaluable learning method in the teaching of other subject areas, is embedded in the National Curriculum English Order and across the curriculum, notably in science, technology, history and modern foreign languages. Where drama can be viewed in its own right, OFSTED proposes that it should be considered under the same two-part framework as art and music:

creating/making and performing drama, and responding and appraising/appreciating drama.

Essentially learning in, and through, drama is to be found in the willing *suspension of disbelief*. Active involvement and identification of pupils in a thinking, feeling response within fictitious situations, is unique to dramatic experience, and is the key to unlocking its power for educational purposes. Drama is important because it offers a way of 'knowing' and through which children can come to terms with the world in which they live. Because drama is rooted in a way of knowing that is natural for children, i.e., *play*, it draws on what is already there – the ability to speak, move, feel, and the compelling desire to find form to communicate with others.

Drama should be a way in which important issues are explored. However, it is only through constant skilled teacher intervention in helping children to work in, and through, drama, and so come to terms with the disciplined nature of the form, that meanings can emerge from the action, and a natural sense of rightness or truth be achieved. Otherwise a drama lesson is only *play* – an essential activity for your children, but one which needs to be extended into significant dramatic form if collected meanings and understandings are to be achieved.

It is vital that all primary teachers understand, and have skills in, drama if they are to enable children to become fully drama literate; that is able to exploit, and gain, satisfaction from the medium. Learning will take place when pupils experience a relationship between drama *form* and *content*, and make connections between make-believe situations and reality. Ideally, you would be concerned in your drama teaching with both process and performance, primarily focusing on exploiting drama towards educational goals.

There is a strong case for drama in primary education, and for drama specialists, whose overriding aim is to help pupils to develop knowledge, skills and understanding of drama, and who are able to exploit fully dramatic art as a learning tool. Provision for drama in the new National Curriculum should be a whole school issue, reviewed regularly to ensure that it makes appropriate demands on pupils of different ages and abilities, and is manageable in terms of the time, resources and professional expertise available to schools. Drama should be used as a learning medium across the primary curriculum, and taught as a discrete practical, artistic subject in its own right.

References and Annotated Suggested Reading

THE ARTS COUNCIL OF GREAT BRITAIN (1992) *Drama in Schools*, ACGB, London.
(*This booklet offers some excellent advice on drama in the National Curriculum, including a curriculum model. The booklet includes suggested programmes of study and end of Key Stage statements.*)

BOLTON, G. (1979) *Towards a Theory of Drama in Education*, London, Longman.
('*Type "d" drama' was a category used by Bolton to describe drama which resulted in a change*

of understanding which, although it might blend 'dramatic playing', 'exercise' and 'theatre', was different in quality from them.)

DAVIS, D. and LAWRENCE, C. (1986) 'Drama in Education – a reappraisal', in G. BOLTON, *Selected Writings*, London, Longman.

DES (1989) *Drama from 5 to 16*, HMI Curriculum Matters 17, London, HMSO.

FLEMING, M. (1994) *Starting Drama Teaching*, London, Fulton.
(An excellent book on the theory and, more particularly, the practice of drama teaching in primary schools. This book is aimed primarily at teachers and student teachers who are new to drama.)

HORNBROOK, D. (1991) *Education in Drama: Casting the dramatic curriculum*, London, Falmer Press.
(There are no prescribed Attainment Targets for drama in the new National Curriculum. However, along with the Arts Council's report, Drama in Schools, *Hornbrook's book will help you note levels of attainment which might be expected by the end of Key Stage 2.)*

KEMPE, A. (1990) *GCSE Drama Coursebook*, Oxford, Basil Blackwell.
(This book offers a clear discussion of the relationship between form and content, an issue which is discussed further in, Bolton, G. (1992) New Perspectives On Classroom Drama, *Hemel Hempstead, Simon Shuster.)*

The poster published by the National Curriculum Council in 1991, *Drama in the National Curriculum*, identified the references existing at the time to drama within the Orders for core and foundation subjects. The poster showed both how drama can be used to deliver elements of the National Curriculum subjects and where drama appears as part of National Curriculum Programmes of Study.

NATIONAL CURRICULUM COUNCIL (1990) *The Arts 5–16: A Curriculum Framework*, London: Oliver Boyd.
(This booklet offers a clear and concise argument about how, through sharing the essential processes, different art forms relate to each other.)

NEELANDS, J. (1990) *Structuring Drama Work: A Handbook of Available Forms in Theatre and Drama*, edited by Tony Goode, Cambridge University Press. See also, O'NEILL, C. and LAMBERT, A. (1982) *Drama Structures: A Practical Handbook for Teachers*, London, Heinemann.

O'TOOLE, J. (1992) *The Process of Drama*, London, Routledge.
(Drama in education is defined, not as the whole corpus of work in drama which takes place in schools, but specifically as the form of dramatic activity centred on fictitious role-taking and improvisation. See also Bolton, G. (1984) Drama as Education, *London, Longman. This publication provides a useful historical overview of the development of Drama in Education. For further definitions of drama see, DES (1989)* Drama 5–16, *London, HMSO. The definition given by HMI is usefully unpacked in* NEELANDS, J. (1992) *Learning through Imagined Experience, London, Hodder and Stoughton.)*

O'TOOLE, J. and HASEMAN, B. (1987) *Dramawise – An Introduction to GCSE Drama*, London, Heinemann.
(Essential reading if you really want to understand the bones of drama.)

READMAN, G. and LAMONT, G. (1994) *Drama: A Handbook for Primary Teachers*, London, BBC Educational Publishing.
(Combined in one volume are suggestions for planning, implementation and assessment. As well as practical examples, this handbook shows how drama can enhance the National Curriculum, and deepen personal and social skills.)

SOMERS, J. (1994) *Drama in the Curriculum*, London, Cassell.
(This book provides a very detailed account of drama methodology used across the curriculum. See also WOOLAND, B. (1993). The Teaching of Drama in the Primary School, *London, Longman.)*

WAGNER, B.J. (1976) *Dorothy Heathcote: Drama as a Learning Medium*, Washington, D.C., National Education Association.

15   Building an Inclusive Curriculum

Barry Carpenter

Introduction

Emily, Michael and Tim worked enthusiastically creating their information sheet on the town's historic church. This was part of a 'Tourist Office' project that class 5 (9–10-year-olds) at Hilltown Primary School were engaged in. The town in which the school was located was full of local history, and often frequented by tourists.

The children in the class were asked to select a feature of the town (i.e., the church, market square, meadows, etc.) that they would like to investigate. They were then grouped according to the feature of the town they wished to explore.

The classteacher was particularly keen to encourage collaborative group work amongst her pupils. She chose to try a jigsawing technique that she had read about (Rose, 1991). Each child in a group was given a specific task to undertake: without the contribution of each group member the overall goal, in this case to create an illustrated tourist information sheet, would not be achieved.

On their visit to the church Emily chose to write down her thoughts and feelings about the church: that 'the windows were made of stained glass that shone like jewels'; that there was a high ceiling 'with stones in different shapes'. She decided to find a book in the school library about churches that would explain to her why the church ceiling was designed like this.

Michael's greatest pleasure was drawing. He took a variety of pencils with him to the church and sketched some of the objects he saw on the altar. He was particularly keen to do some rubbings of the old tombstone. His teacher obtained permission for him to do this and, with Tim and Emily holding the paper still for him, he set about taking a rubbing of a tombstone dating back to the sixteenth century.

Tim was fascinated by the size of the church, and walked around, gently touching the various surfaces: the wooden pews with ornate carvings at each end; the tomb of a local landowner with a stone figure lying along it. As he explored each of these features, Tim recorded his comments into a small tape recorder, not afraid to say exactly what he thought – 'It's cold and it smells!'

Back at school the three children pooled their findings about the church. Michael suggested that they use the computer to create their information fact sheet. They discussed this idea with their teacher. The children took their idea one step further and decided to create an interactive information sheet. This involved using an A3 concept keyboard in conjunction with the computer.

Michael set about transforming his sketches and rubbings into an overlay, and with the help of the teacher blocked areas of the concept keyboard to correspond with each overlay picture.

Tim and Emily combined their written and oral observations into a description of various aspects of the church. They wrote up their findings directly on to the computer, using the 'Writing with Symbols' computer program (Banes, Coles, Detheridge and Newton, 1994). This programme had a symbol accompanying each word in the text. Emily thought this would be particularly good for foreign visitors who may not be able to read English, but could decipher (even guess) what the symbols were.

Eventually their information sheet was complete. By pressing Tim's sketch of the altar on the concept keyboard, the description of the altar, compiled by Tim and Emily, came up on the computer screen. The contribution of each individual enabled the group to accomplish its task in a creative and innovative manner.

Enquiry Task

Consider the above project case study of Michael, Emily and Tim. Which aspects of the Key Stage 2 Programmes of Study do you think would be covered by this activity?

Make a list for yourself.

The Children Inside the Case Study

On the surface Michael, Emily and Tim may appear like any 9- or 10-year-olds in a primary school, but when you delve more deeply you discover that they each have unique individual needs.

Michael is on the Local Education Authority (LEA) Register of More Able Pupils. He has been nominated for his exceptional artistic ability. Once a term he is invited to attend a Saturday Art Workshop in a local secondary school. Local artists conduct the workshop, engaging the children in a variety of techniques and media. Michael meets other children of the same age who find art as exciting as he does. His teacher consults regularly with the LEA advisory teacher for more able pupils, and borrows resources for the classroom that match her schemes of work, but which will challenge Michael, and encourage him to use his talent.

Emily's mother died last year. Since then she has changed from an outward-going girl at the centre of a group, to a withdrawn child preferring her own company to that of others. Whilst her work in class has not deteriorated significantly, her teacher is concerned that Emily has become so withdrawn. The teacher talks to the school special educational needs (SEN) coordinator about Emily and has met with Emily's father who is equally concerned about his daughter. They have agreed that the classteacher will keep an observational diary regarding Emily's behaviour over the next three months. As such, Emily is deemed to be at stage 2 of the Code of Practice under the 1993 Education Act. If they are still concerned after this time then the SEN coordinator will ask the headteacher to make a referral to the Educational Psychology Team, which runs a counselling service: stage 3 in the Code of Practice.

Tim has Down's Syndrome. He attends Hilltown Primary School for four afternoons per week. The remainder of the time he attends The Beeches, a neighbouring school for children with severe learning difficulties, which shares a campus with Hilltown and the local secondary school. Both schools are part of the Partnership Network of Schools which agree to support the integration of pupils from the Beeches into local mainstream schools.

Tim's placement at Hilltown is part of a shared learning project for several primary age pupils from The Beeches. His involvement in this project has been planned jointly between his classteacher from The Beeches and the Hilltown Year 5 teacher. Tim used to be supported on his visits to Hilltown by a Learning Support Assistant, but as he has grown in confidence this is no longer necessary.

Tim can write his name and a few other words. As his verbal skills are good, tape recording his oral observations of the church was the most effective strategy. Also, as Tim could not read unfamiliar vocabulary such as 'altar' or 'font', Emily suggested he use his symbols computer program.[1] She has seen him using this in other lessons. As each word is accompanied by a pictographic symbol, Tim was able to not only access the text, but create sentences too. For example:

The church is big and cold.

Tim's involvement with the Year 5 class at Hilltown was planned on the basis of the targets set in his Individual Educational Programme (IEP). His teachers from the two schools examined these and asked, 'Which school environment is best able to facilitate each of these targets?' Consequently there was shared ownership of Tim's curriculum programme, with cross-school record-keeping strategies in place.

A Curriculum for All?

When the National Curriculum (NC) was first launched it was hailed by the government as an entitlement curriculum for all pupils. It soon became obvious that insufficient thought had been given to the design and structure of the NC if pupils

---

Enquiry Task

List the ways you think that this project met some of the individual needs of the three children involved?

- Michael
- Emily
- Tim

---

with special educational needs (SEN) were to make meaningful learning gains through it. Hence a range of initiatives were launched by the National Curriculum Council (NCC) to convince teachers that this was a 'Curriculum for All':

> NCC wishes to reaffirm the principle of active participation by the complete range of pupils with SEN . . . whether they are in special, primary, middle or secondary schools, with or without statements. (NCC, 1989a)

Subsequently *Curriculum Guidance 2: A Curriculum for All* (NCC, 1989b) articulated the need for teachers to ensure access to the NC for pupils with SEN. At this stage there was little curriculum guidance in planning to meet SEN within the NC. Gradually as each subject appeared with draft consultation Orders the guidance for the inclusion of pupils with SEN became more explicit; the consultation document on Physical Education (PE) (DES, 1991) remains a rich resource of information for teaching PE to pupils with SEN.

Specific projects such as the NC Development Team (Severe Learning Difficulties) produced useful guidelines for curriculum planning and teacher professional development through *Curriculum Guidance 9* (NCC, 1992a and 1992b).

Similarly LEAs have endeavoured to illuminate curricular access for pupils with SEN through curriculum guidelines to schools (Humberside LEA, 1990; Solihull LEA, 1991). It has been from the commercial market that the most useful materials have emerged. Lewis (1991) has provided a seminal text in *Primary Special Needs and the National Curriculum*, whilst others have addressed the specific application of the NC to children with learning difficulties (Ashdown, Carpenter and Bovair, 1991). Subject-specific materials enabled teachers to interpret the Programmes of Study within a broad framework that could absorb the needs and interests of the majority of their pupils: for example in technology (Mount and Ackerman, 1991), history (Sebba, 1994), religious education (Brown, 1995 – in preparation).

Perhaps the most useful points to emerge from the NC to date are the common curriculum principles of breadth, balance, relevance and differentiation. These are fundamental to the child with SEN in ensuring his or her right to a curriculum equal in quality to that of their peers.

SEN should not be synonymous with a narrow curriculum. The range of learning experiences should be diverse and challenging; for our most and least able pupils the curriculum should be enriching. Balance within the overall curriculum for the child with SEN needs to be addressed. In the past, because a child has had difficulties in either English or mathematics, we have tended to give them more of the same (and often through the same teaching style). The raised curriculum profile of subjects such as science and technology has, since the advent of the NC, brought about an awareness amongst teachers for the potential for open-ended, problem-solving tasks which may engage the child with SEN without necessarily being reliant on good reading or writing skills.

The older the child with SEN is, the more of an issue the relevance of curriculum experience becomes. An 11-year-old who is attaining only Level 1 in English does not want reading material designed for 5- or 6-year-olds: they have probably had such materials several times over already. They require materials matched to their interest, as well as their ability level. Age-inappropriate curricula do not dignify the learning of the child with SEN. Dignity in learning, like education itself, should be a fundamental right of all children.

Though our audit of the curriculum we will come to realize the potential of differentiation as the key to a whole range of curriculum experiences for all children: differentiation is about meeting the needs of all learners and requires a concern with the pupil, the task and the learning context. No longer must we view differentiation as solely the territory of those who teach the less able. All learners are different and all teaching needs to be differentiated. It is through the strength of differentiation that all children will be given access to the curriculum, and that continuity and progression will be ensured.

Enquiry Task

Identify the significant gains for pupils with SEN since the implementation of the National Curriculum. What have been the disadvantages?

The 'New' National Curriculum and Pupils with Special Needs

Whilst the NC may have undergone a radical review, the overarching principles of the Education Reform Act have not. The principles are:

- to promote the spiritual, moral, cultural, mental and physical development of pupils at school and in society;
- to prepare such pupils for the opportunities, responsibilities and experiences of adult life.

At times it has been hard to achieve this within the existing NC due to the rigid application of certain level bands within the NC to prescribed key stages. However this difficulty was acknowledged by Sir Ron Dearing when he stated:

What the National Curriculum should and must do is allow teachers and schools to meet particular needs of pupils with special educational needs in ways which they judge to be relevant. Only when this is the case can we justifiably claim that the National Curriculum is a curriculum for all. (Dearing, 1993, paragraph 6.2)

The Dearing Report recommended some measures be taken in order to achieve participation at Levels 1 and 2 by pupils of any age. Firstly, the working groups advising the School Curriculum and Assessment Authority (SCAA) were asked to rewrite the Key Stage Programmes of Study for each subject, so that it became easier to identify elements which can be taught at Level 1. Secondly, provision is made at the end of each Key Stage for pupils with SEN to work from earlier Key Stage Programmes of Study. It was heartening that a representative from the field of SEN was included on each of the subject working parties for the Dearing review.

The Dearing Report also stated that the SCAA would investigate ways in which the small steps of progress that some pupils make are assessed, recorded and reported positively. This holds the promise that pupils who are unable to achieve Level 1 need not be labelled as 'working towards Level 1' for the whole of their school careers. In fact, this is a term that emerged largely from the assessment process advocated by School Examination and Assessment Council (SEAC). Conversely the National Curriculum Council (NCC) used the term 'working within Level 1'. This is a far more inclusive approach to the delivery of a curriculum for all. SCAA has now commissioned National Foundation for Educational Research (NFER) to survey good practice in assessment, reporting and accreditation, with particular reference to those pupils working within Levels 1, 2 and 3 but who, age-wise, are outside of Key Stage 1. It is hoped that from this survey models of good practice will emerge that will inform teachers' practice.

Altogether these are positive measures and should facilitate access to the NC and the appropriate assessment of progress. It remains to be seen how effectively the SCAA will assist teachers through non-statutory support and guidance, and whether SCAA will address teachers' concerns. Some commentators are already claiming that the review of the NC has to be considered a qualified triumph from the point of view of pupils with SEN (Byers, 1994). The simplification and clarification of the Programmes of Study will make the construction of coherent schemes of work easier. The move from Statements of Attainment to Level Descriptions will promote a less cumbersome, more flexible and pupil-centred reporting process, hopefully to the benefit of children with SEN.

The new policies on access and enablement represent a significant move forward. In the subject proposals made by SCAA, subject-specific access statements were included. For example, in music, pupils with hearing impairments should have access to equipment and resources which visually record and display sounds. Similarly in science, when dealing with the topic of light, visually impaired pupils who retain a degree of sensitivity to light can gain access to this part of the Programme of Study through adapted means. In science, when considering the topic of sound, hearing impaired pupils should be supported in their access to this part of the

Programme of Study by the use of visual demonstrations of the property of sound. e.g., through the use of oscilloscopes, sound-level meters, speech trainers or musical instruments.

In the consultation on the review of the NC (Dearing, 1993), the majority of respondents felt that the statements supporting access in the proposed new NC would help teachers in planning appropriate work for pupils with SEN. It was stressed that the starting point, in planning the curriculum for all pupils, should be the Key Stage Programme of Study appropriate to the pupil's age. However, the flexibility to supplement content by using material for earlier Key Stage programmes was widely welcomed.

More able pupils were also considered in this consultation, and respondents here welcomed the enabling statements, as they felt they offered valuable support for teachers of able pupils. The statements encouraged teachers to use material from higher Key Stage Programmes of Study if appropriate to the individual's needs. Whilst this is a useful strategy, again the age-appropriate context should be born in mind when enriching and extending the NC for able pupils.

The key strategy for addressing the individual needs of the least and most able was again identified as differentiation, with teachers requesting help concerning how to differentiate work and use Level Descriptions to assess pupils' performance when they may not meet all elements of a Level Description. So let us consider now the important curriculum concept of differentiation.

Differentiation – The Key to Good Practice?

Whatever subject or Programme of Study we are considering, differentiation will be the key strategy for insuring that children's individual needs are met. All children are different, they learn in different ways and through different strategies. Teachers too are very different and teach in a variety of ways. Thus, we should seek curriculum match, not mismatch. Our teaching styles should address the needs of the child at their point of learning.

We need differentiated teaching and learning strategies to rectify some of the curriculum imbalances that might otherwise exist, and seriously disadvantage some children's capacity and opportunity to learn. Imbalance in the curriculum occurs when teachers use only written outcomes from an experience, adopt closed tasks (only one right answer) and/or continually employ whole class teaching. The antidote to these three approaches might be to balance written outcomes with drama, oral presentation, drawing, construction or collage; to balance closed tasks with open-ended tasks; and to ensure that in addition to whole class teaching there are opportunities for collaborative small group work and individual teaching when necessary.

Defining Differentiation

Lewis (1991) states that 'differentiation is the process of adjusting teaching to meet the learning needs of individual children'. Her point has been echoed by other authors who have all fundamentally agreed that differentiation is a process whereby teachers match the need for progress through the curriculum by the selection of appropriate teaching methods for an individual child within a group situation (Dickinson and Wright, 1993; Peter, 1992; Visser, 1993). This may seem a daunting task, but Alexander, Rose and Woodhead (1992) were quick to point out that 'the idea that at any one time learning tasks in nine subjects can be exactly matched to the needs and abilities of all pupils is a class is hopelessly unrealistic.'

Differentiation has been identified as a key feature of effective teaching and learning. Elements of differentiation include:

- teaching based on the assessed capabilities of the learner
- children working at their own pace
- provision of alternative learning activities for individuals
- opportunities for children to learn in cooperative groups
- children taking some responsibility for their learning
- development of children's reflectivity about their learning.

Any of these points could be embodied in how we plan differentiated teaching. For example, do we differentiate tasks according to the child's pace of learning: do we always have the same starting points in a task for all children or are there different access points? Does the sequence and structure of a task have to be exactly the same for all pupils?

The above points very much reflect a child-centred approach to teaching and learning. What strategies do we have in place for self-differentiation? Have we designed open-ended tasks that will enable the child to plot their own learning route? Many teachers claim, and rightly so, that they would not have time to plan individually for all thirty pupils in their class, but in a classroom that offers structure, cooperation and freedom it is possible for the child to map their own individual learning route. Through self-differentiation, the child is able to develop an appropriate level of challenge for themselves providing them with a sense of earned success. It is a process that can be undertaken by the child to fulfil their own needs. Self-differentiation involves the child assessing their own needs, and adapting or extending activities or choices appropriately in relation to selected targets, or searching out alternative means of achieving goals, fulfilment or recognition.

Effective Differentiation

Many teachers wonder if they would recognize effective differentiation in their own classrooms. OFSTED have prepared, in their *Handbook for the Inspection of Schools* (1994), a section on quality teaching which matches the principles of differentiation. These indicators for each classroom could also be translated thus:

- short-term targets (in the context of long-term targets/broad aims)
- clearly identified learning experiences (What are the knowledge, skills and concepts we want the children to put into practice?)

Enquiry Task

Consider the attached list, 'Elements of Differentiation'. Consider the ten points made on this list and note how in your classroom or school any of these aspects of differentiation maybe observed.

Elements of Differentiation

Differentiation . . .

- . . . is premised on diversity
- . . . is multi-dimensional
- . . . applies to individuals
- . . . applies to all learners
- . . . is diagnostic
- . . . challenges expectations
- . . . challenges classroom relationships
- . . . is in an integral aspect of effective learning
- . . . is relevant for all teachers
- . . . requires a long-term, whole school strategy.

- enables a celebration of achievement
- provides information on continuity and progression
- an atmosphere which has an expectation of success.

Differentiation, then, is fundamentally the process of enabling pupils of all abilities to show what they know, understand and can do. In constructing a scheme of work, you will need to have a clearly identifiable common core in which the essentials of each session must be covered by the least and most able. For the most able pupils this would mean that there would be extension activities, perhaps around resource-based learning where pupils could access a variety of books and media to explore and investigate a topic for themselves. In addition to this, extra content may be available which challenges the pupil in the realms of higher order skills. Those pupils with SEN would need opportunities for reinforcement of the key concepts, skills and content contained in the core of the scheme of work. This may involve introducing different, or more appropriate materials, perhaps offering concrete first-hand experiences to ensure reinforcement.

Much has been said about differentiation by task and outcome. We have possibly undersold ourselves as a profession by not acknowledging differentiation by input. The many hours that teachers spend thinking about the pupils that they teach, mentally mapping out activities for the pupils, and then the hours that they actually spend writing out schemes of work and lesson plans: all of this is differentiation by planning. Following this, comes differentiation in practice whereby the task is offered, the range of resources to support the task made available, and the teaching strategies employed. The pupil engages as an active learner in the task. It is so important that children are not peripheral participants in the learning experience: standing on the side lines, observing others engaged in learning, will in the long term be of no cumulative benefit to the child. In considering the outcomes of differentiation it is fairly obvious that with thirty pupils in the class there will potentially be thirty different outcomes. The onus here should be on how the teachers record those outcomes – differentiated assessment.

Differentiated assessment is a relatively new concept. Falconer-Hall (1992) identified a range of differentiated assessment strategies that were already embodied in the practice of teachers. These included such things as unfocused observation, focused observation, check lists, *aide memoires*, individual target plans, tests, reports and records of achievement.

The process of differentiation can be diagnostic. As the teacher more closely matches the learning tasks to a child's needs so he or she gains more intricate knowledge about that child and his or her pattern of learning. The following sequence may help you to construct and individualize a programme for a child.

Assessment for Differentiation

- Establish a baseline.
- Concentrate on what the child can do.
- Assess within the context of the classroom or school environment.
- Assess through samples of everyday work.
- Ensure that children are involved in their own assessment.
- Do not restrict your evidence to written work alone.

A word of caution here: by recommending an individualized programme for a child I am not suggesting that it should be necessarily individual and delivered to the child on a one-to-one basis. 'Individual and individualized' approaches are both strategies for meeting individual needs. The former is differentiation by isolating the learning experiences of individual children; the latter is differentiation of a learning experience within the group context, a matching of the individual child and the task within the group context (Hammond and Read, 1992). As Dickinson and Wright (1993) state: 'Differentiation is not a single event, it is a process.' This process involves recognizing a variety of individual needs within the class, planning to meet those needs, providing appropriate delivery and evaluating the effectiveness of the activities in order to maximize the achievements of individual students. Thus, a differentiated curriculum is one that has been planned to meet those individual needs and through systems of recording and reporting allow pupils to demonstrate their knowledge, skills and understanding. The underpinning principle has to be that every child achieves something worthwhile and that this should be celebrated. It is a skilled teacher who can unlock the achievement in every child, allow that child to demonstrate his or her talents, can cherish, harness, and then, with the child, celebrate those talents, through their achievements.

Enquiry Task

Think about the various forms of recording and reporting you use currently in your classroom.

- Do these recognize individual attainment of pupils?
- Do you have systems in place for celebrating achievement in your classroom? In your school?

Choose an activity that you use in your classroom. Design an observation sheet that would enable you to record individual achievements within a group context.

Extended Programmes of Study

The Programmes of Study, as they stand within each of the NC subjects, will not address the individual needs of all pupils in your class. It will be necessary to offer additional or supplementary experiences to some pupils. In this sense, it is useful to visualize the curriculum as a spiral that spins out through stronger and stronger differentiated teaching strategies, to embrace each child at their point of learning need.

Extended Programmes of Study (EXPOS) are a useful form planning. You would take the essential elements of a Programme of Study for a topic and would add extension activities for the more able pupils and support activities for the pupils with SEN. EXPOS have particular features. The list below identifies some of those features.

- Carefully structured.
- Contain small steps in learning.
- Individualized approaches are identified within a group context.
- Curricula access is evident for all pupils.
- Specific teaching approaches are identified.
- Programme matches learning pattern of the child.
- Learner objectives are clearly identified.
- Supplementary activities are included.
- Creative activities are offered through imaginative presentation.
- Challenge and expectation is still implicit (i.e., the curriculum is not watered down).
- Interest levels remain high.
- The learning experience is enriched.
- Possibilities for learning are extended.

Another approach to planning EXPOS is through a curriculum ladder (Lewis, 1991). In this approach, a teacher specifies what the end goal of a project may be. He or she then identifies activities on the ladder of progression from which a pupil ideally can select. These activities would be generated through pupil-teacher discussion. Whatever activity is chosen it enables that pupil to participate actively as a member of a group working towards the end goal. In this approach degrees of access are offered to the child.

The Differentiation Spiral: Planning an Extended Programme of Study

Not all pupils will be able to access a task at the same level. Establish a core activity, and from there identify how it could be extended for the most able pupils, or support offered to those pupils with SEN (start with an easy activity such as 'writing their full name', until you are familiar with the planning model).

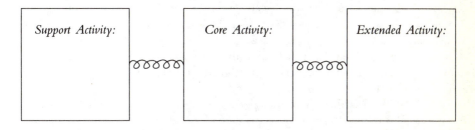

Support Activity: *Core Activity:*   *Extended Activity:*

The Differentiation Spiral approach ensures that learning activities do not become fragmented. All pupils continue to engage in the core activity or dimensions of the core. We are not presenting pupils with something that is different – rather it is differentiated. This model can be described as inclusive; the lesson is designed in such a way that all pupils are included in the body of activity generated by the lesson. Access points for all are specified acknowledging the diversity of ability and need within any primary classroom.

Enquiry Task

Plan an EXPOS by answering the following questions:

- What prior knowledge can the children bring to this Programme of Study?
- What do the NC Programmes of Study themselves offer?
- What is the core content that I need to include in this Programme of Study?
- How can I modify, adapt or supplement activities to offer support to pupils with SEN?
- How can I extend the content to offer challenge to the more able pupils?
- What individual targets do I need to embed in the programme for specific pupils?
- How will the pupils record the outcomes of their work?
- What various assessment and recording strategies will I use to register the attainments of each and every pupil?

Using the Whole Curriculum

We must remind ourselves that there are other dimensions to a child's learning, not solely the specified NC subjects. If we have a genuine concern for relevance in the curriculum, it is through differentiation that we will deliver that relevance to the whole child. The whole child needs a whole curriculum.

The NCC produced a range of Curriculum Guidance documents (numbers 3 to 8) pertaining to the 'whole curriculum' (NCC, 1990a). These documents offer a context against which the NC in the primary school must be set. The status of these documents remains the same even with the implementation of the new NC. It is worth examining what these have to offer to primary children.

Curriculum Guidance 3: The Whole Curriculum (NCC, 1990a) illuminates through its discussion of cross-curricular skills, themes and dimensions the possibilities for a whole curriculum. The need for all elements of the Curriculum to contribute to the Personal and Social Education (PSE) of all pupils is stressed in this document. PSE has a major role to play in the education of all children, but for the child with special needs it is vital that it is dealt with thoroughly and in considerable depth. The cross-curricular elements afford enrichment and variety to the overall curriculum experience.

The skills identified within this document as having cross-curricular application may also be highly pertinent to the individualized learning goals that a teacher may have either negotiated with pupils, or, in the case of a statemented pupil, may be embedded in their Individual Education Programme. These skills can be fostered across the whole curriculum and comprise communication, numeracy, problem solving, personal skills and information technology. The development of these skills in young children is directly aligned to preparation for adulthood.

> What is beyond dispute is that in the next century these skills, together with flexibility and adaptability, will be at a premium. (NCC, 1990a)

The themes outlined by the NCC are particularly noteworthy for the primary teacher. The cross-curricular skills, dimensions and themes should form the bedrock on which we set the core and foundation subjects of the NC. In the documents explaining careers education and guidance, economic and industrial understanding, etc., we find many of the curricular activities we have considered crucial to the education of pupils with SEN. For example, *Curriculum Guidance 6: Careers Education and Guidance* (NCC, 1990b) recommends that pupils in Key Stage 1 complete a visit to a workplace (local factory, farm, fire station, cafe, bus depot), decide upon the information needed, devise questions to ask and items to be collected (timetables, pictures, leaflets). What is more, these activities are given status, and are accepted in their own right as valid and valuable.

Conclusion

All children deserve the best education we can offer them. The challenge to the teacher is always how to do this? Whilst the new NC removes some barriers to participation in the curriculum for pupils with SEN through the access and enabling statements, without effective teaching these principles will never be seen in practice. They will never present to the child the quality learning experiences they were intended to liberate.

This chapter has argued that differentiation is the major curriculum tenet that will inform teaching and engage the child in meaningful learning. As such differentiation is the key, but it is the teacher that holds that key. Only when that door to learning is unlocked will children with SEN find themselves included in the dynamic and exciting learning opportunities that typify many primary classrooms. Our task now is to take the new NC, differentiate it according to individual need, and build an inclusive curriculum.

Acknowledgement

The contribution of the Westminster College BEd Differentiation Elective groups for 1993/94 and 1994/95 in sharing their thoughts on EXPOS is duly acknowledged.

Note

1   The 'Writing with Symbols' computer program is available from Widgit Software, 102 Radford Road, Leamington Spa, Warwickshire.

References

ALEXANDER, R., ROSE, J. and WOODHEAD, C. (1992) *Curriculum Organisation and Classroom Practice in Primary Schools: A Discussion Paper*, London: HMSO.

ASHDOWN, R., CARPENTER, B. and BOVAIR, K. (1991) *The Curriculum Challenge: Access to the National Curriculum for Pupils with Learning Difficulties*, London: Falmer Press.

BANES, D., COLES, C., DETHERIDGE, M. and NEWTON, W. (1994) 'Writing with symbols – the Meldreth suite', *British Journal of Special Education*, 21, 1, p. 20.

BROWN, E. (1995 – in preparation) *Religious Education for All*, London: David Fulton.

BYERS, R. (1994) 'The Dearing review of the National Curriculum', *British Journal of Special Education*, 21, 3, pp. 92–6.

DEARING, R. (1993) *The National Curriculum and its Assessment: An Interim Report*, London: NCC/SEAC.

DES (1991) *Physical Education for Ages 5 to 16: Proposals of the Secretary of State for Education and Science*, London: HMSO.

DICKINSON, C. and WRIGHT, J. (1993) *Differentiation: A Handbook of Practical Strategies*, Coventry: NCET.

FALCONER-HALL, L. (1992) 'Assessment for differentiation', *British Journal of Special Education*, 19, 1, pp. 20–3.

HAMMOND, C. and READ, G. (1992) 'Individual vs. individualised: into the 1990s', in K. BOVAIR, B. CARPENTER and G. UPTON (eds) *Special Curricula Needs*, London: David Fulton.

HUMBERSIDE LEA (1990) *Science for Special Educational Needs*, Humberside: LEA.

LEWIS, A. (1991) *Primary Special Needs and the National Curriculum*, London: Routledge.

MOUNT, H. and ACKERMAN, D. (1991) *Technology for All*, London: David Fulton.

NCC (1989a) *Circular 5: Implementing the National Curriculum – Participation by Pupils with Special Educational Needs*, York: NCC.

NCC (1989b) *Curriculum Guidance 2: A Curriculum for All*, York: NCC.

NCC (1990a) *Curriculum Guidance 3: The Whole Curriculum*, York: NCC.

NCC (1990b) *Curriculum Guidance 6: Careers Education and Guidance*, York: NCC.

NCC (1992a) *Curriculum Guidance 9: The National Curriculum and Pupils with Severe Learning Difficulties*, York: NCC.

NCC (1992b) *The National Curriculum and Pupils with Severe Learning Difficulties: INSET Resources*, York: NCC.

OFSTED (1994) *The Handbook for the Inspection of Schools*, London: HMSO.

PETER, M. (ed) (1992) *Differentiation: The Way Forward*, Stafford: NASEN.

ROSE, R. (1991) 'A jigsaw approach to group work', *British Journal of Special Education*, 18, 2, pp. 54–8.

SEBBA, J. (1994) *History for All*, London: David Fulton.

SOLIHULL LEA (1991) *Circular 4: Special Educational Needs*, Solihull: Council Press.

VISSER, J. (1993) *Differentiation: Making it Work*, Stafford: NASEN.

16   Conclusion

Kate Ashcroft and David Palacio

Within this book, the chapter authors have analysed each of the subjects in the new National Curriculum for England, and have demonstrated some of the ways that this curriculum can be implemented. From this analysis, it is clear that the various authors are generally optimistic about the process of implementation and believe that it offers a number of opportunities for creativity and development.

The new National Curriculum does not require you to abandon your present plans or schemes of work. Much of the content of the original curriculum is retained, though it is sometimes expressed differently, or is included now under a different subject of the curriculum. Where some content is eliminated from the statutory curriculum, you remain at liberty to include it, if you feel that it continues to have value.

The section, *Beyond the National Curriculum*, makes the point that the National Curriculum is not the whole curriculum. The new National Curriculum will not, of itself, meet the needs of every child or class. As you take the opportunity to go beyond the framework and to cover other issues and subjects, we hope that you find implementing the new National Curriculum to be an empowering experience. Schools and teachers are back in the driving seat. It is *you* who now decides the additional curriculum that is most appropriate and relevant to your children's interests and particular needs. For instance, there is now scope for you to include areas of interest and knowledge that you have acquired, but that are not part of the statutory curriculum.

While there are major areas of similarity between the old and the new National Curriculum, there are some changes in emphasis. For instance, technology has been separated from information technology and retitled design and technology. This change is to be welcomed since it makes clearer the importance of the creative and decision-making processes within the subject now called design and technology.

In general, you remain free to choose the teaching and learning methods that you think most appropriate, but in some subjects, such as mathematics and science, you will find that the specifications of the National Curriculum Order determines some of the teaching approaches that you must use. For example, it is difficult to see how it is possible to fulfil the requirements of each of these two Orders without adopting an investigative/problem-solving approach to learning. This, in turn, requires you to use active learning techniques in your classroom.

Chapter authors have pointed out the changes in the assessment methods within the new National Curriculum. These are likely to be seen by most primary teachers as more 'teacher friendly' since the spurious 'objectivity' and the recourse to excessive detail, seen in the previous assessment requirements, have been abandoned. This very welcome change will enable you to modify your methods of record keeping so as to move away from checklists and, possibly, move towards a largely word-based system, perhaps founded upon assessments that are made in the course of your day-to-day work. This implies that record keeping and assessment has the potential to become not only a continuous and integrated process but also one that is manageable within the context of most primary classrooms.

Cross-curriculum themes, except for information technology and English (and Welsh in Wales) are not now part of the compulsory curriculum. Unfortunately, the School Curriculum and Assessment Authority has decided that the very helpful non-statutory guidance will be provided no longer. However, all is not lost since, as with other aspects of the curriculum, there is no reason why you should not continue to use the documents that previously supported these aspects of the curriculum. Many of the chapter authors have suggested that much valuable material and guidance is still contained within them.

The issue of children who have special educational needs is taken much more seriously in the new National Curriculum. Teachers are now provided with more flexibility, and the opportunity to provide a challenging and progressive curriculum for all children. Furthermore, specified within each subject Order is the requirement for schools to make appropriate provision for children with physical and other disabilities. For example, in science, provision now has to be made for sight, and hearing, impaired children to have access to the Programme of Study for light and sound.

Much has remained constant between the old and new National Curriculum. The existing subjects remain (with the addition of information technology as a separate subject), as does the concept of Key Stages. As has been the situation in the past, the statutory aspects of each subject are listed within the Orders but for Key Stages 1 and 2 all subjects are contained now within a single document that includes both Programmes of Study and Attainment Targets. Curriculum content has been streamlined and duplication between subjects has been eliminated. The assessment requirements have been made more manageable, with Level Descriptions, or End of Key Stage Descriptions, replacing the previous complex assessment requirements.

In conclusion, although we argue with the detail of some of the changes, overall, we feel that the new National Curriculum should allow you more freedom and opportunities for the exercise of professional judgments. The National Curriculum now provides each child with a minimum entitlement to a broad and balanced curriculum (which, of course, is what the 1988 Education Reform Act intended should happen) and, at the same time, provides teachers, schools, parents and the community with the necessary information concerning children's achievements and progress. It is interesting to note that the process of evaluation, consultation and holistic planning has led to a considerable improvement to the curriculum that you are now able to offer your pupils. We hope that many lessons have been learned from this process about the management and implementation of large-scale change and that governments have learned that the planning of such change needs a longer time frame than the usual Parliamentary Term of Office. If such a change is to succeed, it seems that it must be based on a fairly general climate of acceptance and consent. Innovation as an imposed process, even when heavily promoted, and presented as the heroic defeat of vested interests, has been found to fail on too many occasions.

List of Contributors

Kate Ashcroft is Professor and Dean of the Faculty of Education at the University of the West of England. Formerly Head of the School of Education at Westminster College, Oxford and Principal Lecturer at Oxford Polytechnic, she has extensive primary teaching experience as a class teacher, Deputy Head and Advisory Teacher. She has a distinguished research and publication record in the area of educational management.

Pat Booth is Senior Lecturer in Mathematics and Mathematics Education at Westminster College, Oxford. She previously taught at Brighton Polytechnic and Bulmershe College of Higher Education. She worked in a number of schools as a class teacher and as a Head of Mathematics Department. She is presently undertaking research into the psychodynamics of mathematics classrooms.

Carolyn Boyd is Senior Lecturer in Language Education and Teaching Studies at Westminster College, Oxford. Previously, she gained teaching experience as class teacher in Australia. In the UK, she has been a class teacher, Curriculum coordinator and Advisory Teacher within the area of inner city early years education. She has published and presented a number of conference papers in the area of Early Years Language.

Barry Carpenter is the Director of the Centre for the Study of Special Education at Westminster College, Oxford. Formerly an Inspector of Schools and a Head of a Special School, he has a distinguished research and publication record in the area of Special Educational Needs.

David Coates is Senior Lecturer in Science and Design and Technology in Primary Education at Westminster College, Oxford. Previously, he worked as the Design and Technology Coordinator in a primary school. He has a range of publications in the areas of Science, Design and Technology and mentoring in primary schools in the UK and abroad.

Jennifer Gray is Lecturer in Physical Education at Westminster College, Oxford. She has extensive experience of school teaching and of educational consultancy. She has published a number of books and articles on teaching swimming and diving.

John Halocha is Principal Lecturer in Geography Education and Teaching Studies and Professional Studies Coordinator on the BEd at Westminster College, Oxford. He has taught in primary and middle schools and was Deputy Head Teacher of two schools. He is currently closely involved in partnership work with schools in initial teacher education.

Chris Higgins is Senior Lecturer in Information Technology and Head of Mathematics at Westminster College, Oxford. He is a member of the Editorial Board of *Information Technology for Teacher Education* and has taught extensively within primary and secondary teacher education courses on Information Technology in the classroom.

Margaret Jones is Senior Lecturer in Mathematics Education at Westminster College, Oxford. She has previous experience as a secondary and primary teacher, as a Head of Mathematics Department and as an Advisory Teacher in Mathematics. She was a member of the General Committee of the *Association of Teachers of Mathematics*. She has extensive experience of the development of curriculum materials in Mathematics and has published a number of articles about Mathematics Education.

Gwyneth Little is Lecturer in Religious Education at Westminster College, Oxford. Formerly Advisory Teacher in Religious Education in Leicestershire and Head of Religious Education within a secondary school, she is a regular contributor to the journal *Religious Education Today*.

Peta Lloyd is Senior Lecturer in Language and Early Years Education at Westminster College, Oxford. She has extensive experience of nursery and infant teaching within multicultural settings. She has worked as a class teacher, Curriculum Support Teacher and Advisory Teacher for the *Language in the National Curriculum* project. She has published a number of articles in the area of Early Years Education.

Cliff Marshall is Principal Lecturer in Science and Science Education and is BEd Course Leader at Westminster College, Oxford. He has previous experience as a primary school teacher and as a Deputy Head Teacher. He has published a number of papers in journals and at conferences on Primary Science.

David Menday is Senior Lecturer in Art and Art Education at Westminster College, Oxford. He was previously a teacher within mainstream and special schools. He worked on the *National Curriculum Arts in Schools* project and is Deputy Director of the *National Foundation for Arts Education*. He has published a number of books and articles on Art and Arts Education.

Carrie Mercier is Senior Lecturer in Religious Education and Head of the Religious Education Centre at The College of Ripon and York St John. Previously Lecturer in Religious Education at Westminster College, Oxford, she has also taught extensively in the USA and UK. She is the author of several books on Religious Education.

Helena Mitchell is Senior Lecturer in Language and Literacy and Early Years Coordinator of the PGCE course at Westminster College, Oxford. She has experience of Early Years education at class teacher and Deputy Head Teacher level. She has published in the area of Language and Literacy and is completing a research project into early reading.

Jenny Monk is Senior Lecturer in Language Education and Teaching Studies at Westminster College, Oxford. Previously she worked in primary schools as a class teacher, a Deputy Head Teacher and a Language Advisory Teacher. She has contributed to a number of books on Language and Learning.

David Palacio is Head of Research and Science Subject leader at Westminster College, Oxford. He has taught in primary and secondary schools and has published extensively in the areas of Science Education and assessment.

Maureen Roberts is Senior Lecturer in Teaching Studies and Primary Geography at Westminster College, Oxford. She has studied Interdisciplinary Studies in the USA and Comparative Education in the UK. She has experience as a Geography Curriculum Support Teacher within UK and USA inner city primary and nursery schools.

John Siraj-Blatchford is Senior Lecturer in Primary Education at the University of East London. Previously he was Senior Lecturer in Design and Technology at Westminster College, Oxford. He has wide experience of Design and Technology and Science as a class teacher and as a Curriculum Coordinator. He has a distinguished publication record in Science, Design and Technology and Anti-Racist Education.

Paul Taylor is Senior Lecturer in History and Humanities Education at Westminster College, Oxford. He has taught in a range of schools and has published a number of articles in books and journals about History and Humanities Education.

Patricia Thompson is Head of Teaching Studies and Principal Lecturer in Music and Music Education at Westminster College, Oxford. She has a range of experience as a class teacher and Head of Music Department. She has an international profile in the world of Music Education and adjudicates at music festivals and contributes to conferences across the world.

David Tilley is Senior Lecturer in Drama Education at Westminster College, Oxford. Previously he was Advisory Teacher in Drama in Oxfordshire and Gloucestershire. He has taught Drama and Theatre Arts in a variety of schools in Canada and the UK.

Index